Dying to win

Doping in sport and the development of anti-doping policy

2nd edition

Barrie Houlihan

French version

La victoire : à quel prix ?
Le dopage dans le sport et l'élaboration de politiques contre le dopage
ISBN : 92-871-4774-4

Note on the cover photo :

European sports fans were dramatically alerted to the issue of drug abuse in sport by the death of Tom Simpson, aged 29, during the 1967 Tour de France. The first Englishman to wear the yellow jersey, he was recognised as a leading cyclist of his generation, known for his courage and determination in one of the most gruelling sports.

Simpson's autopsy revealed that his heart had collapsed and traces of amphetamine and methyl amphetamine were found in his blood supply. While the amount of stimulant was insufficient to have killed him, it led him to go beyond the normal limit of his strength and stamina. The capture on television of his death increased world interest in doping.

Cover photo : Tour de France, 1967, Mont Ventoux © Presse Sports
Cover design : Graphic Design Workshop

Council of Europe Publishing
F-67075 Strasbourg Cedex
http ://book.coe.int

ISBN 92-871-4685-3
© Council of Europe, May 2002
Printed in Germany

For Jacqui

Contents

Gold medals and world records – But at what cost?

The battle against doping in sport is every athlete's fight. Ideals of dignity, human excellence and fair play are not unique to the Olympic movement, but apply to the very nature of sport – to be the best an athlete can be. But at some point, a line must be drawn between being the best through hard work, perseverance and certain levels of biological luck and that of taking extraordinary means. Doping, winning at all costs, cannot be accepted, least of all by athletes.

There are any number of reasons why doping must be banned and even more reasons why athletes should lead that charge. Every athlete has the right to a level playing field. A field on which he or she can compete with equals and succeed as champion because he was faster, she jumped higher or, simply, he was the best. All things being equal, each champion should be able to say, "I worked hard, I deserve this," on the merits of his or her own achievements, rather than on the back of illegal substances. All athletes should be able to go into competition with the same advantages as his or her competitors. That is the Olympic ideal of fair play. Athletes must face the challenge of doping in order to see the concept of fair play become the accepted practice rather than just a lofty ideal. We must preserve the reputation of sport and our accomplishments.

Athletes are role models for the children of their time. Children everywhere idolise athletes for their strength, grit, determination and unflappability under stress. They emulate their heroes by taking up their sports, changing the way they compete and striving for excellence. At some point, athletes must hold themselves responsible for the image they project to sponsors, sport federations, other athletes, their fans, and the youth and children who cheer them to success and admire them. It may seem trite to expect athletes to set good examples, but one has an obligation to the young, to ensure that we lead them on a sound path and give them the tools of success. By speaking out against doping and espousing the ideals of excellence and fair play, we can serve our youth by triumphing in the war against doping.

One would expect that health concerns related to doping alone would be enough to deter an athlete whose body is a finely tuned machine from taking harmful and dangerous chemicals that could end their careers, not to mention their lives. That is of course not the case. Everyday, athletes risk their health in taking any number of banned substances. Winning at any cost, it seems, includes heart disease, arrhythmia and blood pressure problems. By working to eliminate doping in sport, athletes have the opportunity to educate themselves and pass on this knowledge on the health perils of banned substances to others.

With more opportunities to be involved in decision-making processes, athletes are now looked upon not only as athletic achievers, but also as global leaders of today and tomorrow. Athletes are in a greater position to make decisions with regard to the development of their sports and are looked on as role models for the young. Athletes have a voice and we have the ear of the public and of the world's youth. We have the power to effect change: to clean up our own sports and to complete each race, each competition, with excellence, dignity and fair play. In every competition, athletes are expected to win, but the costs of that victory can be too high. Athletes should not be dying to win.

Johann Olav Koss

Chapter 1

The value of sport

Olympia
in the courses where speed is matched with speed
and a man's force harsh at the height.
And the winner the rest of his lifetime
keeps happiness beside him sweeter than honey.

Pindar[1]

The Olympic Games epitomise modern sport. The three or four years preparing the bid followed, if successful, by a further six or seven years of planning and construction by the host city, the hundreds of television companies that broadcast the Games, the thousands of participants, coaches and officials that attend, and the hundreds of millions who watch the events from all points of the globe provide ample testimony to the prestige, popularity and global coverage of modern international sport. But it is not just the scale of the Olympic Games that sticks in the mind. The Olympics also provide an insight into the hold that sport has on the popular imagination. To reflect on the most memorable events of the last two or three Games provides a rich range of images of triumph and despair, unanticipated success and unexpected failure, and breathtaking good fortune and heart-breaking bad luck.

This range of images and emotions could be found in any major international sports competition such as the soccer World Cup, the Paralympics, the Tour de France and the World Athletics Championships. More importantly, these images and emotions can also be found, and for many of us experienced, in the vast array of sport played by those whose sporting aspirations are far more modest. Yet sports participation provides a powerful thread that links the Olympic gold medalists Stephen Redgrave and Matthew Pinsent and the Saturday afternoon rowers, Sonia O'Sullivan, Haile Gabresilasie, and Hicham El Guerrouj and fun-runners in the Berlin marathon, and Luis Figo and Gabriel Batistuta and the thousands playing in the Sunday morning soccer leagues. In addition to the many millions throughout the world who participate in sport, there is also the enormous number who experience the excitement of sport vicariously through spectating either at live events or through the media, especially television.

---

1. *Odes of Pindar,* translated by R. Lattimore, 2nd edn., Chicago: University of Chicago Press, 1976.

The extensiveness and intensity of popular involvement in sport and its capacity to arouse an astonishing depth of passion both in participants and spectators is only part of the reason for sport's unique place in modern society. The particularity of sport in the modern world is also based on the fact that sport is a cornerstone of the global corporate media provision and is the subject of intense governmental interest. In addition, modern sport is also remarkable for the degree to which it stirs, on the one hand, associations with a classical past and, on the other, a belief that sport occupies a privileged position in society.

The deliberate association of sport with a classical past, especially through the Olympic Games, continues to provide a rich basis for the assumption of continuity with what many consider to be a time when sport was practised in a purer form and was less tarnished by its current association with excessive commercialism, professionalism, violence and drug abuse. For the founder of the modern Olympics, Pierre de Coubertin, the ancient Olympic Games provided a profound and powerful source of inspiration. The description of ancient games found in Homer's poems, *The Iliad* and *The Odyssey*, provides a sharp insight into the interweaving of the athletic achievements of the warrior élite with the celebration of sport as an integral part of Hellenic culture. More importantly Homer also made clear the extent to which games and sports reflected a cultural ideal based on the complementarity of physical and intellectual excellence. The emphasis on the development of mind and body was based on a belief that true excellence was the product not just of physical prowess but of moral and intellectual qualities as well, and provided "a profoundly original conception and a philosophy of life"[1] that still resonates in our modern world and is particularly clearly reflected in the Olympic Charter. As McIntosh notes, "[that] sport in the days of Homeric heroes was noble there is no doubt", but he also draws attention to the fact that in later years "the religious and cultural functions of the Olympic Games and of other pan-Hellenic festivals were obscured and then destroyed by specialism and commercialism" and that "success in the Games was sought for narrow political ends both by states and by individuals".[2]

The desire to maintain continuity between ancient and modern sport, albeit based on a selective reading of the history of the ancient games, in part explains the strong tendency to see modern sport as either outside normal society or at least as occupying a privileged position in society. At one extreme, sport is seen as providing an oasis within the modern world where higher standards of morality, often the product of a romanticisation of late Victorian middle-class values, are practised when compared to the dubious

1. Segrave, J.O. & Chu, D. (eds.), *The Olympic Games in Transition*, Champaign, Ill: Human Kinetics Books, 1988.
2. McIntosh, P., *Sport in Society*, revised edn., London: West London Press, 1987, pp. 20 and 22-23.

and compromised character of everyday social, political and business behaviour. In part, this view is based on a belief that it is possible to sustain values within sport that are not simply a reflection of those to be found in wider society and thus exhortations to "fair play" and that "participating is more important than winning" are realised in competitive sport. Some substance is given to this assertion by emphasising the central place in sport of rules and their strict application. Much of modern sport is organised on a strictly meritocratic basis where quantification not only ensures that he or she who jumps higher, runs faster or throws further wins but also provides part of a clear and transparent set of rules of competition that, far from producing athletes that are "indoctrinated, regimented and repressed",[1] provide liberation from prejudice and bias.

If aspiration to a higher morality is part of the explanation for the distinctive position of sport in modern society then an equally powerful contribution is made by the long association between amateurism and sporting excellence. In most European and North American countries, the commitment to amateurism that dominated the bulk of the present century has left an indelible imprint on contemporary sport. For many, the legitimacy of sport's claim to higher moral values was reinforced by a definition of amateurism that attempted to protect competitive sport, and especially Olympic sport, from the corruption that prize money was thought to create.

Unfortunately, these views of modern and ancient sport are both highly inaccurate. Being generous one might argue that to see modern sport as characterised by simple straightforward values which provide a model for wider society is not only to read selectively the history of ancient Greece, but also to romanticise the motives for the defence of amateurism in the nineteenth and twentieth centuries. A harsher, but more accurate explanation is that the promoters of modern Olympic sport sought, in the history of the early Olympics, a rationale which would legitimise their preferred model of athletics which was designed to maintain the social position and interests of a privileged leisured class. It is indisputable that the pattern of sport that develops in a society is the product of that society in exactly the same way as the commercial and political systems are the product of deeper social values and attitudes. However, the suggestion that sport is as much the product of society as business and politics is not to detract from the desire that many involved in sport have to aspire to a set of values frequently less visible in other sectors of society. If sport has a contribution to make to the moral development of society it is in the persistence of an optimistic view of human nature and belief that sport and major sports events are capable of demonstrating the viability of higher moral standards in modern complex societies. There is no better example of the seriousness of the challenge facing sport than the protracted campaign to eradicate doping from competitive sport. The

---

1. Brohm, J.-M., *Sport, A Prison of Measured Time*, London: Pluto Press, 1978, p. 112.

anti-doping campaign can be seen as an acid test for the moral aspirations of national and international organisations involved in sport. Needless to say, the existence and strength of these aspirations must be explored through an analysis of the evidence rather than relying simply on assertion.

A selection of recent episodes associated with major sports events provide ample illustration of the place of sport and doping in the contemporary world. The first episode concerns six Finnish skiers who, at the Lahti World Skiing Championship in February 2001, tested positive for the plasma volume expander Hemohes and were subsequently banned for two years as well as being stripped of four medals including the gold medal that the men's team had won in the relay and the silver won by the women's relay team. Among those banned were Mika Myllyla, a winner of thirteen Olympic and world championship medals, and Harri Kirvesniemi, winner of six Olympic medals and one of Finland's sporting heroes. Apart from the status of the athletes involved what also made this case notable was, first, Finland's reputation as a leader in anti-doping efforts and, second, that members of the athletes' entourage were also punished. The head skiing coach and the coaches for the men's and women's teams were all dismissed and banned for life and two doctors who were also implicated were cautioned by the Finnish Medical Association. Perhaps the most notable aspect of this episode was that after the second positive result was made public, the World Anti-Doping Agency (WADA) conducted unannounced tests on twenty-seven of the remaining twenty-nine members of the Finnish squad. In response to the positive tests, the Finnish Government declared that it intended to review the financial allocation to the sport's governing body while the commercial sponsors also announced an intention to review their link with the Finnish Ski Association.

On the one hand, this episode illustrates that no country, however committed its government and governing bodies are to drug-free sport, is immune from doping. That the six skiers should include a number of national sporting heroes made the affair all the more shocking in Finland. On the other hand, the episode did highlight a number of more positive aspects from which the supporters of drug-free sport can take heart: first, there was the decisive attitude towards members of the athletes' entourage with both the coaching staff and doctors being held accountable for their part in the affair; second, the intervention of WADA is further evidence of the momentum that the new organisation developed during the Sydney Olympic Games; third, the attitude of the government in declaring its intention to hold the domestic governing body responsible for actions of its athletes; and, fourth, the expressions of disapproval from the commercial sponsors.

The second episode, which dates from the 1996 Atlanta Olympic Games, relates to the behaviour of four Russian athletes. Since the collapse of communism, central and eastern European countries have been faced with an uphill struggle to live down their reputation for relying on state-sanctioned doping for their dominance of many events in the Olympic Games between the 1960s and the late 1980s. For the former German Democratic Republic and the former Soviet Union the evidence was especially damning. At Atlanta four Russian athletes, a sprinter, two swimmers and a wrestler, tested positive for bromantan a substance apparently developed to help Soviet soldiers stay alert during the Afghan war and which acts, not only as a stimulant, but which may also be used as a masking agent for other drugs. The initial response of the International Olympic Committee (IOC) was to strip the wrestler Zafar Guliyev of his bronze medal and to indicate that a similar decision would be made regarding the bronze medal winning swimmer, Andrei Korneyev. However, the defence utilised by the Russians, in their appeal to the Court of Arbitration for Sport, was not to deny drug use, nor allege errors in the laboratory analysis, nor indeed to rely on any of the other standard defences employed by those testing positive: the Russians simply argued that bromantan was not a banned substance. The argument of the Russian team was successful: the IOC decision was overturned and the two bronze medals were reinstated. Although the IOC considered the drug to be a stimulant and a masking agent, the committee's position was undermined because bromantan had not, at the time of the Atlanta Games, been added to the list of proscribed substances. In February 1997, the drug was added to the IOC list of banned substances and practices but unfortunately too late for the two athletes who were denied a bronze medal in the wrestling and in swimming events by bromantan-using Russian athletes. This episode draws attention to the need for a fast and efficient process by which newly identified drugs can be added to the IOC list without delay. However, what is particularly significant about this episode is what it reveals about the attitude of athletes and officials to the spirit of the IOC anti-doping policy. The IOC rules on doping appear to have been perceived as an impediment to success rather than as a reflection of Olympic values. The continuing association between the Olympic Games and doping was confirmed when the Australian customs service announced that it had made a record 1 268 seizures of performance enhancing drugs in fiscal year 2000/01 with 44% of seizures being between July and the start of the Games in mid-September.

More recently, at the 2001 World Athletics Championships in Edmonton, Canada, there was a further illustration of the problems of establishing an effective anti-doping policy. The 5 000 m runner Olga Yegorova tested positive for the drug erythropoietin at the Golden League meeting in Paris in July 2001. However, the test was later declared invalid by the International Amateur Athletics Federation (IAAF) because the French authorities had failed to take a blood sample as well as a urine sample. Consequently, Yegorova was eligible to compete in the 5 000 m final, which she duly won. In contrast to the previous example there was no dispute that the drug identified in the urine sample was on the list of banned substances, but, as with the previous case, administrative inadequacies prevented a thorough investigation of the actions of the athletes concerned. The Yegorova case highlights the technical complexity of current anti-doping procedures and the caution of international federations due to the risk of legal action by aggrieved athletes.

The complexity surrounding the issue of doping is not just confined to the Olympic Games or major track and field competitions. The investigations that followed the police search of the Festina team vehicle during the 1998 Tour de France and particularly the testimony of the leading French cyclist Richard Virenque and the Festina team *soigneur*, Willy Voets, at the subsequent trial provided ample evidence of the extent of doping in one of the world's major sports. The investigation by the French authorities led to the trial in Lille of Virenque, Voets, Bruno Roussel, the Festina team manager, and Joel Chabrion, the team public relations manager. Virenque, whose court confession enabled him to avoid criminal prosecution, was suspended from competition for nine months by the Swiss federation with whom he was registered, while the other three received suspended prison sentences and fines for supplying and inciting the use of drugs. The events surrounding the 1998 Tour de France were dramatic in themselves, but their true significance was in the strong intervention by the French public authorities reflecting, in large part, the growing frustration among some governments at the apparent inability or unwillingness of some of the major sports federations to take a leading role in challenging the deeply embedded culture of doping in sports such as professional cycling. The French action prompted similar parallel investigations in Belgium, Switzerland and Italy, and, more significantly, removed the inhibitions felt by some governments towards "interfering" in high-profile cycling competitions. In 1999, Italy's leading cyclist, Marco Pantani, was excluded from the Giro d'Italia because of a high haematocrit level (a possible indicator of the use of EPO) and was subsequently found guilty of "sporting fraud". Two years later, the Giro was subject to a massive police raid of riders' hotels in San Remo, providing further evidence of the increased concern of public authorities to challenge doping in sport.

The above episodes taken collectively help to illustrate the modern context for high performance sport, which can be characterised as an intensely commercialised and professionalised activity, in which governments and public authorities are taking an ever-increasing interest and where winning rather than taking part is considered by many athletes to be the only priority. In addition, there are a significant proportion of athletes who are willing to cheat in order to win or remain competitive at the élite level. To treat these characteristics of modern sport as representing in some way a fall from grace would be to grossly over-romanticise the past. As will be shown in Chapter 2, doping has a long history. The intention in the sections that follow is to identify the major elements of the social, economic and political context within which sport, doping and doping control takes place. It is only through an understanding of the context of modern sport that the problems facing those concerned with the effective development and implementation of anti-doping policy can be appreciated.

Sport, government and nationalism

There is a temptation to equate governmental intervention in sport for political purposes with the period of the cold war. It is also common in the west to suggest that governmental manipulation of sport was a phenomenon found only in the countries of the former communist bloc. Not only are both these assertions false but they also mislead in suggesting that governmental involvement in sport is a recent phenomenon. Indeed, it is likely that governmental involvement in sport is as old as organised sport itself. In their review of the ancient Olympics, Finley and Pleket argue that there was "hardly a limit to the ways in which the passion for athletics and for victories could be capitalised on for ends that were in a broad sense political".[1] One of the examples they give is the desire of rulers to enhance their status through association with successful athletes, a desire which led, on occasion, to attempts to "buy" or "transfer" élite athletes. Such behaviour has its modern parallels as an increasing number of sportspeople have been encouraged to change nationality. The South African athlete Zola Budd was granted UK citizenship in record time in order that she could compete for her new country in international athletics. There are also examples of Ethiopian-born athletes competing as naturalised Turks and Sudanese-born athletes competing as naturalised Qataris. Mohammed Mourhit, previously of Morocco, won bronze in the world 5 000 m cross-country title in 2000 in Seville for Belgium and then posed, wrapped in a Moroccan flag, with his former team-mate Salah Hissou.

Other examples of the use by politicians of successful sports events or sportspeople include the recruitment of élite athletes as ambassadors and the use of athletic achievement in the Olympics to provide the foundation for a future political career. The close involvement of the Spanish royal family in the Barcelona Olympic Games, the visit to Wembley stadium by Helmut Kohl for one of Germany's matches in the Euro '96 soccer competition, and the journey by Charles Haughey, the Irish Prime Minister, to Paris to be able to welcome Stephen Roche as he crossed the finish line to win the 1987 Tour de France all testify to the persistence of the Greek belief that association with successful athletes enhances political status and popularity. The decision by the British government to send Roger Bannister on a tour of the United States following his sub-four-minute mile is one of many post-war examples of the use of successful athletes as ambassadors.

For many governments, apart from occasional interventions to regulate sport, their most consistent involvement has been through support for school sport. However, few governments until very recently saw school sport as part of a broader sport strategy – for most governments, school sport was defined by its relationship to an education agenda which justified the inclusion of

1. Finley, M.I. & Pleket, H.W., *The Olympic Games: The First Thousand Years*, London: Chatto & Windus, 1976.

sport and physical education in the curriculum in terms of the beneficial impact on discipline and "character", on the one hand, or health and hygiene, on the other. It is only comparatively recently that governments have incorporated the funding of sport and recreation within a broadening conception of the role of the state, a conception that has extended beyond the regulation of sport to an acceptance of sport (and recreation) as an important part of the quality of life of developed societies.

For many developed industrial countries, even those such as the United States with a tradition of limited government, the provision of sport and recreation services by government has become gradually accepted. Almost uniformly across Europe and North America, local government has expanded the provision of sports facilities and, increasingly, the provision of staff acknowledging that sport and recreation are important elements in the range of local services. For most countries, the expansion of state involvement in sport and recreation services has been the result of a steadily widening conception of the role of the state to embrace a general responsibility for the quality of life and a much more broadly defined notion of welfare. Within democratic states, the interplay between political parties and sports interest groups has also been supported by the attractiveness to the electorate of high quality sport and recreation facilities, and international sporting achievement.

In some countries, the steady expansion of local provision has frequently taken place with the permission of central government rather than as a result of its explicit encouragement. However, for a number of other countries central government has frequently intervened to shape local provision where it defines sport as a useful policy instrument to solve specific social, economic or political problems. In many countries in western Europe, sport has been used as a palliative for a series of social problems including unemployment, juvenile delinquency and community fragmentation. In the United Kingdom, for example, sport has been seen as one of the solutions to the "problem of leisure" caused by the emergence of a generation of young males in the early post-war period who, by comparison to earlier generations, enjoyed relatively high wages and relatively short working hours which provided a substantial amount of free time.

The most notable change in the relationship between government and sport over the last fifty years or so has been the shift away from occasional involvement by the former in sport to a situation where governments are now an integral part of the sports infrastructure in almost all countries in Europe and in most countries throughout the world. Indeed, until the early 1960s sport was of only marginal interest to most governments prompting sporadic, though occasionally forceful, interventions in reaction to specific problems such as urban disorder, poor standards of health in urban areas or military requirements. Intervention by government was rarely the consequence of the recognition of sport and recreation as a distinct policy area. Nevertheless, in most countries there are a series of recurring themes that provide a significant degree of continuity and similarity in the pace and character of government involvement in the policy area.

One theme concerns the intervention by government to determine which sports are played and who can participate in them. Legislation was often used to preserve class privileges and property rights under the guise of humanitarianism. In seventeenth-century England, the Game Laws were used to restrict access to particular field sports such as hunting. Similar laws existed in France, up until the revolution, which reserved all forms of game hunting, with the exception of rabbits, for the nobility.[1] Later, in 1835, Britain passed the Cruelty to Animals Act, which clearly reflected the exercise of power to preserve aristocratic and middle-class privilege. The act outlawed bull- and bear-baiting, which were both predominantly urban working class "sports", but left the sports of the rich – fox and stag hunting – unrestricted. Similar examples could be drawn from the history of disputes over access to the countryside.[2] Apart from protecting class interests, governments have also been motivated by a sense of propriety and a view that, for example, the participation of women in sport contravened moral standards or the boundaries of religious acceptability. Indeed there are still many countries where governmental prohibitions on women's participation persist. Controlling gambling provides a further motive for many governments to intervene in sport.

A second theme in the development of sport policy is a sporadic concern with the health benefits of recreation and sport. In the nineteenth century, the stimulus for concern was the appalling conditions in the rapidly expanding industrial towns and cities. Most countries in Europe passed public health legislation that helped to lay the basis of an urban infrastructure for sport. The Baths and Wash-houses Act, which was passed by the UK Parliament in 1846, gave powers to local authorities to build facilities to improve the standards of personal hygiene of the urban poor. Later, in 1936, the Public Health Act gave explicit recognition to the recreational role of public baths by enabling local authorities to build baths exclusively designed for swimming. A similar pattern of the adaptation of public health legislation for sport and recreational purposes can be traced through the history of the development of urban open spaces and parkland. Created initially as the lungs of the new industrial cities, parkland rapidly became the location for pitches for soccer, cricket and rugby, bowling greens and tennis courts.[3] In the mid-twentieth

---

1. Holt, R., *Sport and Society in Modern France*, London: Macmillan, 1981, p. 18.
2. Donnelly, P., "The Paradox of Parks: The Politics of Recreational Land Use Before and After the Mass Trespass", *Leisure Studies*, Vol. 5.2, 1986; Shoard, M., *This Land is Our Land: The Struggle for Britain's Countryside*, London: Grafton Books, 1987; Holt, 1981, op. cit.; and Gorn, E.J. & Goldstein, W., *A Brief History of American Sports*, New York: Hill & Wang, 1993.
3. See Cuneen, C., "Hands Off Parks: The Provision of Parks and Playgrounds" in Roe, J. (ed.), *Twentieth-Century Sydney: Studies in Urban and Social History*, Sydney: Hale & Iremonger, 1980; Crantz, G., *The Politics of Park Design: A History of Urban Parks in America*, Cambridge, Mass: MIT Press, 1982.

century, government intervention reflected the growing concern among physical educators and health professionals with the consequences of an increasingly sedentary lifestyle. More recently, governments have become more aware of the health issues associated with increasing drug use in sport. As will be discussed in more detail below, governmental concern is not limited to the use of performance enhancing drugs in competitive sport, but also encompasses the increasing prevalence of drug use in activities such as body building and weight management.

A third motive for government involvement relates to the attempt by government to use sport as a means of social integration. In Britain, sport was seen as a vehicle for instilling discipline among urban working-class males with schools being encouraged in the early part of the twentieth century to include physical training and military drill as part of the curriculum. In the 1950s and early 1960s, the traditional fear of the destabilising potential of the urban working class was reflected in a series of reports which sought to address the problem of "too much leisure". The Wolfenden Report, for example, published in 1960, suggested that there was an association between the shortage of sports facilities and the rise in delinquency. More recently, the British Government responded to a series of serious urban riots in the early 1980s with the provision of more recreational facilities and the initiation by the Sports Council of the "Action Sport" project, which was designed to put sports leaders into local communities with the aim of fostering the integration of disaffected social groups. Public investment in sport has also been used in Northern Ireland in an attempt to bridge the sectarian divisions in the province although, in general, these policy efforts have only tended to fuel the exploitation of sport by sectarian interests. From the late 1960s, the Canadian Government has also attempted to use sport to bridge the gap between its anglophone and francophone communities with, at best, mixed results.

The expectation that sport can provide a focus for community regeneration or development is widespread. In France, for example, the Vichy Government of the wartime period identified sport, particularly gymnastics, as a means of "social discipline and a means of regenerating French youth".[1] An awareness of the "serious risk of social problems as a result of social tensions in the suburbs of some cities" led the French Government in the 1980s to seek solutions through investment in sports facilities and programmes.[2] Similar examples may be drawn from Australia and the United States where the strength of the "muscular Christian" movement in the nineteenth century established a strong association between sport and recreation, on the

1. Holt, 1981, op. cit., p. 58.
2. Poujol, G., "Leisure Politics and Policies in France" in Bramham, P. et al. (eds.), *Leisure Policy in Europe*, London: CAB International, 1993, p. 23.

one hand, and the maintenance of social integration and stability, on the other.[1]

Governments have also intervened in sport when there was a need to strengthen the military preparedness of the country. In the late 1930s and early 1940s, many governments introduced legislation or programmes in an attempt to improve the level of fitness among potential conscripts. This fourth policy motive is evident not just among the major European governments but also in Australia and Canada. For all these governments, their interest in sport was marginal to their preoccupation with reducing the high rejection rates of military recruits that they experienced during the first world war.[2]

A fifth, and particularly important contemporary, motive for government involvement in sport is the use of international sporting success as a convenient and relatively cheap way of enhancing the country's prestige and as a means of expanding the repertoire of diplomatic tools available to government. It is in relation to these two overlapping motives that the temptation is strongest among governments to sanction the use of drugs or, at least, to turn a blind eye to their use. Governments are increasingly aware of the high media profile of international sport and the potential of sport to reflect and enhance, but also to undermine, the prestige of the country. For many western European and North American countries the startling success of the then German Democratic Republic and Soviet Union in the early 1960s was a significant challenge to the comfortable assumptions of western sporting superiority and prompted a series of debates about the threat to national prestige resulting from communist domination of major sports events. The concern with the decline in sporting performance relative to the GDR and USSR was one of the factors that led the British Conservative Government to appoint an Advisory Sports Council in the mid-1960s and also prompted one of the rare interventions by the United States Federal Government in sport when, exasperated at the inability of the American sports bodies to organise themselves effectively for Olympic competition, it supported the passage by Congress of the Amateur Sports Act in 1978.

While the dramatic improvement in the performance of sportsmen and women from communist countries was important in providing a source of

---

1. See Boag, A., "Recreation Participation Survey: Activities Done Away from Home" in *Department of Arts, Sport, the Environment, Tourism and Territories*, Ideas for Australian Recreation: Commentaries on the Recreation Participation Surveys, Canberra: Australian Government Publishing Service, 1989; Cashman, R., *Paradise for Sport: The Rise of Organised Sport in Australia*, Melbourne: Oxford University Press, 1995: p. 57 for comments on Australian policy; Lewis, G., "The Muscular Christian Movement", *Journal of Health, Physical Education and Recreation*, No. 5, 1966; Gorn & Goldstein, 1993, op. cit.; Crantz, 1982, op. cit., p. 231; and Swanson, R.A., "The Acceptance and Influence of Play in American Protestantism", Quest, 11, 1968, regarding the United States.
2. See Houlihan, B., *Sport, Policy and Politics: A Comparative Analysis*, London: Routledge, 1997, Chapter 3.

motivation in many countries, for others the motivation lay more in the perceived need to enhance the profile of the country on the international stage. Especially for ex-colonies, the problems of establishing an identity within the international community were substantial. In Canada, for example, from the early 1960s the government, through the Fitness and Amateur Sport Act 1961, sought to achieve the dual aim of improving the level of fitness of the general population and meeting the government's "concern about national prestige and the success of élite athletes".[1] By the 1970s, the Canadian Government had established a dominant presence within the organisations responsible for élite sport development often using specialist task forces to target particular problems, events or sports. France adopted a similar interventionist policy when in 1984 the government decided to restructure the administration of sport and give responsibility for élite development to the Ministry of Youth and Sport.

One of the clearest examples of the deliberate exploitation of sport for purposes of international prestige or diplomatic advantage concerns the former German Democratic Republic (GDR). The example also provides one of the clearest illustrations of government-sanctioned drug use by athletes and is a powerful reminder of the extent to which governments are tempted to treat sport and sportspeople as instruments for the achievement of non-sports policy objectives. The nascent GDR Government quickly recognised the utility of sport in helping to fulfil the twin policy objectives of, first, obtaining diplomatic recognition as an independent state and not simply the soviet zone of Germany and, second, reconstructing east German culture following the nazi period.

The East German Government established a powerful sports bureaucracy under the control of the Deutscher Turn und Sports Bund (DTSB) whose long-serving president, Manfred Ewald, was also the president of the GDR's national Olympic committee. The initial emphasis of sport policy was on the contribution of sport to "the democratic revival of our nation"[2]. However, during the 1950s the emphasis began to shift from the development of mass participation in sport as a basis for civic re-education to the cultivation of élite success as a focus for the emergence of a new East German national identity. According to Sutcliffe, the élite sport policy was intended to realise three objectives: first, the achievement of diplomatic recognition; second, the enhancement of the status of the GDR within the communist bloc; and,

1. Franks, C.E.S. & Macintosh, D., "The Evolution of Federal Government Policies Toward Sport and Culture in Canada: A Comparison" in Theberge, N. & Donnelly, P., Sport and the Sociological Imagination, Fort Worth, Tex: Texas Christian University Press, 1984; Macintosh, D. & Hawes, D., Sport and Canadian Diplomacy, Toronto: McGill-Queen's University Press, 1994; and Helmes, R.C. "Ideology and Social Control in Canadian Sport: A Theoretical Review" in Sport and the Sociocultural Process, 3rd edn., Hart, M. & Birrell, W.C., Dubuque Iowa: Brown & Co., 1981.
2. Quoted in Hardman, K., "The Development of Physical Education in the German Democratic Republic, Physical Education Review, Vol. 3.2, 1980, p. 124.

third, the demonstration to non-communist countries of the superiority of the communist system.[1] Elite sport success and membership of sports organisations such as the IOC and the major international federations were central to the GDR strategy regarding diplomatic recognition. Sustained élite success by its "diplomats in tracksuits"[2] made it increasingly difficult for the Olympic movement and the major international federations to ignore the claims of the GDR to be treated as a country distinct from the Federal Republic.

Table 1.1: East Germany's Olympic Success: 1968-88

Year	Gold	Silver	Bronze	Position in medals table
1968	9	9	7	5th
1972	20	23	23	3rd
1976	40	25	25	2nd
1980	47	37	42	2nd (boycott by USA and others)
1984	Los Angeles games boycotted by GDR and others			
1988	37	35	29	2nd

From the late 1950s to the late 1980s, athletes from the GDR dominated many sports events producing, for example, seventy-seven European champions in track and field, and numerous Olympic champions (see Table 1.1). Elite success was established and maintained through the employment of almost 600 full-time coaches working within an elaborate structure of specialist sports schools and colleges at a cost estimated at approximately 1.5-2% of GDP. Following reunification, the performance of former GDR athletes declined sharply. In women's swimming, which the East Germans dominated for much of the post-war period, their success dipped abruptly in the early 1990s. Whereas in the 1986 World Championships, the GDR swimmers won twenty-four medals of which thirteen were gold, the performance of former East German women swimmers in the 1991 World Championships resulted in only six medals, none of which was gold. It is now widely acknowledged that systematic state-sanctioned drug abuse made a substantial contribution to the GDR's sporting (and diplomatic) success.[3] Such was the scale and the effectiveness of the doping programme that one senior GDR sports official

---

1. Sutcliffe, P., "The German Democratic Republic: an Overview" in Hardman, K. (ed.), *Physical Education and Sport under Communism,* Manchester: Manchester University Press, 1988.
2. Comment made by GDR officials to their athletes departing for competition abroad. Quoted in Strenk, A., "Diplomats in Tracksuits: The Role of Sports in the Foreign Policy of the German Democratic Republic", *Journal of Sport and Social Issues,* Spring/Summer, 4.1, 1980.
3. See Berendonk, B., *Doping Dokumente: Von der Forschung zum Betrug,* Berlin: Springer-Verlag, 1991. A summary of evidence is provided in English in Franke, W.W. & Berendonk, B., "Hormonal Doping and Androgenization of Athletes: A Secret Program of the German Democratic Republic Government", *Clinical Chemistry,* 43.7, 1997, pp. 1262-79.

was reported as observing that "Drug-taking was the only field in which the planned economy really functioned".[1]

A similar picture of substantial state use of sport as a diplomatic resource can be found within a wide number of countries. Peppard and Riordan,[2] referring to the former Soviet Union and the United States, illustrate the long history of government use of sport for diplomatic ends. Both countries used sport as a surrogate for their ideological rivalry, as a way of attempting to generate good relations with potential supporters and allies, and as a way of cementing links with their allies. Macintosh points to the role adopted by Canada in shaping British Commonwealth policy on South Africa over apartheid and the use of sports development aid to poorer countries as a way of achieving its leadership on policy within the Commonwealth Heads of Government Meetings [3]. Australia too was not averse to using sport for diplomatic purposes. For example, Prime Minister Menzies encouraged the Australian Cricket Board of Control to undertake a cricket tour of the West Indies in the mid-1950s in order to enhance his standing in the Commonwealth.[4] More recently, in October 2001, the French Government sought to use an international soccer match with Algeria as an opportunity to improve relations with the Algerian Government and also with the large immigrant population of Algerian origin now living in France. The match was the first time that the two countries had played each other, apart from a low level game in the Mediterranean Games in the 1970s, in the forty years since Algeria won its independence as a result of a long and bitter war. The French sports minister, Marie-Georges Buffet, and Prime Minister, Lionel Jospin, attended the match, which Mourad Bouchemia, head of the Algerian Football Association, said was "a match that goes way, way beyond a simple sporting encounter" (Guardian, 6 October 2001, p. 21). Unfortunately, the hope that the match might be a step towards better international and community relations was undermined as the match was abandoned twelve minutes from time and riot police were called in to restore order in the stadium. The problems at the match were a reminder that while sporting contact can build upon already improving relations it can also provide confirmation of just how poor existing diplomatic or community relations are.

The final example of the range of motives that prompt government intervention in sport concerns the contribution that sport can make to economic

1. Quoted in The Times, newspaper (UK), 16 January 1991, p. 40.
2. Peppard, V. & Riordan, J., Playing Politics: Soviet Sport Diplomacy to 1992, Greenwich, Conn: JAI Press Inc; see also Hulme, D.L. Jnr., "The Political Olympics: Moscow, Afghanistan, and the 1980 US Boycott", New York: Praeger, 1990; and Riordan, J., "Soviet Sport and Soviet Foreign Policy" in Lowe, B., Kanin, D.B. & Strenk, A. (eds.), Sport and International Relations, Champaign, Ill: Stipes, 1978.
3. Macintosh, D., "Sport and the State: The Case of Canada" in Landry, F. et al. (eds.), Sport... The Third Millennium, Sainte-Foy: Les Presse de l'Université de Laval, 1991; see also Macintosh, D. & Hawes, D., 1994, op. cit.
4. Cashman, R., 1995, op. cit.

regeneration. During the economic depression of the 1930s, the United States and Canada provided the clearest examples of the development of public works projects as a form of employment generation many of which made valuable contributions to the sports infrastructure of communities. However, the benefits for sport and recreation were inadvertent rather than part of a planned sports resources strategy. More recently, sports investment has been seen by governments as making a valuable contribution to both the local and the national economies. At the local level, stadium development has, for many years, featured as an element of a number of urban regeneration schemes.[1] Crantz argues that in the USA, urban parks and recreation facilities were "advocated as a way to revitalise neighbourhoods economically and stimulate the surrounding business district".[2] Macintosh, commenting on the Canadian situation, noted that both the federal and provincial governments were providing major subsidies for prestigious stadium developments on the grounds that the policy "provides jobs and incentives for profits for the private sector as well as stimulating the local economy by bringing tourists and spectators to the community".[3]

In the United States and Canada in particular, but also in Britain, Australia, Spain, Japan, Germany and France, the longer established motive of civic "boosterism" (the development of major sports facilities as civic status symbols) has been augmented by a recognition of the potential economic return of major stadium and indoor sports facility development. At a national level, the perception of hosting major sports events as a drain on public expenditure and as requiring substantial and often long-term subsidy has been replaced by regarding events such as the soccer World Cup and the Olympic Games as significant sources of inward investment in the form of tourism expenditure and as a net benefit to the economy. Ever since the Los Angeles Olympic Games generated a surplus of over 220 million dollars and particularly since Barcelona used the hosting of the Olympics as a vehicle for regenerating the city, the number of cities bidding to host future Games has steadily increased.[4] It is also argued that the "economic impulse" stimulated by hosting the Games helps to create not only short-term, but also long-term

1. See for example, Baade, R. & Dye, R., "Sports Stadiums and Area Development: A Critical Review", *Economic Development Quarterly,* 2 (August), 1988, pp. 265-75; Johnson, A.T., "The Sports Franchise Relocation Issue and Public Policy Responses" in Johnson, A.T. & Frey, J.H. (eds.), *Government and Sport: The Public Policy Issues,* Totowa, NJ: Rowman and Allenheld, 1985; Johnson, A.T., *Minor League Baseball and Local Economic Development,* Chicago: University of Illinois Press, 1993; Reiss, S.A., *City Games: The Evolution of American Urban Society and the Rise of Sports,* Urbana, Ill: University of Illinois Press, 1989, for discussions of the phenomenon in the United States; and McCormack, G., "The Price of Affluence: The Political Economy of Japanese Leisure", *New Left Review,* No. 189, 1991, pp. 121-34, for a discussion of Japan.
2. Crantz, 1982, op. cit., p. 208.
3. Macintosh, D., 1991, op. cit., p. 271.
4. Preuss, H., *Economics of the Olympic Games: Hosting the Games from 1972 to 2000,* Sydney: Walla Walla Press, 2000.

23

employment.[1] As Table 1.2 shows, the investment in sports and general urban infrastructure can be considerable.

Table 1.2: Urban investment through the Olympic Games[2]

Rome 1960	New sports facilities, roads, water supply system and airport
Tokyo 1964	New sports facilities; two new metro lines; new road link plus twenty-two other road schemes
Munich 1972	280 hectares of land reclaimed for new sports facilities; historic quarter pedestrianised; improvements to roads, metro, underground car parking
Montreal 1976	New Olympic Park and village; 20 km of new metro; new roads, hotels and airport
Moscow 1980	Twelve new sports facilities; new hotels and airport terminal; new television and communications centre
Seoul 1988	New sports facilities and Olympic Village; three new metro lines; forty-seven new bus routes; new arts centre, Classical Music Institute, and museum; refurbishment of shrines; renewed refuse collection system and water supply system; de-pollution of the Han and Chamsil Rivers
Barcelona 1992	Fifteen new sports venues and new airport link; new ring road and railway station; new beaches and marina; office development and conference centre; Olympic village which became general housing as part of revitalised historic quarter; energy conservation scheme
Sydney 2000	New sports facilities on reclaimed land; Olympic village for later housing use

In Britain, it is estimated that the annual value of sports tourism to the economy is £1.5 billion, Van Puffelen et al., estimated that sport and sports events contributed 1.8% to the Dutch economy, while it has been estimated that the Sydney Olympics will help reduce Australia's current account deficit by 1.25%.[3] For the city of Sheffield, the first round matches of the Euro '96 soccer competition generated around £5.8 million of expenditure. It was calculated that the 26 000 supporters who visited the city during the ten-day period spent between £50 and £100 each day. It is estimated by the

1. See footnote 4, p. 25 *ante*. Ibid.
2. Sources: Collins, M., "Sport, Recreation and the Environment" in Houlihan, B. (ed.), *Sport, Politics and Social Issues,* London: Sage, forthcoming; Essex, S. & Chalkley, B., "Olympic Games: Catalyst of Urban Change", *Leisure Studies,* Vol. 17, 1998, pp. 187-206; and Preuss, 2000, op. cit.
3. Van Puffelen, F., Reijnen, J. & Velthuisjen, J.W., De Macro Economische Betekenis Van Sport, Stvhting voor Economisch Onderzoek der Universitient Van Amsterdam, Netherlands, 1988. Quoted in Robinson, L., "The Business of Sport" in Houlihan, B., *Sport, Politics and Social Issues,* London: Sage, forthcoming.

Australian Tourist Commission that the Sydney Olympic Games would attract an additional 2.1 million visitors between 1994 and 2000 due to the city's raised profile and contribute over 4 billion Australian dollars to an aspect of the economy which already, in 1993, accounted for 11% of exports. This expectation is based on assessments of Australia's previous experience in bidding for and hosting major sports events. For example, it was estimated that the hosting of the 1987 America's Cup generated expenditure of 464 million Australian dollars and the equivalent of 9 500 full-time jobs. Even Brisbane's failed bid for the 1992 Olympic Games provided a significant boost to the local economy as it focused "world-wide attention on Australia, its tourism potential, its excellent sporting facilities and its professional sports administration".[1]

With the growing perception that the hosting of major events is no longer a financial burden has come the parallel perception that the chances of a successful bid are greater if a country has a strong sporting élite. The desire to host major events thus becomes one more pressure on national sports organisations and government agencies to "guarantee" élite success. One clear policy adopted by an increasing number of governments is to fund the establishment of an élite training centre. The Australian Institute of Sport at Canberra has become the model for many countries and similar centres now exist or are planned in Canada (Ottawa), the United States (Colorado Springs), the United Kingdom (a number of regional centres), France (Paris), the Netherlands (Arnhem) and Ireland (Limerick). Unfortunately, a number of these centres, most notably those in Ottawa and Canberra, have been tainted with drug abuse scandals, reflecting in large part, the intense pressure of expectations that these élite institutes are under.

With the ending of the cold war, there were grounds for expecting that the "peace dividend" of declining public expenditure on weapons and the armed forces would be matched by a similar decline in public expenditure in surrogate areas of superpower competition such as sport. No such decline took place. Indeed, over the last twelve years government investment in élite sport has increased in all the major industrialised countries indicating the continuing attractiveness and adaptability of sport. Governments continue to use sport to help achieve a range of non-sporting and occasionally sporting objectives and have moved from a position where they were content to approach sport policy development and implementation through a process of consultation or negotiation with relatively independent national sports organisations to a position where governments are much more directive and also more likely to introduce state agencies into the policy area. One concern must be the capacity of national sports organisations to remain effective actors in the policy process; a problem compounded by the increasing prominence of commercial interests in sport.

---

1. Australia's Department of Sport, Recreation and Tourism, *Annual report 1986-87*, 1987, p. 49.

Sport, business and money

The intensification of governmental interest and involvement in sport policy is matched only by the similar surge in involvement in sport by business, a development which has brought clear benefits to sport but also problems. It is the growth in the involvement of media businesses that best illustrates the increasing commercialisation of sport. Sport has always been an important element in the schedules of radio and television companies but it is from the mid-1960s that the relationship began to change from one of considerable mutual benefit to one best described as mutual interdependence or symbiosis. The transformation of the relationship is partly the result of technological innovation (the development of geostationary satellites and the consequent capacity for live broadcasts of foreign sports events), partly the effective marketing of international, and especially Olympic, sport as national or ideological clashes, and partly as a result of the success of the Olympics in attracting a huge audience, but one with the higher proportion of female, younger and more affluent viewers sought by advertisers.[1] The importance of sports to the major broadcasting companies is easily illustrated through an examination of the escalation in fees paid for the television rights to the Olympic Games. The European broadcasting companies negotiating through the European Broadcasting Union (EBU) paid $670 000 for the rights to the 1960 Games in Rome; $1.7 million for the 1972 rights; $19 million in 1984; and $90 million for the rights to the Barcelona Games in 1992. There is currently no sign that the fee ceiling has been reached as the EBU agreed a figure of $350 million for the Sydney 2000 Games as part of a $1.442 billion deal securing the broadcasting rights for the five Winter and Summer Games between 2000 and 2008. A similar escalation in the scale of fees that television companies have been willing to pay is evident in the United States where the rights to the 1960 Rome Games were purchased for a mere $400 000. By 1972, the fees had increased to $225 million, rising to $401 million in 1992, and most recently to $793 million for the Sydney Games and $2.3 billion for the 2004, 2006 and 2008 Games.[2]

It is not only in the rapid increase in broadcasting fees that the greater prominence of business in sport is evident. Sponsorship is claimed to be a $20 billion global industry involving contracts with individual athletes, clubs, venues and leagues.[3] Multi-million pound sponsorship contracts for a small number of élite sportspeople are no longer a rarity. Tiger Woods received $40 million to promote Nike while Boris Becker reputedly received £24 million from Puma to promote its products. Soccer clubs are able to negotiate lucrative

1. Klatell, D.A. & Marcus, N., *Sports for Sale: Television, Money and the Fans,* New York: Oxford University Press, 1988; Geraghty, C., Simpson, P. & Whannel, G., "Tunnel Vision: Television's World Cup" in Tomlinson, A. & Whannel, G. (eds.), *Off the Ball: The Football World Cup,* London: Pluto Press, 1986.
2. Neither the figures for the sale of the US rights nor those for the sale of the European rights have been moderated to take account of inflation.
3. Gratten, C. & Taylor, P., *Economics of Sport and Recreation,* London: E & FN Spon, 2000.

sponsorship deals with major companies such as Opel, who paid £2.2 million to advertise on the shirts of the German soccer club Bayern Munich,[1] and Vodaphone, who concluded a £28 million deal with Manchester United. Sponsorship of complete leagues is also common with the brewers Bass sponsoring the English soccer Premier League for four years at a cost of £12 million. While sponsorship is estimated to be growing at about 10% each year, the distribution of income is highly uneven in terms of the sports that benefit, the level of sport that benefits and the regions of the world that benefit. Some sports are less attractive to sponsors. Soccer, track and field, motor racing, tennis and golf are among the main beneficiaries of sponsorship and television revenue. In Britain, tobacco sponsorship of field hockey ended because the sport failed to attract a mass television audience. Squash was dropped by the tobacco company Benson and Hedges, one of the major sponsors of sport, because the image of the sport was considered inappropriate for the product. As the sales promotion manager for Benson and Hedges observed "I always felt I was in the wrong place. You could have a cigarette when playing golf or cricket and even the hockey crowd were a cosmopolitan bunch who enjoyed the odd drink and a cigarette. Squash was more obsessive".[2]

Even those sports that are regular beneficiaries of sponsorship find that business is highly selective in the aspects of the sport they will support. In track and field, finding sponsorship for youth competition, regional events and even national championships is difficult. Sponsors are also generally keener on supporting sprint and middle distance track events than field events and generally prefer men's to women's events. More worrying is the fact that with one or two minor exceptions, sponsorship flows to sports, events and athletes in the more affluent parts of the world. Athletes in poorer countries often have to rely on the meagre sports development budgets of Olympic Solidarity ($121.9 million for the period 1997-2000) or the major federations such as the IAAF. Alternatively, poorer athletes rely on the provision of sports scholarships, often provided by universities in the United States or, if they play soccer, transfer to European and Japanese clubs.

According to the IAAF, the gap between rich and poor countries in relation to sport has three primary dimensions: élite programmes, development planning and programmes for mass participation. In addition, there are also substantial deficiencies in the areas of sports science and medicine, qualified coaches and officials, equipment and facilities and opportunities for competition.[3] Very few countries are able to offer a substantial proportion of the full

---

1. In addition to its sponsorship of Bayern Munich, Opel also sponsors the soccer clubs AC Milan and Paris St Germain, and the Swedish national soccer team as well as being involved in sponsorship of basketball and motorsports.
2. Quoted in Wilson, N., *The Sports Business: The Men and the Money*, London: Judy Piatkus, 1988, p. 163.
3. Wangemann, B., Report to the IAAF Development Department, London: IAAF, 1988.

range of summer Olympic sports with the poorer countries frequently offering only one or two to any significant level of competition. The degree of inequality of participation at the highest levels of competition is easily illustrated by reference to recent Olympic Games. At the Los Angeles Games in 1984 only sixteen countries entered athletes in sixteen or more sports while ninety countries had athletes participating in five or fewer events, of which seventy-eight were developing countries. The pattern was repeated at Seoul where sixty-three national Olympic committees, overwhelmingly in developing countries, entered athletes in fewer than ten events.[1]

The striking flood of money into sport in the richer developed countries and the equally striking lack of even the most basic sports infrastructure for the majority of the world's population have consequences for doping and anti-doping policy. For the rich countries, leagues, clubs and athletes the fear of failure and the loss of the attendant sponsorship puts enormous pressure on athletes, and their coaches and managers to use whatever measures necessary to sustain their current high level of success. Few of the major commercial sports seem prepared to address the issue or use their resources to give a lead on the issue of doping, for example through education and the provision of information. Rather than necessarily indicating a lack of interest in the issue, it might also be a reflection of the tenuous control that a number of federations, both domestic and international, exert over their commercial clubs. The reluctance of clubs to co-operate is often the result of their unwillingness to risk the loss of the services of star team members through suspension. Clubs consequently will exert pressure for financial penalties or short bans even for serious offences such as drug taking. This is most clearly the case in the United States where commercialisation is integral to most sport and where the major sports leagues including basketball and football have been most noticeable in their reluctance to impose substantial bans on drug abusers. However, much the same may also be said of the increasingly commercial English soccer where there is a preference for regarding positive drug tests as a signal for counselling and medical advice albeit during a period of suspension for the player rather than a firmer punishment which would be likely in other sports.

A further consequence of the wealth now available in some sports is that athletes, and their coaches and managers will fight hard to avert any threat to their income from sport. One of the most significant problems facing national sports organisations and their international federations is the risk of costly legal defences of their decisions on positive doping results. Most national sports organisations (NSOs), even in affluent countries, are not rich bodies and few could withstand the imposition of modest damages should an

---

1. Anthony, D., "The North-South and East-West Axes of Development in Sport: Can the Gaps be Bridged?" in Landry et al., 1991, op. cit.

appeal against a ban be successful and it is debatable whether many have the resources to underwrite the cost of a sustained legal challenge.

Although the situation of athletes from poorer countries may appear different, it is in many respects the same as that of their rich counterparts. However, for those on sports scholarships or with contracts with European or Japanese soccer clubs, the fear is the loss of the opportunity to break through into the élite or to retain membership once it has been achieved. As a result of these pressures, the use of drugs is not a problem confined to a particular group of athletes but is a ubiquitous problem in modern commercialised sport.

Sport, health and personal glory

The rapid growth and intensification of governmental and commercial interest in sport has added greatly to the pressures facing sportspeople in high-level competition. Yet, significant though these changes undoubtedly are, there have been other developments which have been equally critical in shaping the character of modern sport. Of especial note is the growth in the cult of the body. Generally, it has been possible to equate participation in sport with good health and fitness. There have of course been notable qualifications to this loose equation. There has been a long-standing concern about the level of risk of injury in some, usually full-contact sports such as American football, rugby union and rugby league. There is also an emerging concern with the deliberate over-training of athletes especially in those sports, such as female gymnastics, where the most intensive period of training and competition takes place during or before puberty.

More recently the ability to generalise about the complementarity of sports participation and good health has been questioned by those social analysts who see sport as increasingly incorporated into a consumer culture which encourages a high degree of self-absorption and a pre-occupation with an idealised version of femininity and masculinity. Much of the recent analysis focuses on the effects of modernity on the female body and the way in which self-perception of women is influenced by a culture and by a sports and leisure industry that values women's bodies in terms of male desire.[1] The current western cultural stigmatisation of fatness is frequently seen as being the root cause of eating disorders such as anorexia nervosa and responsible for the growth in obsessive concerns with fitness. As Rojek claims, "Western culture associates fat bodies with indiscipline and indulgence; by contrast, thin bodies symbolise asceticism and self-control".[2] Being thin and fit is one way of publicly demonstrating one's "social and moral worth"[3] – one's right to a

1. Boskind-Lodhal, M., "Cinderella Stepsisters: A Feminist Perspective on Anorexia Nervosa", *Signs*, Vol. 2.2, pp. 342-56; and MacLeod, S., *The Art of Starvation*, London: Verso, 1981.
2. Rojek, C., *Decentring Leisure: Rethinking Leisure Theory*, London: Sage, 1995, p. 63.
3. Hughes, B., "Medicalised Bodies" in Hancock, P. et al., *The Body, Culture and Society: An Introduction*, Buckingham: Open University Press, 2000.

place in modern society – with the wearing of sports clothing in non-sporting situations being a further way of demonstrating one's credentials for membership of today's world. Although the feminist analysis has its critics, there is a more general acceptance that within contemporary culture the image of women's bodies constructed by men, a climate of narcissism and a more general idealisation of the female body has helped to foster an increase in participation in fitness activities that is motivated less by a desire for empowerment and the building of self-esteem or a desire to be fit to play sport, and more by an inability to cope with the pressures of contemporary culture.[1]

The incidence of sports participation as pathological behaviour is not limited to women. Although less well researched, it is clear that men are not immune to the pressures of modern society. For men, the development of an idealised physique is an expression of empowerment and self-confidence within a society that, on the one hand, has given economic and political priority to the individual over society but, on the other hand, appears increasingly dismissive of individual worth. For an increasing, yet still small, number of young men the path to their desired physique involves not only hours on the fitness equipment of the gymnasium but also the use of anabolic steroids. Although the volume of empirical data is small those that exist indicate that a surprisingly high proportion of steroid users have a cosmetic and non-sport motive. In a 1988 study by Pope et al., 2% out of a total sample of 1 010 college students admitted taking steroids.[2] More interestingly, just under half (42%) of the steroid users claimed they were taking the drug for the sake of appearance or body building. George reports that in Britain there is "anecdotal evidence to suggest that anabolic steroid abuse is higher in areas with a macho culture, ample male leisure time (that is, unemployment), low self-esteem and proximity to … a suitable location to parade the results of your body building".[3]

While the emergence of steroid abusers who take the drugs for reasons of vanity and self-esteem rather than to gain a competitive edge may be deemed a further consequence of the spread of drug abuse in sport, it also needs to be seen in the context of an increasingly pill-dependent society. It is unrealistic to expect athletes to insulate themselves from a culture which expects pharmacists and doctors to be able to supply medicines for all their ills whether physical or psychological. It is also unrealistic to ignore the importance of legitimate drugs in the intensely scientific training regimes of most, if not all, élite athletes in the 1990s. The use of dietary supplements and

1. Bruch, H., *The Golden Cage: The Enigma Anorexia Nervosa,* Cambridge, Mass: Harvard University Press, 1977.
2. Pope, H.G., Katz, D.L. & Champoux, R., "Affective and Psychotic Symptoms Associated with Anabolic Steroid Use", *American Journal of Psychiatry,* Vol. 51, 1988, pp. 487-90.
3. George, A., "The Anabolic Steroids and Peptide Hormones" in Mottram, D.R. (ed.), *Drugs in Sport,* 2nd edn., 1996.

vitamins is routine, and the willingness of athletes and their coaches to experiment with untested herbal concoctions defies common sense but also indicates the desire, indeed desperation, of many athletes to find a means of giving them an edge over their rivals. As Lipsyte wryly notes, "By the time [athletes] have made the pros, most athletes have been given so many pills, salves, injections, potions, by amateur and pro coaches, doctors and trainers, to pick them up, cool them down, kill pain, enhance performance, reduce anxiety, that there is isn't much they won't sniff, spread, stick in or swallow to get bigger or smaller, or to feel gooooood (sic)".[1]

Conclusion

The feeling of shock that most sports enthusiasts experience when another drug scandal is revealed is not simply the reaction to an example of duplicitous behaviour but is also a feeling of being personally cheated: the private emotions that a spectacular medal winning performance generated have been publicly betrayed. It is possible to mock the disillusioned spectator or participant as being naive in expecting all sportspeople to adhere to a higher moral code than the rest of society. However, such a response would be churlish as it would fail to acknowledge the salience of sport in modern society and to belittle the motives of the majority who devote their time to sport, much of it given without financial reward, as coaches, administrators and participants to promote sport as an oasis within society where a higher morality can be aspired to. Yet while such aspirations are laudable they must be tempered by an awareness of the changes that have taken place in the context of sport over the last thirty years. While it is still possible to expect sportspeople to subscribe to high moral standards, it is unreasonable to expect them to be immune from social change. The challenge facing sports organisations and governments in attempting to eradicate drug abuse is an increasingly daunting one. As will be shown in the chapters that follow, governments are often ambiguous regarding the question of drug abuse, and commercial interests frequently appear content to ignore the issue. Against this background, sports drug agencies have to cope with increasingly sophisticated drugs, the rapid growth in élite competition and a high level of geographical mobility of sportspeople.

---

1. Lipsyte, R., "Baseball and Drugs", *The Nation,* 25 May 1985, p. 613.

Chapter 2

The evolution of doping

Early examples of drug use

It is a commonplace to state that doping, along with other forms of cheating, is not new. Yet, it seems necessary to preface any discussion with this reminder as there is a tendency for many involved in sport as spectators, participants, coaches or officials to imagine a past sporting world dominated by the noble of spirit and the pure of heart. The long history of doping should put modern policy makers on their guard against seeking an easy solution to the problem. But the history of doping is also instructive not just in demonstrating the continuity or intractability of the problem. Of equal importance is the value of history in making clear the modern dimensions of the problem which require ingenuity and commitment from policy makers.

In general, wherever and whenever the outcome of a sporting competition has involved status, money or other similar rewards, attempts have been made to seek an advantage through doping. From the standpoint of the beginning of the twenty-first century, the methods and substances seem crude and of questionable value but the motive provides an indelible link between the centuries. In the third century BC, Greek athletes were taking varieties of mushroom to improve their performance,[1] and were also reported as training on special diets which included dried figs. Egyptians had confidence in the properties of the ground rear hooves of the Abyssinian ass while Roman gladiators were reported to take stimulants to overcome fatigue.[2]

More recently during the nineteenth century, there were many accounts of athletes using a variety of substances to enhance their performance including strychnine, nitro-glycerine, opium, alcohol and caffeine.[3] In the mid-nineteenth century, there were reports of competitive swimmers in Amsterdam taking an opium-based drug. In 1869, there were reports of cycling coaches preparing heroin and cocaine mixtures for their riders in order to increase their endurance during continuous 144-hour races. Belgian cyclists were reported to have taken ether-soaked tablets, the French caffeine tablets while the British allegedly relied on a range of drugs including strychnine, heroin, brandy and cocaine as well as inhaling pure oxygen.[4] Throughout the

---

1. Puffer, J., "The Use of Drugs in Swimming", *Clinical Sports Medicine,* Vol. 5.77, 1986.
2. Finley & Pleket, 1976, op. cit.; Hanley, D.F., "Drug and Sex Testing: Regulations for International Competition", *Clinical Sports Medicine,* Vol. 2, 1983, pp. 13-17; Meer, J., "Drugs and Sports" in Snyder, S.H. (ed.), *The Encyclopedia of Psychoactive Drugs,* New York: Chelsea House, 1987.
3. Puffer, 1986, op. cit.
4. Voy, R., *Drugs, Sport and Politics: The Inside Story about Drug Use in Sport and its Political Cover-up,* Champaign, Ill: Leisure Press, 1991.

last twenty years of the nineteenth century, there were rumours of fatalities due to the use of some very dangerous drugs such as strychnine which tested the limits of human tolerance.[1] However, despite the clear risks, reports of doping continued to appear throughout the remaining years of the century.

Drug use in the twentieth century

Apart from the American athlete Tom Hicks' infamous involvement in the marathon at the 1904 St Louis Olympics where he collapsed following the use of a strychnine-brandy cocktail, the early part of the twentieth century was not marked by any major escalation or development in drug use. There continued to be examples of the use of crude drugs and preparations often administered more in hope than with any certainty that they would aid performance. In the 1930s, for example, there were reports of athletes using a mixture of powdered gelatine and orange juice in the expectation of enhanced performance.[2] The next phase in the history of drug use came later in the century when the synthesis and mass production of drugs became more common (see Table 2.1). However, the crucial catalyst for the widespread use of drugs in sport came with the extensive and frequently unregulated experimentation with drugs during the second world war. The use of amphetamines and steroids in particular by the military not only greatly increased scientific knowledge about the properties of the various drugs but also demonstrated the widespread opportunities for the use of the drugs outside a therapeutic context.

Amphetamines

In the early post-war period evidence about drug abuse continued to accumulate, as indeed did the deaths. Amphetamine and its derivatives rapidly replaced the earlier cruder preparations, such as strychnine, as the preferred drug of athletes, especially those involved in explosive and endurance events. Not surprisingly, throughout the 1950s cyclists continued to be identified as the main group of athletes thought to be heavily involved in drug abuse, though drug taking was also considered to be rife in professional boxing and several speed-skaters became ill through the over-use of amphetamines during the 1952 Helsinki Olympics. But it was not until a series of deaths in the 1960s that sports organisations were prompted to move from a stance of condemnation and dismay to a more interventionist position. In 1960, the Danish cyclist Knud Jensen collapsed and died at the Rome Olympic Games during the 175 km team time trials following his use of

---

1. Dyment, P.G., "Drug Use and the Adolescent Athlete", *Pediatric Annals,* 13 : 602, 1984. Donohoe, T. & Johnson, N., *Foul Play : Drug Abuse in Sports,* Oxford : Basil Blackwell, 1986, p. 3, suggest that Linton did not die during or close to competition but in fact died many years later from typhoid.
2. Asken, M.J., *Dying to Win : The Athlete's Guide to Safe and Unsafe Drugs in Sport,* Washington DC : Acropolis Books, 1988.

Table 2.1 : History of drug use and doping practices in sport (major drugs and practices only)

Drug	Approximate date of discovery	First use in sport	Extent of use	Major sports affected	Peak of use	Current level of use
Amphetamines	1920s	1940s	Heavy use between the mid 1950s and the late 1970s	Cycling, American football	Late 1960s to early 1980s	Light, due to ease of identification and availability of alternatives
Ephedrine and related stimulants	c1940s	1970s	Heavy use from mid 1970s to the present	Most Olympic sports and many major team sports	Yet to be reached	Heavy
Caffeine	Pre-19th century	Early 19th century	Heavy in 19th century then declined, only to increase in use from 1970s to the present day in combination with ephedrine and as a diuretic	Most Olympic sports and many major team sports	19th century, then from the mid 20th century to the present	Heavy, but mainly in conjunction with other drugs
Blood doping and rEPO	Blood doping 1970s rEPO Mid 1980s	1970s / Late 1980s	Moderate / Light in later 1980s but rising (rEPO)	Endurance sport such as long distance cycling, running, swimming and cross-country skiing	1980s / Still rising (rEPO)	Moderate / Moderate but rising (rEPO)
Barbiturates	Early 20th century	1970s	Moderate	Modern Pentathlon (shooting)	1970s	Light
Beta-blockers	1960s	1970s	Moderate use in small number of sports	Shooting, archery and snooker	Late 1980s	Moderate, but use not completely banned by IFs and IOC
Anabolic steroids and anabolic agents	1930s	1950s	Heavy between the late 1960s and the late 1980s	Most Olympic sports and many major team sports	Mid 1980s	Heavy
Cocaine	Pre-17th century	Late 19th century	Heavy between the late 1960s and the present day	American football	1980s	Moderate
Human growth hormone	Mid 1980s	Late 1980s	Moderate and mainly confined to the United States of America (?)	Body building and a similar range of sports that attract anabolic steroid users	Yet to be reached	Small but rising
Diuretics	Synthetic diuretics 1960s	1970s ?	Moderate to heavy in early 1970s	Weight related sports, but all sports when used as a drug to flush others out of the body	mid 1970s	Light, due to ease of identification.
Genetic manipulation	1970s	No confirmed cases	Rumours and speculation, but no evidence of use	Potential to affect all sports	Any significant level of use of genetic manipulation is still five to ten years away.	None to negligible

35

amphetamines and nicotine acid. Jensen's two team-mates, who had taken the same mixture, also collapsed but later recovered in hospital. Tom Simpson's death in the 1967 Tour de France brought on by excessive use of methyl amphetamine was caught on television and dramatically raised the profile of the issue in Britain. Simpson's death was followed the next year by the death of the French cyclist Yves Mottin a few days after he had won a gruelling cross-country cycling event.[1] Despite the focus of attention on the implications of the growing use of amphetamines and the increasing number of fatalities, there was also a continuing use of heroin and a steady increase in the number of deaths. The hurdler Dick Howard died at the Rome Olympics from heroin; the same drug that was found in the body of the boxer Billy Bello, who died three years later.

By the mid-1930s scientific experimentation with amphetamines had resulted in its adoption for therapeutic use, for example in the treatment of narcolepsy and, though less successfully, in the treatment of nasal congestion and obesity,[2] but had also alerted the German military authorities to the potential uses of the drug in overcoming fatigue during combat. Evidence of the use of amphetamines in sport began to emerge in the late 1950s with the drug beginning to become fashionable among young people as a social drug in the mid-1960s. As with all attempts to plot accurately the development and extent of drug use, the history of the spread of amphetamine use in sport must be tentative. A 1984 study in the United States found that 8% of university students admitted using amphetamines within the previous twelve months with one-third of the total using the drug to enhance their sports performance.[3] Use was especially high among football players who, in the 1970s, replaced cyclists as the groups of athletes giving greatest cause for concern. According to Mandell et al., approximately two-thirds of the sample of professional football players interviewed had used amphetamines, half of whom admitted to regular use. Dosages ranged from 5 mg to 200 mg per game: dosages at the mid to upper end of this range have been associated with manic behaviour.[4] In 1984, Dyment claimed that "amphetamines are probably the principal drug misuse problem in athletics", but the early to mid-1980s probably marked the high point of abuse as the drug began to be

---

1. It is interesting that the long association between drug use in general and amphetamine use in particular in cycling has not led to a significant discussion about the nature of some events in the sport, such as the Tour de France and Giro d'Italia. It can be argued that the unrelenting intensity of endurance cycling makes it difficult for athletes to participate without assistance from drugs. In other words, it is the sport which is unnatural rather than the drug-using competitors.

2. George, A.J., "Central Nervous System Stimulants", *Baillière's Clinical Endrocrinology and Metabolism,* Vol. 14.1, 2000; Delbeke, F.T., From Amanita Muscaria to Somatotropine: The Doping Story, *Biology of Sport,* Vol. 17.2., 2000.

3. Anderson, W.A. & McKeag, D.B., The Substance Use and Abuse Habits of College Student Athletes, Research Paper #2: General Findings, Michigan: Michigan State University, 1985.

4. Mandell, A.J., Stewart, K.D. & Russo, P.V., "The Sunday Syndrome: From Kinetics to Altered Consciousness", *Federal Proceedings,* Vol. 40: 2 693, 1981.

replaced by caffeine and steroids and also as it became much more easily detectable.[1]

Although drug use has been accused of altering the character of some sports, it is probably more accurate to argue that drug use has exaggerated certain aspects of particular sports, often those aspects that already give rule makers greatest cause for concern. American football is a good example as it is a sport that many claim has been seriously undermined by the extensive abuse of drugs, such as amphetamines and steroids. At its best, American football as a contact sport relies on a combination of athleticism, creativity, determination and bravery for its excitement. Yet, many clubs and sportsmen involved in the sport have trodden a fine line between athleticism and aggression, creativity and formula, determination and brutality, and between bravery and recklessness. In the early years of the sport, one of the most pressing problems facing the nascent governing body for the sport was the need to control the level of violence. The high number of deaths in the 1905 season prompted President Theodore Roosevelt to call a meeting in an attempt to persuade the three major universities, Harvard, Yale and Princeton, to reform the sport. The impact of the presidential intervention was negligible as football remained an, at times, harsh and brutal sport fulfilling the role in American society of "defining and testing physical and psychological masculinity ... Though football carried fewer risks than military combat, players invested it with many of the same feelings".[2] Almost one hundred years later, little has changed in the social significance of the sport or in the spirit in which it is played. The effect that access to drugs has had is to make it more difficult for the sport's governing authority to ensure that the attributes of athleticism, creativity, determination and bravery are protected from those who aspire only to aggression, formula, brutality and recklessness. Mandell recounts in graphic detail the huge quantities of amphetamines taken by players on a regular basis: "I imagine what it is like to gulp down thirty pills at one time. The result is a pre-psychotic paranoid rage state. A five-hour temper tantrum that produces the late hits..., the unconscionable assaults on quarterbacks, that are ruining pro-football".[3] The use of steroids has much the same effect, inducing in the user what has been termed "road rage", which is essentially an inability to control aggression. With extensive and sustained steroid use, the loss of judgment is compounded by the added danger arising from the increase in the bulk and the consequent capacity to inflict more serious injuries on opponents. Thus, rather than changing sport, drug abuse has the effect of exaggerating those elements that have long proved a threat to the integrity of the sport and the delicate balance of attributes that mark out the great spectator and participant sports.

---

1. Dyment, P.G., "Drugs and the Adolescent Athlete", *Pediatric Annals*, Vol. 13.8, 1984, pp. 602-4.
2. Gorn & Goldstein, 1993, op. cit., p. 163.
3. Quoted in Goldman, 1992, op. cit., p. 52.

Ephedrine and related stimulants

Ephedrine, along with pseudoephedrine and phenylpropanolamine, are examples of a family of drugs which mimic the effects of amphetamines. These "look-alike" drugs (prototypic sympathomimetic amines) are similar to amphetamines in that they are stimulants which act on the central nervous system. Drugs from within this family are present in many proprietary medicines, most commonly in cold remedies and nasal decongestants, and can be bought over the counter without a medical prescription in many countries and are usually available in combination with caffeine. They first emerged as drugs used by athletes in the 1970s when countries were achieving greater success in restricting the availability of amphetamines.

The first occasion on which the drug came to the public attention was during the 1972 Munich Olympic Games when the American swimmer Rick DeMont tested positive for ephedrine. Despite having informed officials that he was using an anti-asthma drug (Marex), he was stripped of his gold medal for the 400 m freestyle and was disqualified from participating in the remaining events for which he was entered. Some twelve years later, the British-Canadian athlete Ronald Angus was given a life ban by the British Judo Federation after traces of sympathomimetic amines were found in his urine sample. The traces were from the drug whose proprietary name was Sudafed, a nasal decongestant, prescribed by his doctor. Unlike DeMont, Angus successfully appealed against the imposition of a life ban and was reinstated in time to compete in the trials for the 1984 Los Angeles Olympics.[1]

Stimulants from the sympathomimetic amine family, especially pseudo-ephedrine, are still regularly found in the urine samples of drug abusers in sport. The main problem facing the enforcers of the doping regulations is how to respond to the frequently voiced defence that the drugs were taken inadvertently as part of a cold or cough remedy bought at the local pharmacy. The challenge facing the testing authorities has been to establish a level of mild sympathomimetic amine which would distinguish between normal therapeutic use and doping. It is expected that the IOC will introduce such a reporting level in the next few years. At the 1988 Olympics, a British athlete was prevented from competing in a relay event due to a positive test which showed traces of pseudoephedrine in the urine sample. The athlete had previously tested negative on seven occasions but was taking ginseng. Forgo, in an experiment with ginseng capsules administered to a control group for fourteen days, found no traces of banned substances in their urine but Watt et al., have drawn attention to the dangers of contaminated ginseng in many commercial preparations. Linford Christie, in one memorable illustration of the problem, tested positive for an extremely small trace of pseudoephedrine at the Seoul Olympics. Christie successfully argued that the trace was due to

---

1. Donohoe & Johnson, 1986, op. cit.

an ingestion of a cold cure preparation where pseudoephedrine was not mentioned in the ingredients. That Christie was not banned illustrates not only the care that athletes need to exercise in taking any substance or preparation where the ingredients are not clearly listed, but also the fact that many test results for drug abuse do not produce unequivocal evidence of a doping infraction. Rather than the answer to the question "Have the federation's doping regulations been broken?" being "Yes" or "No" it is often "Maybe" or "We are not sure".

Ephedrine appears to be widely used with data from Poland showing not only its prevalence but its rising popularity (see Table 2.2).

Table 2.2 : Positive samples by year and by drug

Year	Samples	Positives	AAS (Anabolic androgenic steroids)	Other	No. of "other" from the ephedrine family	Ephedrine family as % of all positives	Ephedrine family as % of "other"
1987	748	27	13	14	0	0	0
1988	1 401	58	30	28	1	2	4
1989	1 060	5	4	1	0	0	0
1990	1 007	11	7	4	4	26	100
1991	1 228	31	23	8	2	6	25
1992	973	12	11	1	0	0	0
1993	1 591	45	40	5	3	7	60
1994	1 053	18	13	5	4	22	80
1995	1 785	32	24	8	6	19	75
1996	2 061	44	31	13	11	25	85
1997	2 008	23	16	7	5	22	71
1998	2 170	48	16	32	12	25	38

Source : adapted from Kwiatkowska et al[1].

The use of ephedrine is considered to be especially common among cyclists. In the study in Belgium by Delbeke, the test results for 4 374 cyclists were analysed between 1987 and 1994.[2] Table 2.3 shows the pattern of drug abuse over the period and the consistency with which ephedrine and norephedrine, in particular, occur regularly throughout the period.

1. Kwiatkowska, D., Grucza, R., Chrostowski, K. & Smorawinski, J., "Doping Cases in Polish Athletes, *Biology of Sport,* Vol. 17.2, 2000.
2. Delbeke, F.T., "Doping in Cyclism: Results of Unannounced Controls in Flanders", *International Journal of Sports Medicine,* Vol. 17, 1996, pp. 434-8.

Table 2.3 : Incidence of selected doping substances in cyclists (1987-94)

	1987	1988	1989	1990	1991	1992	1993	1994	Total
Ephedrine	6	18	21	20	22	13	15	10	125
Norephedrine	5	26	8	14	20	7	10	7	97
Nandrolone	15	29	8	13	12	4	6	6	93
Amphetamine	8	18	13	10	11	11	9	8	88
Prolintane	2	5	1	1	3	3	6	2	23
Pseudoephedrine	0	1	2	2	3	1	6	2	17
Testosterone	1	1	2	0	0	3	4	3	14
Pemoline	0	4	2	2	0	2	3	0	13
Number of tests	230	464	550	650	587	500	637	656	4374
Number of positives*	30	70	54	50	57	39	61	40	401
% positives	13.0	15.1	9.8	7.7	9.7	7.8	9.6	6.1	9.2

* Includes refusals and fraudulent tests.
Source: adapted from Delbeke (1996), ante.

For the period as a whole, the average figure for positives was 7.8%, which is a very high proportion and one which climbs higher when the number of refusals is added giving an average for the period of 9.2%. More significantly, there is relatively little variation in the proportion of positive results throughout the period. The table also shows the continuing popularity of amphetamines despite the relative ease with which they can be detected. A final feature of the pattern of doping among Flemish cyclists noted by Delbeke is the incidence of multiple drug use. Particularly popular were combinations of amphetamines and ephedrine, and also amphetamines in combination with steroids.

Caffeine

Caffeine has a long history of both social and medical use. Soon after the drug first appeared in central Europe in the seventeenth century, claims were quickly made regarding its success in curing a broad range of ailments including venereal disease, colds and gout. Although caffeine is present in a number of drinks, the most common source is coffee and as Wadler and Hainline observe "caffeine remains the most widely consumed drug in Europe and America".[1]

The claims for caffeine's healing properties were not lost on athletes who by the middle of the nineteenth century were taking substantial quantities of

1. Wadler, G.I. & Hainline, B., *Drugs and the Athlete*, Philadelphia: F.A. Davis and Co., 1989, p. 107.

caffeine in the belief that it would help their sporting performance. The popularity of caffeine as an ergogenic aid was due in large part to its ease of purchase, its cheapness and its high level of public acceptability. Until comparatively recently, the primary perceived utility of caffeine was as a stimulant. But, as synthetic stimulants have been developed, such as amphetamine and the sympathomimetic amines, the use of caffeine has declined dramatically. However, it also has some utility as a diuretic, a drug which can be used to flush other drugs out of the system. Even this use of caffeine is declining as more effective synthetic diuretics have been developed. None the less, caffeine is still on the list, produced by the IOC, but as a restricted drug rather than a banned substance partly because of its diuretic properties but also because of the ubiquity of the drug and the plausibility of the argument that its presence in a urine sample is the result of social use rather than an attempt to cheat. The weakness of any proven significant utility of caffeine has not stopped large numbers of athletes believing that its use will improve their performance. During the 1972 marathon at the Munich Olympics the gold medal winner Frank Shorter is alleged to have been given regular drinks of decarbonated Coca-Cola.[1] At the 1976 Olympic Games, Laurin and Letorneau found significant amounts of caffeine in the urine samples of athletes.[2] In 1984, for example, the American Federation of Cycling revealed that its team had taken caffeine suppositories before competing in the Los Angeles Olympics, while a survey undertaken by the Canadian Centre for Drug-free Sport found that 26% of a sample of 16 000 11 to 18 year-olds had used caffeine to enhance performance.[3] However, as will be made clear below, for testing authorities to be concerned at the presence of caffeine in a sample the concentration would have to be far in excess of normal social use (that is, over 12 micrograms per millilitre) and there have been only two athletes who have recently tested positive for concentrations of caffeine above the level permitted by the IOC: an American cyclist and an Australian member of the modern pentathlon team, who both tested positive at the Seoul Olympics.[4]

Blood doping: transfusions and rEPO

Blood doping by transfusion refers to the practice of giving athletes transfusions of blood which may be their own or that of a donor. The purpose is to

1. Brown, W.M., "Paternalism, Drugs, and the Nature of Sports", *Journal of the Philosophy of Sport*, Vol. XI, 1984, pp. 14-22.
2. Laurin, C.A. & Letorneau, G., "Medical Report on the Montreal Olympic Games", *American Journal of Sports Medicine*, Vol. 6, 1978, pp. 54-61.
3. Stamford, B., "Caffeine and Athletes", *Physician and Sports Medicine*, Vol. 17, 1989, pp. 193-94; Rogers, C.C., "Cyclists Try Caffeine Suppositories", *Physician and Sports Medicine*, Vol. 13, 1985, pp. 38-40; and CCDS survey reported in Graham, T.E, Rush, J.W.E. & van Soeren, M.H., "Caffeine and Exercise Metabolism and Performance", *Canadian Journal of Applied Physiology*, Vol. 19, 1994, pp. 111-38.
4. Nehlig, A. & Derby, G., "Caffeine and Sports Activity: A Review", *International Journal of Sports Medicine*, Vol. 15, 1994, pp. 215-23.

increase the capacity of the blood to transport oxygen to the muscles and it is based on the principle that the amount of oxygen available to the muscles is determined by the quantity of red blood cells in the body. Therefore, if the number of red blood cells can be increased so too can the volume of oxygen transported to the muscle during competition. One form of blood doping by transfusion is to remove a volume of blood from the athlete, separate the red blood cells from the plasma and freeze-preserve the red blood cells. Following the removal of the blood the number of red blood cells in the athlete's body will gradually return to a normal level at which time the preserved red blood cells can be injected back into the athlete's blood stream in time for competition.

Blood doping is especially effective in the sports that require stamina such as long-distance cycling and running, and cross-country skiing. The first rumours of the practice of blood doping by athletes emerged in the early to mid-1970s and were rife during the 1976 Montreal Olympic Games where the Finnish and East German teams were the targets of considerable suspicion.[1] The celebrated Finnish runner Lasse Viren, who was a specialist at the 5 000 m and 10 000 m events and won gold medals at both the 1972 and 1976 Games, was questioned repeatedly about his possible involvement in blood doping by transfusion; allegations which he strenuously denied. Confirmation of the use of blood doping by transfusion came in 1981 when the Finnish steeplechaser who competed in the European Games of 1971 and the Munich Olympics the following year admitted that he had undergone transfusions prior to Olympic competition. Further revelations came in the mid-1980s when eight members of the United States cycling team, including the winner of a gold medal and a world record holder, admitted blood doping by transfusion two days before competition in the Los Angeles Olympics where the team collected nine medals.[2] Donohoe and Johnson report that "There had been a period of silence following the Games until Mark Whitehead and a colleague from the American team revealed that half of the team had received an infusion of their own or a relative's blood".[3] That the doping had been carried out under the supervision of both the team doctor and trainer made the revelations all the more serious.

Estimating accurately the extent of blood doping is much more difficult than estimating the frequency of other forms of doping and indeed relies on admissions of use as there is currently no reliable test for the practice. It is therefore unsurprising that there have been few public cases and since the mid-1980s there have been no admissions similar to those of the American cycling team. This might mean that the practice is continuing but that users

---

1. Government of Australia, "Drugs in Sport", Interim Report of the Senate Standing Committee on the Environment, Recreation and the Arts, Canberra: Australian Government Publishing Service, 1989.
2. Goldman, 1992, op. cit.; and Mottram, D.R., Drugs in Sport, 2nd edn., London: E & FN Spon, 1996, pp. 24-5.
3. Donohoe & Johnson, 1986, op. cit., p. 118.

are now more discreet or it might mean that the value of the practice is being questioned at least by comparison with other forms of blood doping currently available.

In the last fifteen years, the development of rEPO (recombinant erythropoietin) has provided potential blood dopers with an alternative in drug form. Erythropoietin, a synthetic drug, and human rEPO function by stimulating the production of red blood cells within the bone marrow. The identification of the properties and potential medical applications of rEPO in 1987 was followed rapidly by the first references to the use of the drug in sport. However, because of the difficulty in developing a reliable test for the drug the evidence was circumstantial rather than direct. Accusations of abuse of rEPO again focused on cycling, with a French magazine drawing attention to the large number of cyclists who had died of heart failure, one of the most common risks associated with rEPO use. One claim was that eighteen cyclists were thought to have died as a result of rEPO up to 1991 with a second claim that twelve Dutch cyclists died from cardiac failure between 1987 and 1991.[1] As will be seen from the discussion in Chapter 3, the advent of rEPO is causing considerable problems for anti-doping authorities and it is currently impossible to estimate with any confidence the extent of use. However, the extent of use uncovered at the1998 Tour de France, and the 1999 and 2001 Giro d'Italia make it clear that use of rEPO is still endemic in professional road racing.

Barbiturates and benzodiazepines

Barbiturates are used to suppress the central nervous system and have been in medical use for almost one hundred years. Chloral hydrate was available in 1869 and the first barbiturate derived from barbituric acid was used in clinical medicine in 1903.[2] Although barbiturates were prescribed in huge quantities in the early twentieth century, there was a serious concern about the capacity of the drug to create a physical and psychological dependence among users. Within both medicine and sport, alternatives were sought from amongst the compounds from the benzodiazepine family which were considered as a non-addictive alternative and a set of drugs not proscribed by the IOC, although they are banned by the UIPMB, the international federation controlling the modern pentathlon and biathlon.[3] Unfortunately, the benzodiazepines have also been proved to create dependence.

Within sport, barbiturates and benzodiazepines are considered to reduce anxiety but without any loss of judgment and co-ordination, and have tended to be used most frequently to control muscle tremor in throwing sports, but could also be used in any sport where a steady hand is required such as

---

1. Robert Hartmann, writing in the *Tagesanzeiger* newspaper (Zurich) and the *Observer* newspaper (UK), quoted in Mottram, 1996, op. cit., p. 232.
2. Wadler & Hainline, 1989, op. cit., p. 114.
3. UIPMB (Union internationale de Pentathlon moderne et Biathlon).

shooting and snooker. The most serious abuse of minor tranquillisers occurred at the Munich Olympics of 1972 where more than a quarter of competitors in the modern pentathlon had taken tranquillisers. Accurate information about trends in the use of the minor tranquillisers is unavailable but it is likely that use is declining partly because they have been superseded by beta blockers, discussed below, which have proved particularly popular among marksmen.

Beta blockers

Beta blockers are used to treat a range of medical conditions including migraine, hypertension, angina and a number of anxiety disorders. The effect of the drugs on heart rate and blood pressure make beta blockers of little value in most sports. However, the capacity of the drugs to lower anxiety levels, steady the breathing and reduce hand and arm tremor levels have made them popular in a limited number of sports, primarily those that require a steady hand and great precision such as snooker, darts, bowls, archery and shooting. There is some evidence of limited use of the drug in fencing (a combat sport) and show jumping (a high-risk sport), both sports where relaxation, precision control and concentration are of value.[1]

It was during the 1980s, and largely within the Olympic sport of modern pentathlon, that the debate about the possible misuse of the drugs was at its most intense. Modern pentathlon involves competition in a series of different sports, including cross-country running and shooting and because it was normal to hold these events on different days it was possible for athletes who wished to cheat to tailor their drug use to the needs of the particular sport of the day. At the 1984 Los Angeles Olympics, beta blockers were not prohibited although team doctors had to notify the IOC whenever any of their team members was taking the drug. The fact that a number of team doctors were submitting notification not simply for the isolated squad member but for whole teams involved in shooting events and in the modern pentathlon sounded the alarm bells in the IOC Medical Commission.[2] The use of beta blockers was confirmed also through the IOC's own testing procedures, which identified a number of positives among athletes involved in the modern pentathlon. Because the drug was not on the IOC list of banned substances, the names of the athletes testing positive were not revealed. However, the incident not only concerned the IOC but prompted the UIPMB to lobby hard for the inclusion of the beta blockers on the IOC list. In addition, the Secretary General of UIPMB insisted on the release of the names of the countries whose doctors had notified the IOC of the use of beta blockers by their teams. Eventually, in November 1984, it was announced that at least one competitor from Switzerland and one from the United States had legally

1. Government of Australia, 1989, op. cit., pp. 25-6.
2. At the 1984 Olympic Games the entire Italian shooting team announced that they needed beta blockers in order to take part in their events.

44

used beta blockers at the Olympic Games.[1] Attempts to thwart drug users by holding the shooting event on the same day as the cross-country running only prompted athletes to select a short-acting beta blocker.

It is not just modern pentathlon that has been affected by controversy over the use of beta blockers: the use of the drug in the non-Olympic sport of snooker also prompted considerable debate. Following the newspaper revelation in 1987 that the chairman of the sport's governing body, Rex Williams, had been taking beta blockers for fifteen years, it was also revealed that a large number of élite players, including two former world champions, had used or were currently using beta blockers. The governing body of the sport, the World Professional Billiards and Snooker Association, eventually agreed to ban the drug but continued to allow its use for therapeutic purposes if there was independent medical support.

Anabolic steroids

One of the most interesting aspects of the history of drug abuse in sport is the way in which drugs developed for scientific experimental or medical purposes become recognised as having a value in sport and how they are gradually adapted for use within a sports context. The synthesis of anabolic steroids is especially instructive. As early as the eighteenth century, scientists suspected that the testes were central to the development of male characteristics. In 1849, Berthold conducted experiments on castrated cockerels by transplanting testes to their abdominal cavity which retarded the development of the characteristics normally expected following castration. Later in the nineteenth century, scientists experimented with ways of extracting the chemicals essential to the development of male characteristics from the testes. However, it was not until 1935 that Laqueur successfully isolated testosterone in a crystalline form.[2] Over subsequent years, it became clear that testosterone was one of a family of compounds which possessed a male hormone-like activity; the name of this family of compounds is androgens. The first medical use of the new drug was in the 1930s when it was used to help the recovery of starvation victims. It was also used in the same decade for the non-medical purpose of increasing the aggressiveness and strength of German soldiers. It was not until the early 1950s that reports began to surface that anabolic steroids were being used by athletes. The first reports came from the Soviet Union and coincided with the country's return to Olympic competition when its spectacular success at the 1952 Helsinki Games began three decades of superpower rivalry for Olympic domination of the medal table. As the rumours of steroid use among Soviet athletes multiplied during the late 1950s, two factors coincided to accelerate the spread of steroid use in western Europe and especially in the United States. The first factor was the distortion of values generated by the cold war and, closely

1. Donohoe & Johnson, 1986, op. cit., pp. 85-7.
2. Much of this section uses Wadler & Hainline, 1989, op. cit.

linked to that, the McCarthyite hysteria that swept America. The second factor was the willingness of a number of doctors to abuse their privileged position in society and to supply drugs to athletes. As Goldman notes:

> "When steroids first came on the scene there were many physicians, including the father of anabolic steroids, Dr John Ziegler, who cautiously embraced them, and willingly prescribed them to athletes for whom they were responsible ... [P]atriotism was a factor as well. The feeling of these doctors was that if they could in any way help an American athlete bring home the gold, they had somehow struck a blow for freedom." [1]

Ziegler became aware of the use of steroids by the Soviet team at the 1956 World Games in Moscow where the extent of use was so great that male athletes had to be catheterised in order to pass urine as the use of steroids had enlarged their prostate gland making the passing of urine in the normal way difficult or impossible.[2] As a result and in "conjunction with the Ciba Pharmaceutical Company, Zeigler (sic) developed anabolic steroids for use by weightlifters".[3] The new drug Dianabol was an attempt to develop a steroid which had reduced side-effects associated with the use of straight testosterone. Dianabol rapidly became established in American, and later European, gymnasiums as the preferred drug among athletes. As the number of early anabolic steroid users began to win events, the word soon spread that the route to competitive success was through the use of the new drug.

Initially, the use of the drug was confined to the power disciplines such as weightlifting and the throwing events, but its use soon spread to swimmers and, in the United States, to football players, leading the Czech, and later American, Olympic Gold medal winning athlete and coach Olga Fikotova-Connolly to comment that "There is no way in the world a woman nowadays, in the throwing events ... can break the record unless she is on steroids. These awful drugs have changed the complexion of track and field".[4]

Use of anabolic steroids continued to be a persistent problem among élite sportspeople at least until 1976, when the first reliable tests for the presence of the substance in urine were developed by Manfred Donike. Tests were conducted for steroids at the Montreal Olympic Games where eleven athletes were disqualified, eight of whom were disqualified for the use of anabolic steroids. However, as will be shown below, this landmark in the battle to eradicate steroid use represented simply the first stage in a continuing campaign. Not surprisingly, reliable epidemiological evidence about steroid use is in short supply. Ljungqvist's survey, conducted in the early 1970s, of

1. Goldman, 1992, op. cit., p. 47.
2. Voy, 1991, op. cit., p. 9.
3. Government of Australia, 1989, op. cit.
4. Quoted in Goldman, 1992, op. cit.

male Swedish élite track and field athletes concluded that 31% had used anabolic steroids.[1] Data from the United States collected in the 1980s suggested that use among college athletes was between 15-20% with football players being among the heaviest users.[2] In addition, there has been a steady stream of anecdotal evidence of continuing use among athletes across a wide range of sports.

The 1980, Moscow Olympic Games were dubbed the "Junkie Olympics" by one observer who commented that:

> "There is hardly a medal winner at the Moscow Games, certainly not a gold medal winner, who is not on one sort of drug or another: usually several kinds. The Moscow Games might as well have been called the Chemists' Games ..."[3]

The allegations of extensive drug use at the Moscow Games contrast with the lack of any positive test results. According to Jennings, the Soviet's secret service, the KGB, ensured that no drug scandals would cloud the Soviet organisational triumph.[4] However, when the samples collected at Moscow were re-analysed by Professor Manfred Donike, a senior member of the IOC Medical Commission, he found evidence of a large number of athletes using steroids.

By far the most serious scandal of the early 1980s occurred at the 1983 Pan-American Games held in Caracas, Venezuela, when not only did many athletes withdraw from the Games when they were informed of the new and more rigorous drug-testing regime in place, but nineteen athletes from ten countries including the United States and Canada tested positive for drugs, mainly steroids. In May 1987, thirty-four people, including the British Olympic medalist David Jenkins, were indicted by United States drug enforcement agencies on 110 counts relating to conspiracy to manufacture, smuggle and distribute huge quantities of anabolic steroids. The following year the positive test on the Canadian sprinter Ben Johnson shocked the sporting world. Johnson's breathtaking run in the 100 m made him an immediate international hero. He was lauded in the Canadian and world press as an exceptionally gifted athlete, a perception which was transformed overnight as a result of the announcement of the positive test for the anabolic steroid stanozolol.

By the late 1980s, the use of anabolic steroids had become so widespread that one estimate suggested that of all the positive results at the eighteen IOC accredited laboratories throughout the world, 70% were for anabolic

---

1. Ljungqvist, A., "The Use of Anabolic Steroids in Top Swedish Athletes", *British Journal of Sports Medicine*, Vol. 9.2, 1975.
2. Dezelsky, T.L., Toohey, J.V. & Shaw, R.S., "Non-medical Drug Use Behavior at Five United States Universities: A Fifteen-Year Study", *Bulletin of Narcotics*, Vol. 37. 49, 1985; and Pope et al., op. cit., 1988.
3. Government of Australia, 1989, op. cit., p. 10.
4. Jennings, A., *The New Lords of the Rings*, London: Simon and Schuster, 1996, p. 235.

steroids.[1] More recently, Bahrke et al., in a survey of developments in research into the effects of steroids in the first half of the 1990s, reported a series of cases demonstrating the extent to which steroid use was deeply rooted in élite sport. Among the cases they reported was that of a 14-year-old South African female runner who tested positive, making her probably the youngest athlete to be caught using steroids, and the banning of a para-lympic athlete for steroid use.[2] In a study of body builders in the Flanders region of Belgium, between 38% and 58% of those tested had used steroids between 1988 and 1993.[3] A total of 11% of high school football players in Arkansas high schools were also reported to be taking anabolic steroids.[4] A more recent study revealed steroid use by adolescents of between 3% and 5%, and between 5% and 15% for adults.[5]

Table 2.4 shows that anabolic agents, which include anabolic steroids, have consistently accounted for approximately two-thirds of all substances identified by IOC accredited laboratories.

Table 2.4: Number of substances in the banned classes from IOC-accredited laboratories, 1993-97

	1993	1994	1995	1996	1997
Stimulants	331	347	310	281	356
Narcotics	46	42	34	37	47
Anabolic agents	940 (65%)	891 (62%)	986 (60%)	1131 (68%)	997 (59%)
Beta blockers	11	15	14	6	11
Diuretics	65	63	59	54	90
Masking agents	7	8	3	0	13
Peptide hormones	4	3	9	4	5
Other	48	77	224	155	184
Total	1452	1446	1639	1668	1703

1. Government of Australia, 1989, op. cit., p. 26.
2. Bahrke, M.S., Yesalis, C.E. & Wright, J.E, "Psychological and Behavioural Effects of Endoge-nous Testosterone and Anabolic-Androgenic Steroids: An Update", *Sports Medicine,* Vol 22.6, 1996, pp. 367-90.
3. Delbeke, F., Desmet, N. & Debackere, M., "The Abuse of Doping Agents in Competing Body Builders in Flanders (1988–1993)", *International Journal of Sports Medicine,* Vol. 16.1, 1995, pp. 66-70.
4. Herrmann, M., "Steroids: A Vague Threat", *Newsday,* 30 October 1988.
5. Laure, P., "Epidemiological Approach to Doping in Sport", *Journal of Sports Medicine and Physical Fitness,* 37, 1997, pp. 218-24.

Although the late 1980s may have marked the high point of steroid use as measured by the proportion of the total number of tests that were positive for steroids, the family of drugs still remains the most popular substance abused by athletes. Any decline in the prevalence of steroids is less likely to be due to increased intensity of testing in the wake of the Johnson scandal than the fact that drug-using athletes were moving on to other more sophisticated drugs such as Human Growth Hormone (hGH) and insulin, both of which are impossible to detect. Nevertheless, use of anabolic steroids continued into the late 1990s and into the new century with a number of high-profile athletes testing positive, including sprinter Dennis Mitchell, shot-putter Randy Barnes and tennis player Petr Korda in 1998, middle-distance runners Mary Decker Slaney in 1996 and Dieter Baumann in 2000, shot-putter C.J. Hunter in 2000 and weightlifter Maria Isabel Urritia in 2001.

Cocaine

Of all the drugs used in substantial quantities by modern athletes, cocaine has probably the longest history. The stimulant and anorexiant properties of the leaves of the coca bush, a plant indigenous to Peru, were well known long before the arrival of the European invaders. Among the Incas, coca leaves were regularly used when travelling long distances to increase energy and endurance, and also to reduce hunger. Indeed, "distances were measured by the number of doses of coca leaf needed in a day's travel".[1] By the time of Pizarro's conquest of Peru on behalf of Spain in the 1530s, "abuse of the drug had become uncontrolled and widespread".[2] The properties of the coca leaf were swiftly reported to Europe and scientific analysis of the plants brought back was soon underway. However, it was not until the middle of the nineteenth century that scientists were successful in isolating the alkaloid cocaine from the coca leaf. As with both steroids and amphetamines it was war that created the stimulus for more extensive experimentation with the effects of the drug on human physiology. In the 1880s, the drug was administered to Bavarian troops by the army physician Ashenbrandt as a method of delaying the onset of fatigue.

By the early part of the present century, the use of cocaine was widespread largely as a result of being heavily promoted by Freud in Europe and Halstead in the United States. The drug was claimed to possess qualities that were beneficial in the treatment of a broad range of ailments including cancer and, ironically, morphine and alcohol addiction. Angelo Mariani developed a very popular drink produced by combining two ounces of coca leaf with one pint of wine. So popular was his mixture that it received "testimonials from three Popes, sixteen heads of state, and 8000 physicians".[3] Most famously, the

---

1. Kunkel, D.B., "Cocaine Then and Now Part I: Its History, Medical Botany, and Use", *Emergency Medicine,* 15 June 1986.
2. Walder & Hainline, 1989, op. cit., p. 87.
3. Kunkel, 1986, op. cit., p. 128.

coca leaf was one of the original ingredients in the soft drink, Coca Cola, invented by John Smythe Pemberton in 1886. It was only in 1906 that the company agreed to alter the recipe and find an alternative to the coca leaf.

The emergence of the current problem with the illegal social use of cocaine began in the 1960s, developing first in the United States but spreading quickly to Europe. It is at about the same time that reports of cocaine use among sportspeople began to surface, especially among football players in the United States. The first of a continuing series of deaths associated with cocaine use among athletes occurred in the early 1980s. The death, in 1980, of Terry Furlow, basketball, was followed by Billy Ylvisaker, polo, in 1983, but it was the trio of deaths in 1986 in the United States that drew the attention of sports organisations and the public to the extent and seriousness of cocaine abuse among athletes. In 1986, Larry Gordon (football), Don Rogers (also football) and the bright basketball prospect Len Bias all died.[1] By 1986, there was substantial evidence of extensive use among college and professional athletes. In the survey of over 2000 NCAA (National Collegiate Athletic Association) athletes conducted by the Michigan State University College of Human Medicine in 1984, it was reported that 13% were currently taking cocaine with a total of 17% admitting using cocaine in the previous twelve months.[2] These findings were supported by a later survey of élite women athletes which found that 7% of respondents acknowledged using cocaine.[3]

Human Growth Hormone

Human Growth Hormone (hGH) is one of the newest drugs to be exploited for competitive advantage by athletes. In the mid-1980s, hGH was developed as a replacement for natural growth hormone extracted from the pituitary glands of cadavers when the latter were deemed unsafe due to the possibility of the transmission of infections, such as Creutzfeldt-Jakob disease (CJD). Because the range of medical conditions for which hGH is used is small the amount commercially produced is still limited thus restricting its availability for illicit use by athletes.[4] However, Wadler and Hainline reported in 1989 that since the development of synthetic hGH there have been a large number of enquiries about the drug from athletes.[5] In 1983, it was revealed that athletes competing in Helsinki had been using hGH. Although none of the 200 samples taken tested positive, traces of hGH were found in some of the samples when retested at the IOC accredited laboratory at Cologne.[6] By the late 1980s, there had already been cases of athletes reputedly using hGH at

---

1. Voy, 1991, op. cit., p. 8.
2. Anderson & McKeag, 1985, op. cit.
3. Elite Women Athletic Survey. Hazelden Health Promotion Services, Minneapolis, 1987.
4. According to the Dubin report there is only one legitimate medical use for hGH.
5. Wadler & Hainline, 1989, op. cit.; and Cowart, V.S., "Human Growth Hormone: The Latest Ergogenic Aid", *Physician and Sports Medicine,* Vol. 16.3, 1988.
6. Donohoe & Johnson, 1986, op. cit., p. 113.

twenty times the normal level and one case of a doctor attempting to buy large amounts of the drug and selling it for non-medical purposes.[1]

One of the few recorded examples of misuse of the drug by an athlete was uncovered during the enquiries made at the time of Justice Dubin's investigation of drug abuse by Canadian athletes following the Ben Johnson scandal. During the hearings, the Canadian sprinter Angella Issajenko admitted using hGH along with other drugs. According to the Dubin Inquiry report the fact that the drug is tightly controlled has not prevented it becoming available to athletes. "Notwithstanding the strict control of growth hormone, there was evidence of increased use by other sprinters, body builders, weightlifters, and intercollegiate football players whose sole source of supply has been the black market".[2] The attraction of hGH to athletes is not just that it is thought by many athletes to produce a similar effect to anabolic steroids but, more importantly, that it is currently undetectable. The drug seems to be less attractive to those seeking to build muscle strength and more attractive to those, such as body builders, seeking to improve musculature and to achieve a more sculpted effect.[3] However, the discovery of thirteen vials of hGH in the luggage of a member of the Chinese swimming team on its way to the 1998 World Championships in Perth suggests that the drug is also attractive to those competing in power-based events.

Evidence of the use of the drug has also been found among adolescents who may take the drug for sports-related purposes such as attempting to ensure sufficient growth for height-related sports. Evidence of abuse has also been found among those adolescents seeking to improve their physique simply for cosmetic purposes.[4]

Diuretics

Diuretics are drugs that are used to increase the rate of urine formation. In sport, they are used to achieve rapid weight loss in weight-related sports such as wrestling, judo, weightlifting and boxing. They can also be used to flush out other drugs thus making detection more difficult. A third use of diuretics is to overcome the side-effect of fluid retention resulting from the use of androgenic anabolic steroids. As Mottram notes, the use of diuretics in conjunction with this class of steroids helps body builders, in particular, to achieve a more sharply defined musculature or "cut look".[5]

1. Cowart, 1988, op. cit.
2. Dubin Inquiry, Commission of Inquiry into the Use of Drugs and Banned Practices Intended to Increase Athletic Performance, Commissioner, Charles L. Dubin, Ottawa: Canadian Government Printing Centre, 1990, p. 120.
3. George, A., "The Anabolic Steroids and Peptide Hormones", in Mottram, 1996, op. cit., p 208.
4. Ibid., p. 209.
5. Verroken, M., "Drug Use and Abuse in Sport", in Mottram, 1996, op. cit., p. 35.

Positive tests for diuretics occasionally occur, and one of the first cases involved a Canadian athlete who, in order to make his weight category for an event in Caracas in 1983, "ran outside at noon in two jogging suits, covered with plastic garbage bags, with a hat, trying to sweat off as much weight as he could, as much water as he could and, at the same time, was using diuretics". Not surprisingly, the athlete collapsed.[1] No breach of doping regulations had taken place because diuretics were not, at that time, on the IOC list of banned substances, although they were added in 1985. Since the inclusion of diuretics on the IOC list, there have been a small but regular number of positive results. One of the most serious examples of the abuse of diuretics occurred at the Seoul Olympics where the British athlete Kerrith Brown won a bronze medal in the judo competition but later tested positive for the diuretic frusemide. In the same year, during the 1988 Tour de France, Pedro Delgado tested positive for diuretics which he was using as a masking agent. The scandal was exacerbated by the response of the French Tour organisers who claimed that the international authorities, in monitoring for drugs, had "broken the heart" of the Tour de France.

The impact of doping on sport: the example of swimming

In a study in the mid-1980s, Puffer admits that there was little evidence regarding the particular drugs favoured by swimmers but suggested that there were five categories of drugs that were in common use by swimmers and other athletes involved in aquatic sports, namely anabolic steroids, psychomotor stimulants, sympathomimetic amines, non-steroidal anti-inflammatory drugs, and recreational (social) drugs.[2] As Puffer suggested, the range of drugs attractive to aquatic athletes is broadly the same as those used by the majority of track and field abusers. What distinguishes swimming from other sports is the seriousness of the doping infractions, their persistence and the impact on the sport.

Two episodes are worthy of mention: the first concerns the dominance of Olympic and world championship swimming by the East Germans in the 1970s and 1980s; and the second concerns the much more recent domination of swimming by athletes from the People's Republic of China. Rumours of extensive doping in Olympic swimming first appeared in the early 1970s and gathered pace with the overwhelming dominance of the East German women at the 1976 Montreal Games – a dominance that was maintained throughout the 1980s. As Leonard noted, the impact of the East German success was profound in the United States, which saw itself as the leading swimming nation. "Careers in both swimming and coaching were ruined. Talented athletes retired early ... The head coach of the [1976] US women's

1. Remarks of Dr Pipe, quoted in the Government of Australia, 1989, op. cit., p. 117.
2. Puffer, J.C., "The Use of Drugs in Swimming", *Clinics in Sports Medicine*, Vol. 5.1, 1986.

team was deemed an outright failure. He was never again offered an Olympic coaching position ..."[1]

The early rumours of drug abuse that surrounded the outstanding success of the swimmers from the GDR were rejected at the time as the product of envy rather than evidence. However, evidence soon began to accumulate, first through the testimony of defectors and later from documentary sources following the ending of the cold war. In 1979, for example, Renate Vogel, the 1974 100 m breaststroke world record holder, defected to the West and recounted stories of systematic use of anabolic steroids. Later evidence from GDR Stasi (secret service) files made clear the extent of doping in all Olympic sports and in swimming in particular. Kristin Otto, who won six gold medals at the 1988 Seoul Games, was named as one of the swimmers who had been through the East German doping programme with the files recording that on the day of one world record-breaking 100 m freestyle competition her testosterone-epitestosterone ratio was 18:1 well beyond the acceptable ratio of 6:1.[2]

As regards the attitude of FINA, the international federation for swimming, it can best be described as one of general indifference and even some satisfaction that the constant setting of new world records was helping to raise the profile of the sport with the public and media. There was, as yet, little recognition of the problem that the emerging series of artificially high world records would pose. Leonard charts the inaction of FINA throughout the 1970s when "not a single official word was noted about doping in FINA minutes", the 1980s when the problem was acknowledged but little action initiated and into the 1990s when, at long last, FINA did undertake investigations of allegations of doping, particularly in China, only to conclude that there was a lack of evidence.

The emergence of China (PRC) as a powerhouse in international swimming was even more rapid than that of swimmers from the GDR. At the 1988 Olympics, the PRC women's team collected only four medals, none of which was gold. Six years later at the Rome World Championships, the PRC team collected a startling twelve gold medals out of a possible sixteen events. At the time, some commentators drew attention to the masculine physique of many of the female swimmers, the rapidity of improvement, the fact that the PRC swimmers were dominating in the power events (freestyle and butterfly, rather than the disciplines requiring greater technical sophistication) and the presence in China of coaches from the former East Germany from 1988 to 1990. A further cause of suspicion was the fact that the dramatic improvement was almost completely confined to the female squad despite the declaration by the Chinese that male and females trained as an integrated squad

---

1. Leonard, J., "Doping in Elite Swimming: A Case Study of the Modern Era from 1970 Forward" in Wilson, W. & Derse, E. (eds.), *Doping in Elite Sport: The Politics of Drugs in the Olympic Movement,* Champaign, Ill: Human Kinetics Publishers, 2001, pp. 230-1.
2. Ibid.

53

with a similar training regime. The voicing of these suspicions led to accusations from the Chinese of racism and jealousy on the part of the critics, but the scientific confirmation of these suspicions was quick to emerge.

Four positive tests were recorded around the time of the Rome World Championships, seven a month later at the Asian Games and eight more to follow by March 1995; all but one of the positive test results were for steroids. As Carlile recounts, the evidence was only provided as a result of the application of extremely sophisticated analytic testing methods involving the development by a Japanese laboratory of a method of detecting the presence of dihydrotestosterone (DHT), "a sophisticated, endogenously produced hormone like testosterone – though much more potent and with a faster clearance time".[1] Following the Rome competition and two weeks before the Chinese squad left for the Asian Games, out-of-competition tests were conducted on two swimmers. The results were positive although the results were not made public immediately. Two weeks later, when the Chinese team arrived in Hiroshima three days before the start of competition, a number of swimmers were selected for immediate testing and five more provided positive results with persistent rumours that another seven or more results were borderline. By testing the members of the Chinese team so early, the sampling officers increased the probability of catching those who had tried to cut their clearance period too fine.

The scale of drug abuse by the Chinese is not the only or even the most significant aspect of this episode. Of greater significance is the attitude of the IOC, on the one hand, and the President of the Chinese Olympic Committee, on the other. The IOC was clearly aware of the scale of doping taking place in China in the early 1990s but chose not to inform FINA, the international federation for swimming, of the number of positive results reported to the Chinese authorities. In addition, the President of the IOC, Juan Samaranch, stated "I do not think the Chinese are using drugs" only to be contradicted by Manfred Donike, a leading authority on doping, who stated "There is systematic doping with the substance DHT".[2] Of greater concern was the attitude of the President of the Chinese Olympic Committee who stated that "we will not have foreigners coming into China as investigators, closely examining our sports preparations in such a systematic and probing way".[3]

The spate of positive test results and the mounting evidence of state collusion in systematic doping provoked an outcry among other members of the Olympic movement not only due to the scale of the cheating but also due to a mounting sense of frustration at the apparent inability or reluctance of the IOC and FINA to pull China into line. There was much talk of banning China

---

1. Carlile, F., "Why the Chinese Must Not Swim at Atlanta '96", *Inside Sport,* November 1995, pp. 18-29.
2. Ibid.
3. Ibid.

from participation in all swimming events until it could prove that its athletes were drug free. Indeed, in 1995 FINA agreed the "four strikes rule", according to which "if four of an NGB's [national governing body of sport] swimmers test positive for doping in a twelve-month period, that nation would be suspended for two years".[1] Although there were a number of occasions when FINA should have applied the rule, it failed to do so. FINA's inaction did little to soothe the mounting anger of the number of swimmers who were, in all probability, denied a medal because of the actions of the Chinese. Finally, the international federation is left with the problem of artificially inflated world record times. Given the importance of record-breaking in selling events to the media, inflated records not only defraud legitimate athletes but make a sport less attractive to the much needed sponsors.

Hopes that the issue of Chinese doping had ended with the furore that followed the Rome Championships were proved unfounded when a series of equally serious incidents occurred at the World Championships held in Perth in 1998. On arrival, one swimmer was found to be carrying a flask containing thirteen glass vials of hGH; enough, according to the FINA secretary, to supply the whole squad. The drug seizure was followed by four positive test results on other members of the squad. The net effect was to overshadow the championships and add fuel to the suspicion that systematic doping was taking place in China. Such was the seriousness of the episode that IOC President, Juan Samaranch, commented that the incident had indeed harmed any plans that China might have of bidding for the 2008 Olympic Games. However, the intense publicity and criticism to which the Chinese sports authorities were subject following the discovery of hGH prior to the Perth World Championships may have proved to be a turning point. The prospect of being rejected yet again as host for the Olympic Games may well have encouraged the Chinese sports officials to adopt a more rigorous anti-doping policy. The public announcement, just before the start of the Sydney Games, that twenty-seven athletes had been dropped from the Chinese squad, many because of suspicious blood test results, was interpreted by the IOC as signalling a greater commitment to drug-free sport. Further confirmation of the changed attitude of the Chinese came from the poor performance of their swimmers in Sydney who failed to win a single swimming medal.

Conclusion

EPO and hGH are among the more recent drugs to be adopted widely by élite athletes, but the search for a pharmacological or other advantage which contravenes the IOC Anti-Doping Code is an endless one. Just as anti-doping authorities successfully devise a test for one breach of the code a new challenge emerges. Genetic manipulation is potentially the most significant

---

1. Galluzzi, D., "The Doping Crisis in International Athletic Competition: Lessons from the Chinese Scandal in Women's Swimming, *Seton Hall Journal of Sport Law,* Vol. 10, 2000, pp. 65-110.

threat to the future integrity of élite sport. There are currently no confirmed cases of athletes using genetic modification to improve their performance and the general view is that effective genetic engineering techniques are five or more years in the future. However, the IOC is sufficiently concerned to have already organised expert conferences aimed, in the first instance, at determining the severity of the threat that "gene doping" poses to sport. If genetic engineering is pushing at the frontier of doping science, there is the continual experiment with much more prosaic substances and methods in the search for a competitive advantage, ranging from altitude tents to oxygenated water. Altitude tents are not banned by the IOC and have been used by athletes in a wide range of sports including cycling (Lance Armstrong), swimming (Ed Moses) and middle-distance running (Suzy Favor Hamilton). The use of the tents is intended to create a similar effect on the body as training at altitude or the use of EPO. By sleeping in altitude tents, where the oxygen in the air is reduced from the 21% found at sea level to about 12-15% through the addition of nitrogen, athletes can simulate the conditions found at 9000 feet above sea level.[1] At the more bizarre end of the range of experimentation, some athletes have been using "super-oxygenated water" in seeking a competitive edge demonstrating yet again the mix of gullibility and desperation that motivates many athletes.

The constant search for new substances and techniques is not the only challenge facing anti-doping organisations. There is also the spread of doping practices into new areas of élites sport, such as disability sport, which give rise to a series of new issues and complications. While there were no positive drug tests announced at the Atlanta Paralympic Games, six power-lifters tested positive at the Sydney Paralympic Games demonstrating that élite disability sport is vulnerable to the same pressures to succeed as mainstream sport. The pattern of drug use is likely to be much the same as for mainstream sport although there are already signs that disability sport will pose anti-doping authorities with some distinctive challenges. The team doctor to the British Paralympic Association recently wrote of the attempts by disabled athletes to obtain an inappropriate disability classification by trying to appear more disabled than they actually were. "This is the disability sports equivalent of doping."[2] A different challenge, possibly unique to disability sport, is posed by the practice of the intentional induction of autonomic dysreflexia (the stimulation of high blood pressure) a practice which has been banned by the International Paralympic Committee since 1994. The induction of autonomic dysreflexia by high paraplegic and tetraplegic athletes is designed to increase heart rate and oxygen uptake, and thereby improve performance. Clamping the urinary catheter to produce distension of the bladder, sitting on

---

1. The IOC Medical Commission is to consider whether to ban the use of altitude tents during the 2002 Winter Olympic Games.
2. Firth, F.Y., "Seeking Misclassification: 'Doping' in Disability Sport", *British Journal of Sports Medicine*, 33.3, 1999, p. 152.

the scrotum and excessive tightening of leg straps are all methods that have been utilised to achieve autonomic dysreflexia. However, because the condition can occur naturally, anti-doping authorities have a difficult task in determining whether a breach of doping regulations has taken place.[1]

The steady development and discovery of new drugs and techniques and the broadening of the range of élite sports where doping has been found indicates the tight grip that doping has on modern sport, and also reflects the powerful social and economic forces that support the spread of doping. Although the sophistication and, possibly, the extent of drug use by athletes are features of the last forty years or so, it is the case that doping has been associated with competitive sport for far longer. In the eighteenth and nineteenth centuries, the major commercial and professionalised sports, including boxing, cycling and running, all provided ample evidence of substantial drug use. While an association between two variables is far removed from a causal relationship, the strength of the association is such that commercialisation must be considered as an important element in any discussion of contemporary doping. A further consideration must be the development of scientific capacity to synthesise drugs in the early and middle part of the present century. The dramatic advances made by the pharmaceutical industry enabled athletes to substitute safer drugs for the more dangerous and to select drugs tailored to meet the requirements of particular sports or training requirements.

The advances by the pharmaceutical industry were also given added momentum by the second world war and the blurring of peacetime morality with the expediency of wartime. Wartime not only added urgency to the search for new drugs which would be beneficial to troops but, much more importantly, also changed the moral climate regarding drug use. Wartime was a period during which governments sanctioned and organised drug use by soldiers. The moral ambiguity surrounding the use of drugs in wartime continued into the cold war period and entered the Olympic arena as sport emerged, along with space, as surrogates for military conflict. The power of cold war politics to affect the judgment of those who cared deeply about sport is amply illustrated by the actions of Dr Ziegler discussed above in connection with the use of steroids by the American team.

The involvement of Dr Ziegler in the promotion of steroids in the United States not only draws attention to the significance of the cold war in affecting moral judgment but also draws attention to the central role of medical doctors in the spread of drug use. Dr Ziegler, who, once he realised the destructive potential of steroids for sport as well as individual athletes, campaigned for the rest of his life against doping in sport, was the first of a series of doctors involved in facilitating drug use in sport. Ben Johnson's doping regime was carefully prepared and monitored by his doctor, Jamie Astaphan, who "had

1. Webborn, A.D.J., "'Boosting' performance in disability sport", British Journal of Sports Medicine, 33.2, 1999, pp. 74-5.

been heavily involved for many years in the planning, supervision, and administration of steroid programs for many athletes".[1] In the United States, Dr Robert Kerr "estimated that in the mid-1980s there were at least seventy physicians in the Los Angeles area who prescribed anabolic steroids to athletes. He himself has prescribed them for athletes from the United States, Canada, South America, Australia and the Far East."[2] Dr Ara Artinian of Toronto, who dealt mainly with football players and body builders, prescribed over US$200000 of steroids between 1981 and 1988. The Black committee of the Australian Senate heard that 41% of body builders in Australia obtained their supply of steroids from doctors.[3] Research from the Netherlands also pointed to the key role of doctors with a 1997 survey finding that 70 doctors had prescribed banned substances and a further 210 out of a total of 7000 had considered prescribing banned substances.[4] Patrick Laure uncovered similar results in a study of the process by which French élite athletes obtained their drugs. In the sample of 2000 athletes, 186 admitted using prohibited substances, of which 6% obtained their drugs from doctors – in the majority of cases their local general practitioner. French athletes were therefore not only able to obtain drugs that were guaranteed to be unadulterated, but they also had them paid for through the state social security system.[5]

The depth of involvement of doctors is especially worrying as one would expect the medical profession to adhere to a morality that would exclude such behaviour. Yet, doctors are only the most prominent in a long list of professionals in positions of trust who have systematically abused that trust by encouraging, colluding, or, at best, ignoring the continuing use of steroids. Pharmacists, coaches and officials are all implicated, some due to ignorance and others by intent, in the steady increase in drug abuse in sport.[6] Given the range of sports professionals involved in doping, the question arises of the position of athletes and their degree of culpability. While it is undoubtedly the case that many drug-abusing athletes are responsible for initiating and controlling their use of drugs there are many who, either through intimidation or ignorance, are arguably less responsible. The question therefore arises of whether we should always assume that the athlete is the villain rather than the victim. This question is especially important when the application of penalties is considered. While athletes are the focus for disciplinary action, it

---

1. Dubin Inquiry, 1990, op. cit., p. 285.
2. Ibid., p. 357.
3. Ibid., p. 357.
4. Reported in *Cycling News* (www.cyclingnews.com/results/archives/dec97/dec8.html) accessed on 21 September 2000.
5. Laure, P., "Doping in Sport: Doctors are Providing Drugs, *British Journal of Sports Medicine*, 31, 1997, pp. 258-9.
6. Understandably, much of the evidence regarding the involvement of pharmacists in supplying banned substances is anecdotal, however, one suvey in France revealed that 25% of pharmacists had received requests for information about, or the supply of, banned substances (Laure, P. & Kriebitzsch-Lejeune, A., Retail Pharmisists and Doping in Sports: Knowledge and Attitudes. A National Survey in France, *Science and Sports*, 15, 2000, pp. 141-6.

is still comparatively rare for the coaches and managers who condoned the use of drugs, the doctors who prescribed the drugs and the pharmacists who supplied drugs to face any significant penalties.[1]

The development of an effective policy response to doping depends on an ability to identify accurately all those involved in the supply, distribution, encouragement and use of drugs whether they are individual sportspeople or sports and governmental organisations. There is a danger that athletes are being targeted not just because they are guilty of abusing drugs but also because they are one of the easier targets in what is a much more complex and widespread pattern of culpability.

1. This issue is discussed in Chapter 8.

Chapter 3

Banned substances and practices and their effects

The drugs used by athletes in the nineteenth century and earlier were derived mainly from plants, animals or microbiological sources. From plants came drugs such as cocaine, morphine and digitalis; from animals came steroids; and from microbiology came penicillin and streptomycin all of which contributed significant advances in the treatment of ailments, but which also provided a number of drugs which could be used in the attempt to gain an advantage in competition such as the chewing of coca leaves or the ingesting of sheep's testicles. The mid-twentieth century marked the dramatic increase in the synthesis of drugs from plants and animals and was also the golden age in the development of anti-bacterial drugs from microbial sources.

The mid- to late twentieth century has been a period of intense development and expansion in the pharmaceutical industry as chemists sought and continue to seek to identify and synthesise new drugs and refine existing products. One of the many problems facing anti-doping organisations is attempting to keep in step with the pace of pharmaceutical advance. Until 2001, the IOC remained in the forefront of the co-ordination and direction of the global anti-doping effort. One of the initial, but increasingly complex, problems facing the IOC is the compilation and updating of the list of banned substances and practices. Although there are signs that a number of international federations are refining or tailoring the IOC list to suit the particular characteristics of their own sport, the IOC list remains the most authoritative statement of policy. As will be discussed below, two problems facing the IOC in compiling its list are, first, the difficulty in determining whether a drug contravenes "the ethics of sport and medical science" and, second, the timing of the addition of new drugs to the IOC list.

The second problem will be considered later in this chapter but the first problem may be illustrated by comparing a definition of drugs given by Mottram with the definition of doping provided by the IOC. For Mottram, drugs "are chemical substances which, by interaction with biological targets, can alter the biochemical systems of the body".[1] Mottram's definition is an objective statement, quite properly devoid of any normative aspect. However, Mottram does add, later in his discussion, a reminder that "drugs are designed to rectify imbalances of biochemical systems which have been induced by disease. They are not primarily designed to affect biochemical systems in healthy subjects".[2] Articles 1 and 2 of the IOC Anti-Doping Code

---

1. Mottram, 1996, op. cit. p. 1.
2. Ibid., p. 1.

echo some of the sentiments expressed by Mottram although, as will be discussed later, the IOC definition lacks the clarity and precision of Mottram's statement and may well be legally vulnerable.

Article 1 provides the moral context for the definition of doping: "Doping contravenes the fundamental principles of Olympism and sports and medical ethics. Doping is forbidden. Recommending, proposing, authorising, condoning or facilitating the use of any substance or method covered by the definition of doping or trafficking therein is also forbidden". Article 2 defines doping as "the use of an expedient (substance or method) which is potentially harmful to athletes' health and/or capable of enhancing their performance, or the presence in the athlete's body of a Prohibited Substance or evidence of the use thereof or evidence of the use of a Prohibited Method".[1] Appendix A to the code lists the prohibited classes of substances (stimulants; narcotics; anabolic agents; diuretics; and peptide hormones, mimetics and analogues), prohibited methods (blood doping and pharmacological, chemical and physical manipulation), and classes of prohibited substances in certain circumstances (alcohol; cannibinoids; local anaesthetics; corticosteroids; and beta blockers).

Doping classes

Stimulants

The list of stimulants is considerable and covers those substances designed to achieve some or all of the following: increased alertness, reduced fatigue and increased competitiveness and aggression. Among the most commonly abused stimulants in sport are amphetamines, cocaine, caffeine and other sympathomimetic amines such as ephedrine.

Amphetamines

The category of drugs referred to as stimulants function by stimulating the body's central nervous system. The first stimulants to be used extensively in sport in the post-war period were amphetamines. Amphetamine proved and continues to prove attractive to athletes because it mimics physiologic changes in the body that occur at times of stress and danger. The body's normal response to stress and danger is often referred to as "fight or flight". In these situations, the body's sympathetic nervous system is activated and the changes that occur include an increased flow of blood through the muscles, elevated body temperature, and an increase in concentration and alertness. In these processes, the release of epinephrine by the adrenal glands plays a significant role and "drugs that act in a similar manner are called sympathomimetic".[2] Amphetamine is closely related in structure to epinephrine and

---

1. IOC, Olympic Movement Anti-Doping Code, Lausanne: IOC, 1999.
2. Strauss, R.H., "Drugs in Sports" in Strauss, R.H. (ed.), *Sports Medicine,* Philadelphia: W.B. Saunders, 1984, p. 485.

stimulates the central nervous system to release neurotransmitters from the nerve terminals.

The positive effects of amphetamine are "an increase in physical energy, mental aptitude, ... Subjects ... also report that they feel confident, efficient, ambitious and that their food intake is reduced".[1] The positive effects are balanced by a series of negative effects, which include "anxiety, indifference, slowness in reasoning, irresponsible behaviour, irritability and restlessness, dry mouth, tremors, insomnia and, following withdrawal, depression".[2] Amphetamine has proved attractive to athletes for a variety of reasons and across a wide range of sports. For some, the attraction lies in the capacity of the drug to provide an artificial way in which they can get themselves psychologically prepared for competition. This use of the drug is most common in sports where aggression is an important element, such as in contact sports including American football, ice hockey and rugby, and in explosive sports such as the shot, weightlifting and hammer. Amphetamines are also used in some endurance sports which require sustained consumption of energy, such as cycling, running and swimming. Finally, amphetamines are also used in some weight-graded sports to suppress appetite in order to facilitate weight loss.

In attempting to assess the value of drugs in enhancing performance, the primary stumbling block is the lack of valid double-blind experimental data. Much of the "evidence" for the ergogenic effects of amphetamines is anecdotal rather than scientific. In one of the few scientifically valid studies, it was concluded that the use of amphetamines enhanced anaerobic performance while having little impact on aerobic activity, and overall produced a small improvement in swimming (0.59% to 1.16%), running (1.5%) and weight throwing (3% to 4%).[3] However, even this study was criticised for failing to control variables adequately and there must consequently be concern at the validity of the conclusions.[4] It should also be noted that the ability to generalise from the study is also limited by the fact that the researchers focused on a narrow range of skills applied in sport and that skills prominent in other sports such as hand-eye co-ordination, judgment, timing and steadiness of hand were not evaluated. A more recent study confirmed the value of amphetamine in increasing the athlete's ability to tolerate higher levels of anaerobic metabolism.[5] Interestingly, Mandell highlighted not only the versatility of the drug, but also the sophistication of some users when he found that members of an American football team varied the amount of

1. George, 2000, op. cit., p. 83.
2. Ibid., p. 83.
3. Smith, G.M. & Beecher, H.K., "Amphetamine Sulphate and Athletic Performance", *Journal of the American Medical Association,* 170, 1959.
4. George, 1996, op. cit., p. 91.
5. Wyndham, G.H., Rogers, G.G., Bendade, A.J.S. & Strydan, N.B., Physiological Effects of Amphetamines During Exercise, *South African Medical Journal,* 45, 1971, pp. 247-52.

amphetamine that they took depending on their playing position. Thus, those responsible for giving or receiving passes took smaller doses than those in the more aggressive defensive roles.[1]

Some supporting evidence for the ergogenic value of amphetamines is available from studies on animals which have shown increased endurance in swimming and running.[2] In a survey of existing evidence, it was suggested that amphetamine use can improve performance but that the margin of improvement was only of a few per cent.[3] However, the authors were acutely aware of the significance of that apparently disappointing conclusion, noting that among élite athletes a few percentage points may mean the difference between first and fourth place. More significantly, they conclude that there was "an amphetamine margin" and that "amphetamines can confer a significant competitive edge in sports… Moreover, their versatility is so remarkable that they enhance acute bursts of strength as well as the ability to cope with prolonged challenges to endurance".[4] Most tellingly, they point out that in the one mile race there had only been a 15% improvement in the world record in the 100 years up to 1975 and that it therefore takes between six and seven years to produce a 1% improvement. As a result, anyone who was able to improve a near world record time by 1% would be able to create a world record that would take many years to better.

Overall the evidence is not conclusive as other experiments have suggested a much more variable impact of amphetamine use. One such experiment, for example, was only able to show an improvement in three in twenty athletes and also found a reduction in performance in one in twenty.[5] It would appear that while improved performance is indeed possible, the effect is not uniform across all athletes and, equally importantly, is not uniform across all sports or roles within team sports. One study, for example, found that while amphetamine use improved some aspects of athletic performance it did not result in improved sprinting.[6] Another study of the use of amphetamines, this time of American football players, found that offensive and defensive linesmen often used high doses of the drug, but that the effect was negative in so far as linesmen were often less able to adjust their game to changes in team tactics, frequently being unaware that they were repeating the same positional plays.[7]

1. Mandell, A.J., "The Sunday Syndrome: A Unique Pattern of Amphetamine Abuse Indigenous to American Professional Football", Clinical Toxicology, 15, 1979, pp. 225-32.
2. Bhagat, B. & Wheeler, N., "Effect of Amphetamines on the Swimming Endurance of Rats", Neuropharmacology, 12, 1973; and Gerald, M.C., "Effects of (+)-amphetamine on the Treadmill Performance of Rats", Neuropharmacology, 17, 1978, pp. 703-4.
3. Laties, V.G. & Weiss, B., "The Amphetamine Margin in Sports", Federation of the American Society for Experimental Biology, Vol. 40.12, 1981.
4. Ibid., p. 2 691.
5. Karpovich, P.V., "Effects of Amphetamine Sulphate on Athletic Performance", Journal of the American Medical Association, 170, 1959.
6. Chandler, J.V. & Blair, S.N., "The Effects of Amphetamines on Selected Physiological Components Related to Athletic Success", Medical Science Sports Exercise, Vol. 12, 1980, pp. 65-9.
7. Mandell, Stewart & Russo, 1981, op. cit.

Leaving aside the question of the possible benefits to sporting performance, it must be borne in mind that a "completely non-toxic drug does not exist".[1] The side-effects of amphetamines are substantial with loss of judgment and the development of dependence being the most significant. Indeed, there is evidence that many athletes who have used amphetamines think they have performed much better than they have in reality. Amphetamines engender a mood of heightened optimism which interferes with judgment.[2] A diminution of judgment in endurance races is potentially very dangerous as the athlete may exceed his or her physical limits as the cyclist Tom Simpson did during the Tour de France. Research has confirmed that the use of amphetamines by cyclists impaired their ability to recognise that they were exceeding their toleration of exertion and heat, and thus may explain the high incidence of cardiac problems and heat-stroke in the sport.[3] A similar loss of judgment was found among American football players taking amphetamines who often continued playing after injury and often in considerable pain.[4] Further, an athlete's loss of judgment in a contact sport may result in the unnecessary injury of others through overly aggressive play.

It has also been reported that tolerance of amphetamines develops rapidly leading to a situation where as much as 1 g of amphetamine was required by established users to produce the same effects as 10-30 mg had on new users. Research has further shown that dependence may also lead to psychotic aggression and that withdrawal is associated with mental and physical depression.[5] In addition, amphetamine use has also been known to cause paranoia, anorexia, insomnia, hypertension, cardiac arrhythmias and tremor. In conclusion, it is fair to suggest that the scientific evidence regarding the benefits to athletes of amphetamines is variable and ambiguous. Where amphetamines do have a perceived benefit in some sports or team positions, it may well be that the effect is more psychological than physiological.

Cocaine

Many of the comments made about the properties of amphetamines apply to the other major stimulants discussed in the remainder of this section. Cocaine was, in many respects, the precursor of amphetamine and its history of enthusiastic embrace by the medical profession followed by a steady decline in prescription and a growing awareness of the serious side-effects of the drug broadly anticipated that of amphetamine. Like amphetamine, cocaine operates by affecting the central nervous system and has a powerful effect on mood. Cocaine appears to operate in part through the non-thinking part of the brain which governs reflexes and serves emotional, sexual drive and

---

1. Mottram, 1996, op. cit., p. 10.
2. Strauss, 1984, op. cit.
3. Wyndham, Roger, Benade & Strydan, 1971, op. cit., pp. 247-52.
4. Mandell, A.J., *The Nightmare Season,* New York: Random House, 1976.
5. George is referring to research undertaken by Brookes and is reported in George, 1996, op. cit.

memory functions. "It is the pharmacological manipulation of the 'pleasure brain' that explains neurologically the compulsivity, preoccupation, craving and relapse behaviour so often seen in cocaine users."[1] Although both amphetamine and cocaine create dependence, it is the power of cocaine's addictive properties that distinguishes it from amphetamine. Indeed according to George, "Cocaine is thought to be the most addictive agent known".[2] Apart from providing a short-term feeling of euphoria (estimated to be between ten minutes and three hours depending on method of administration and the extent of habituation) cocaine has a mild local anaesthetic effect, but also raises blood pressure.

Being specific about the physiological effects of cocaine is extremely difficult as there are few reliable scientific studies and much of the qualitative data is anecdotal and, more importantly, based on the consumption of cocaine that is rarely free of impurities or else is based on animal studies. Cocaine, sold illegally, is frequently adulterated with other stimulants, such as caffeine and phenylpropanolamine, local anaesthetics, such as procaine, hallucinogens, such as LSD, depressants, such as diazepam, and other less expensive substances designed to dilute the drug, such as talcum powder, sucrose and sodium bicarbonate.

It has been claimed that, "this powerful stimulant can produce feelings of euphoria and is capable of improving some aspects of performance through prolonged endurance".[3] However, while the limited body of research makes it impossible to draw firm conclusions about the effect of cocaine on athletic performance, such recent research that does exist suggests that cocaine has no beneficial effect on performance in certain sports such as running.[4] The absence of scientific data notwithstanding, it is significant that there is evidence of a perception among athletes that cocaine does possess ergogenic properties.[5] One of the very few scientific studies was carried out by Freud over 100 years ago from which he concluded that intranasal cocaine increased muscle strength for up to three hours: however, this conclusion was contradicted by more recent research.[6] Indeed, a review of the research evidence available prior to 1983 concluded that much of it was poorly designed and generally unreliable.[7]

1. Wadler & Hainline, 1989, op. cit., p. 90.
2. George, 2000, op. cit., p. 86.
3. Donohoe, T. & Johnson, N., *Foul Play: Drug Abuse in Sports*, Oxford: Basil Blackwell, 1986.
4. Conlee, R.K., "Amphetamine, Caffeine and Cocaine" in Lamb, D.R. & Williams, M.H. (eds.), *Perspectives in Exercise Science and Sports Medicine*, New York: Brown & Benchmark, 1991; and Conlee, R.K., Han, D.H., Kelly, K.P. & Barnett, D.W., "Effects of Cocaine on Plasma Catecholamine and Muscle Glycogen Concentrations During Exercise in the Rat", *Journal of Applied Physiology*, 70, 1991, pp. 77-82.
5. Puffer, 1986, op. cit., pp77-89.
6. Ritchie, J.M. & Green, N.M., "Local Anaesthetics" in Gillman, A.G. et al. (eds), Goodman and Gillman's: *The Pharmacological Basis of Therapeutics*, 7th edn., New York: Macmillan, 1985.
7. Conlee, 1991, op. cit.; see also Haddad, L.M., "Cocaine Abuse: Background, Clinical Presentation, and Emergency Treatment", *Internal Medicine for the Specialist*, Vol.7.9, 1986, pp. 67-75.

In practice, most, admittedly subjective, assessments suggest that cocaine use results in a deterioration in athletic performance. Hand-eye co-ordination, general concentration and deterioration in team discipline are all considered to be consequences of cocaine use.[1] However, the anecdotal evidence, particularly from within football in North America, indicates that the growth in cocaine use among athletes has been for recreational rather than ergogenic motives.

As suggested above, the side-effects of cocaine abuse are serious and are not simply limited to the creation of a level of dependence.[2] The list of adverse side-effects of cocaine use is both long and daunting, including cardiac and neuropsychiatric problems. Cardiac problems that may occur include strokes (rupture of the brain's blood vessels) and myocardial infarction. Neuropsychiatric problems include paranoia, psychosis, repetitive behaviour and anorexia. The danger of cocaine use is indicated by the increased incidence of sudden deaths among users. One hypothesis is that athletes may be especially susceptible to a fatal reaction to cocaine as a dose of the drug large enough to produce a seizure combined with their muscle composition may result in a lethal production of heat and lactic acid causing cardiac failure.[3]

Caffeine

Caffeine is also included in the stimulant category and is subject to IOC restrictions. The "physiologic effects of caffeine include diuresis, gastric acid release, smooth muscle relaxation, increased contractility of skeletal muscle, increased lipolysis, and increased heart rate, blood pressure, oxygen consumption and metabolic rate".[4] In addition to the metabolic benefits of caffeine, it is also thought that the specific competitive benefit of caffeine might also be due to its capacity to stimulate the central nervous system.[5]

Caffeine is widely perceived to be an effective source of enhanced athletic performance. In a Canadian study, 25% of 11-18 year-old students had used caffeine in an attempt to enhance their sports performance.[6] The current IOC restrictions on the use of caffeine identify the threshold for a doping infraction to be 12 micrograms per millilitre (about 4-8 cups of coffee in a period of two or three hours). Caffeine, as an ergogenic aid, is claimed to increase endurance and to result in heightened alertness and improved concentration. But the effect varies according to dosage and sport, and scientific opinion is

1. See footnote 7, p. 69 *ante*. Ibid., p. 96
2. George, 1996, op. cit., p. 97.
3. Giammarco, R.A., "The Athlete, Cocaine and Lactic Acidosis: A Hypothesis", *American Journal of Medical Sciences*, 294, 1987, pp. 412-14.
4. Scwenk, T.L., "Psychoactive Drugs and Athletic Performance", *The Physician and Sports Medicine*, Vol. 25.1, 1997, pp. 33-46.
5. Rall, T.W., "Central Nervous Stimulants – The Methylxanthines" in Gillman et al., 1985, op. cit.
6. Canadian Centre for Drug-Free Sport, "National School Survey on Drugs and Sport", Ottawa: Government of Canada, 1993.

far from a consensus. Even with the ingestion of doses below the IOC threshold there is a discernible, though extremely slight, effect on athletes involved in short duration high-performance events, but the effect of larger doses in endurance events and in some short-term high-intensity sports is defined as significant.[1] Supporting evidence suggests that work output can increase up to 7% and the duration of exercise time can increase by 19%.[2] In addition, there is evidence that the administration of modest amounts of caffeine (equivalent to two-and-a-half cups of coffee) in controlled experiments have increased the endurance of athletes and non-athletes when cycling to exhaustion.[3] However, the evidence is not conclusive. In a review of current research, it was reported that a number of studies conclude that caffeine "had no ergogenic effect on muscle strength and fatigue, output, work capacity, [and] maximal swimming speed".[4] Ergogenic effects on other capacities and skills required in sport do not seem to be present: steadiness and reaction time appear to be either unaffected or adversely affected by caffeine.[5] There are many possible reasons for the contradictory nature of experimental results, including the lack of standardisation in experimental conditions, the complexity of the impact of caffeine on the body, and the significance of the athlete's use of caffeine prior to administration for experimental purposes. Moreover, it is possible that caffeine is of ergogenic value only in a limited number of sports and in precise conditions.[6] A review of existing evidence in 1991 suggested that there were six factors that might affect the impact of caffeine on athletic performance: dose, exercise type, exercise intensity, pre-exercise fuel intake, previous caffeine use and training status.[7]

Despite the legality and widespread social acceptance of caffeine, it does have some negative side-effects. For the habitual user denial of access to caffeine, even for a short period of a day, can result in the development of withdrawal symptoms such as headaches, dysphoria and insomnia.[8] For the athlete seeking ergogenic advantage, the side-effects are relatively mild and include insomnia, gastrointestinal upset, tremor and anxiety. The diuretic properties of caffeine make its use in endurance competitions problematic.[9] But, it is only at

1. Sinclair, C.J.D. & Geiger, J.D., "Caffeine Use in Sports: A Pharmacological Review", *Journal of Sports Medicine Physical Fitness,* 40, 2000, pp. 71-9, ; and Dodd, S.L., Herb, R.A. & Powers, S.K., "Caffeine and Exercise Performance", *Sports Medicine,* Vol. 15.1, 1993, pp. 14-23.
2. Graham, T.E. & Spriet L.L., "Caffeine and Exercise Performance", *Sports Science Exchange,* Vol. 9, 1996, pp. 1-6.
3. Costill, D.L., Dalsky, G.P. & Fink, W.J., "Effects of Caffeine Ingestion on Metabolism and Exercise Performance", *Medical Science Sports Exercise,* Vol. 10, 1978, pp. 155-8.
4. Nehlig & Debry, 1994, op. cit., pp. 215-23.
5. Franks, H.M., Hagedorn, H., Hensley, V.A. & Starmer, G.A., "The Effect of Caffeine on Human Performance Alone and in Combination with Ethanol", *Psychopharmacologia,* Vol. 45, 1975, pp. 177-81; and Tarnopolsky, M.A., "Caffeine and Endurance Performance", *Sports Medicine,* Vol. 18.2, 1994, pp. 109-25.
6. Nehlig & Debry, 1994, op. cit.
7. Conlee, 1991, op. cit.
8. Rall, 1985, op. cit.
9. Tarnopolsky, 1994, op. cit.

very high doses that there is there a risk of seizure and delirium.[1] Sinclair and Geiger suggest that ergogenic benefits are discernible at levels below the current IOC limits and that the threshold should be reduced.[2]

Ephedrine

Ephedrine and phenylpropanolamine are sympathomimetic amines or "look-alike" drugs because they mimic the effects of amphetamines. Their use increased substantially in the 1970s and coincided, first, with the increase in a number of countries of legal controls over amphetamines and, second, with the growing concern among doctors at the serious side-effects of amphetamine use. As one would expect, ephedrine affects the central nervous system in a very similar way to amphetamine. Physiologically, ephedrine and phenylpropanolamine increase blood pressure and the pulse rate, and, psychologically, they may produce "euphoria and increased alertness".[3]

Ephedrine and similar sympathomimetic amines are widely used in competitive sport due to the widespread perception that they have ergogenic properties. It is believed that they are capable of enhancing endurance and of depressing appetite, and are therefore used by athletes involved in long-distance cycling, swimming and running events, and also by those involved in weigh-related/graded sports, such as judo and wrestling.

The evidence of ergogenic effect is weak. In a double-blind study of twenty-one males using ephedrine or placebo, it was concluded that ephedrine had no effect on a broad range of sports-related variables including strength, endurance, hand-eye co-ordination, speed of recovery from exercise and perception of exertion.[4] A survey of existing studies of ephedrine concluded that the results, from the admittedly small number of studies, suggested that when administered at either therapeutic or twice therapeutic doses, "it appears that ephedrine is not ergogenic".[5]

The side-effects of ephedrine are also similar to, but less common than, those for amphetamine and include, at the extreme, hallucinations, psychosis and compulsive behaviour. Phenylpropanolamine has been associated with some cases of extreme hypertension, but the identification of the specific side-effects of the drug are difficult as it is often taken in combination with other drugs such as caffeine or non-steroidal anti-inflammatory preparations.[6]

---

1. Strauss, 1984, op. cit.; and Stillner, V. et al., "Caffeine-Induced Delirium During Prolonged Competitive Stress", *American Journal of Psychiatry*, Vol. 135, 1978.
2. Sinclair & Geiger, 2000, op. cit.
3. Wadler & Hainline, 1989, op. cit., p. 102.
4. Sidney, K.H. & Lefcoe, W.M., "The Effects of Ephedrine on the Physiological and Psychological on Submaximal and Maximal Exercises in Man", *Medical Science Sports*, Vol. 9, 1977.
5. Clarkson, P.M. & Thompson, H.S., "Drugs and Sport: Research Findings and Limitations", *Sports Medicine*, Vol. 24, 1997, p. 372.
6. Pentel, P., "Toxicity of Over-The-Counter Stimulants", *Journal of the American Medical Association*, 252, 1984.

Narcotic analgesics

Drugs within the narcotics category include diamorphine (heroin) and methadone. From the sixteenth century to the middle of the nineteenth century, opium, from which morphine is derived, was used extensively for its hypnotic and analgesic properties. Early in the nineteenth century, the German pharmacist Sertürner isolated and described morphine, the first of a number of alkaloids of opium which were discovered during the second half of the nineteenth century. The use of the alkaloids rapidly replaced the use of opium in medical treatment.

Narcotic analgesics act primarily on the central nervous system, depressing particular centres and causing a reduction in levels of perception of pain, fear and anxiety as well as reduced powers of concentration. By acting on opiate receptors in the brain, morphine and heroin "appear to be mimicking the effect of certain endogenous opiates, known as endorphins and enkephalins which are thought to control pain".[1]

There is little evidence that narcotics have any ergogenic properties and they have generally been used in sport to enable athletes to continue in competition after injury and also to desensitise athletes participating in contact sports where the risk of injury is high.[2] This pattern of use also constitutes the most significant, though indirect, side-effect of narcotics as the exposure to greater risk of serious injury arising from the power of the drug to raise thresholds of pain beyond the natural level enables athletes to continue to compete when injured thus putting them at risk of further injury or the compounding of the initial injury. Short-term use may result in a number of adverse effects including nausea, constipation, dysphoria and dizziness, although the intensity of the effects will depend on the dose administered.[3] There are also a number of side-effects that result from extended use of narcotic analgesics, the most serious of which is the rapid production of physical dependence manifest through a number of symptoms including sweating, yawning and running eyes followed by muscular cramp, diarrhoea and vomiting, and also a psychogenic dependence where the user experiences an irresistible craving for the drug. Long-term use also leads to the depression of centres in the brain that govern the respiratory system and may, in extreme cases, result in death.

Anabolic agents

Anabolic androgenic steroids (AAS)

There is much evidence of a long-held belief that the testes were the source of male characteristics and in particular were responsible for increased vigour

---

1. Mottram, 1996, op. cit., p. 43.
2. Rounsaville, B. et al., "Neurophysiological Functioning in Opiate Addicts", *Journal of Nervous Mental Disorders,* Vol. 170, 1982.
3. Wadler & Hainline, 1989, op. cit., p. 156.

and strength. As outlined in the previous chapter, the isolation of testosterone was soon followed by the derivation of a series of synthetic anabolic steroids. The increased availability of anabolic steroids in the late 1960s introduced a set of drugs to sport that remain one of the most serious problems for anti-doping agencies to tackle.

Testosterone itself has two central properties: first, it is androgenic, that is it has the effect of developing masculine characteristics and, second, it is anabolic, that is it has a tissue-building effect. One motivation for the development of such a large number of synthetic steroids has been the attempt to separate the two effects and produce a steroid which is anabolic without also being androgenic. The search has so far proved fruitless and all steroids have both properties and are therefore properly referred to as androgenic anabolic steroids (AAS).

The role of testosterone in developing male sexual characteristics occurs in two stages. During the early stages following conception, testosterone is responsible for the development of primary male characteristics while during puberty it affects the development of secondary sexual characteristics, such as the development of pubic hair, enlarged testes and penis, a deeper voice and facial hair. Testosterone also has an effect on the behavioural characteristics associated with aggression. One of the main medical uses of AAS has been to treat problems associated with male development at puberty and thereby restore normal male secondary characteristics and normal male sexual behaviour. AAS have therefore been administered to accelerate the pubertal growth spurt, and they have also been used in the treatment of anaemia, renal failure and osteoporosis, as well as being used in the management of burn victims and to aid the recovery of patients from debilitating illnesses where there has been a loss of weight and strength.

The generally accepted view of the way in which steroids affect the body is that they increase protein synthesis. In brief, strength is proportionate to muscle bulk as measured by changes in the cross-sectional diameter of the muscle being evaluated. Muscle tissue is produced by the conversion of amino acids which are not produced by the body but are obtained by ingesting protein-rich food. Increasing the capacity of the body to create protein is only one of a number of theories which attempt to explain the real or imagined ergogenic effect of steroids. Other hypotheses include the suggestion that AAS enable a more effective utilisation of protein possibly through the increased production of insulin or growth hormone; that they enable more intense exercise to be undertaken which has the effect of stimulating muscle growth; or that the drugs are not inherently ergogenic but create a psychological state where harder and longer training is possible.

Steroids are almost certainly the most widely used drug in modern sport whether measured in terms of the number of countries where abuse has been discovered, the range of sports, and related activities, in which steroids are deemed ergogenic, and the range of levels of competition where their use is apparent. Although steroids were first used by those sportspeople involved in sports that required strength or muscle mass, such as weightlifting, shot-put and discus, it was not long before the drug became common in the explosive events where athletes sought to increase their power. The perception that steroids provide an ergogenic advantage is widespread and deeply held and is best summed up in the report of the Dubin Inquiry:

> "The overwhelming evidence at this Inquiry is that anabolic steroids enhance athletic performance. Witness after witness spoke of increased strength and size; of a greater ability to train intensely, to resist the pain of workouts, and to recuperate; of improved performances; and of new feelings of confidence, physical well-being, and enthusiasm. Coaches and physicians, who had the best opportunity to observe the athletes, were also unequivocal about the performance-enhancing effects which were evident primarily in events requiring weight and strength (including upper and lower body strength in sprinters)."[1]

Providing scientific corroboration for the widely held belief that steroids aid performance is difficult given that the quantities of steroids taken by athletes far exceeds that which would be ethically allowable in any controlled experiment. Use by athletes is often at levels ten to forty times the therapeutic level and may involve "stacking", a practice in which the athlete uses a number of steroids with different pharmacological profiles usually in the hope of benefiting from assumed synergy between the drugs or else in the hope of avoiding the development of tolerance and therefore maintaining the drugs' impact. In a recent survey, it was found that 88% of steroid users practised "stacking".[2] Other regimes are referred to as "cycling" and "pyramiding". The former practice involves periods of intensive steroid use alternating with periods of abstinence, and is designed to avoid some of the side-effects of continuous steroid use. The latter practice is a variation on cycling and involves the gradual build up of drug use and an equally gradual decrease in use during each cycle.[3]

The evidence from scientific experiment indicates that steroids produce both physiological and psychological effects. There is a considerable volume of experimental data concerning the physiological effects of steroids particularly regarding the effects on endurance, bulk and strength. While there seems to be a consensus that steroids have no impact on endurance,[4] there is a

---

1. Dubin Inquiry, 1990, op. cit., p. 103.
2. Evans, N.A., "Gym and Tonic: A Profile of 100 Male Steroid Users", *British Journal of Sports Medicine*, Vol. 31, 1997, pp. 54-8.
3. George, 1996, op. cit., pp. 182-3.
4. Fahey, T.D. & Brown, C.H., "The Effects of Anabolic Steroids on the Strength, Body Composition, and Endurance of College Males When Accompanied by a Weight Training Program", *Medicine and Science in Sports*, Vol. 5, 1973, pp. 272-6.

marked lack of consensus regarding the impact on bulk and strength. There have been numerous studies that have concluded that steroids do increase strength,[1] but an equal number claiming no significant increase.[2] A review of studies of the effects of steroids carried out between 1965 and 1977 concluded that there was "no substantial evidence" that steroid use in conjunction with progressive weight-resistance training led to increased lean muscle bulk and greater strength".[3] "On the contrary, there is a substantial body of evidence that will stand very close scrutiny to indicate that anabolic steroids will not contribute significantly to gains in lean muscle bulk or muscle strength in healthy young adult males."[4] The conclusions of the survey suggested that the key factor undermining the ergogenic effect of steroids is the fact that the body compensates for any increase in steroid use by depressing the level of testosterone production. However, these conclusions are challenged by those of Haupt and Rovere who argue that under particular circumstances steroids can be effective in increasing strength. Improvements will result, they claimed, if the athlete engages in intensive weight training before and during the course of steroids; consumes a high protein diet; and measurement of change is through single-repetition weight techniques.[5] A similar conclusion was reached as a result of a survey by the American College of Sports Medicine, also produced in 1984, which concluded that anabolic steroids can contribute to increases in lean mass and body weight if their use is supported by an adequate diet. The college claimed that muscular strength could also be increased through the use of steroids if coupled with an intensive training regime and proper diet. The college also concluded that steroids do not increase aerobic power.[6] It is also suggested that the physiological effects of steroid use may, in part at least, be due to a placebo effect. In other words, when athletes start taking steroids they expect to be able to train longer or lift heavier weights and consequently push themselves that much harder attributing the improved performance to the effects of the steroids rather than to their own determination and increased effort. Just such an effect was found in a study with experienced weightlifters who they told were being given methandrostenolone, but were in fact receiving a

1. Stamford, B.A. & Moffatt, R., "Anabolic Steroid: Effectiveness as an Ergogenic Aid to Experienced Weight Trainers", *Journal of Sports Medicine and Physical Fitness*, Vol. 14, pp. 191-7, 1974; and Ward, P., "The Effect of an Anabolic Steroid on Strength and Lean Body Mass", *Medical Science Sports*, Vol. 5, 1973, pp. 277-82.
2. Hervey, G.R., & Knibbs, A.V. et al., "Are Athletes Wrong About Anabolic Steroids?", *British Journal of Sports Medicine*, Vol. 9, 1975, pp. 74-7; and Loughton, S.V. & Ruhline, R.O. "Human Strength and Endurance Responses to Anabolic Steroids and Training", *Journal Sports Medicine and Physical Fitness*, Vol .17, 1977, pp. 285-96.
3. Ryan, A.J., "Anabolic Steroids are Fool's Gold", *Federation of American Society for Experimental Biology*, Vol. 40.12, 1981, pp. 2 682-88.
4. Ibid., p. 2 684.
5. Haupt, H.A. & Rovere, G.D., "Anabolic Steroids: A Review of the Literature", *American Journal of Sports Medicine*, Vol. 12.6, 1984, pp. 469-84.
6. American College of Sports Medicine, "Stand on the Use of Anabolic-Androgenic Steroids in Sport", Indianapolis: American College of Sports Medicine, 1984.

placebo.[1] It is interesting to note that a very high proportion of illegally obtained steroids, which is a substantial proportion of the total used, is either fake or significantly adulterated. One survey found that 26% of a sample of thirty-four illegally obtained steroids tested contained no steroids, 53% were mislabelled and 85% contained the wrong dose.[2] These figures highlight the need for caution in accepting the conclusions of any study which is based on the self-reporting by illegal steroid users.

The extended use of steroids has been associated with numerous side-effects which range from the minor to the severe and which affect a variety of bodily systems. Because steroid use in men tends to depress the natural production of testosterone, there are a number of side-effects that affect sex organs and sexual behaviour. Testicular size tends to decrease as does the production of sperm.[3] In one study, a fall of 73% in the sperm count was noted with three of the subjects exhibiting a complete absence of sperm.[4] The sex drive may also be affected, although the effect is variable often producing an enhanced sex drive in the early stages of use but a diminished sex drive after sustained use.[5] A number of steroid users also take human chorionic gonadotrophin in an attempt to counteract testicular atrophy and/or diminished libido.[6] Additional problems may include the development of breast tissue.[7] Changes may also be experienced in the level of blood pressure and in the balance between high-density and low-density lipoprotein cholesterol: such changes have been identified as increasing the risk of cardiovascular disease.[8] While there is not sufficient evidence to draw a firm conclusion that changes in the cholesterol balance lead to increased cardiovascular risk due to the absence of long-term studies, it is the case that "in a review of sudden deaths among competitive athletes, three out of twenty-nine could be

1. Ariel, G. & Saville, W., "Anabolic Steroids: The Physiological Effects of Placebos", *Medicine and Science in Sports*, Vol. 4, 1972, pp. 124-6.
2. Walters, M., Ayers, R. & Brown D., "Analysis of Illegally Distributed Steroid Products by Liquid Chromatography with Identity Confirmation by Mass Spectrometry or Infrared Spectrophotometry". *Journal of the Association of Analytical Chemistry*, Vol. 73.6, 1990, pp 904-26.
3. Jackson, H. & Jones, A.R. "The Effects of Steroids and their Antagonists on Spermatogenesis", *Advanced Steroid Biochemistry and Pharmacology*, 1972, Vol. 3.
4. Quoted in Mottram, D.R. & George, A.J., "Anabolic Steroids", *Baillière's Best Practice and Research: Clinical Endocrinology and Metabolism*, Vol. 14.1, 2000, pp. 55-69.
5. Strauss, R.H., Wright, J.E, Finerman, G.A.M. & Catlin, D.H., "Side-Effects of Anabolic Steroids in Weight-Trained Men", *Physician and Sports Medicine*, Vol. 11, 1983, pp. 87-101.
6. Ibid., p. 258.
7. Strauss, R.H., "Anabolic Steroids" in Strauss, R.H. (ed.), *Drugs and Performance in Sports*, Philadelphia: W.B. Saunders, 1987.
8. See Rockhold, R.W., "Cardiovascular Toxicity of Anabolic Steroids", *Annual Review of Pharmacological Toxicity*, Vol. 33, 1993, pp. 497-520, for a discussion of the evidence on the effect of steroids on blood pressure; Strauss, R.H., Wright, J.E, Finerman, G.A.M. & Catlin, D.H., "Anabolic Steroid Use and Health Status Among Weight-Trained Male Athletes", *The Physician and Sports Medicine*, Vol. 13, 1985; McKillop, G. & Ballantyne, D., "Lipoprotein Analysis in Bodybuilders", *International Journal of Cardiology*, Vol. 17, 1987, pp. 281-6; and Chrostowski, K., Kozera, J. & Grueza, R., "Medical Consequences of Anabolic Steroids Abuse", *Biology of Sport*, 17.2, 2000, pp. 133-52.

attributed to coronary atherosclerosis".[1] Another side-effect associated primarily with men is damage to tendons, possibly be due to the failure of tendon strength to keep pace with muscle strength, the possibility that steroid use inhibits the collagen which is an important element in tendons or the reduction in tendon plasticity arising from steroid use.[2] A recent review of the evidence regarding the ergogenic value of anabolic steroids concluded that due to "variability in subject selection; type, dose, frequency and duration of steroid use; control of dietary and training factors; and ethical considerations ... it is unlikely that conclusive evidence for the androgenic potential of anabolic steroids will ever be achieved".[3] Nevertheless, the authors noted that the lack of evidence has not stopped the perception of the utility of steroids becoming deeply entrenched.

For both men and women there have been reports of a risk of jaundice and liver damage, and also the danger that the self-administration of steroids may result in the transmission of diseases such as hepatitis B and Aids. A further concern is that steroid use may contribute to the likelihood of developing cancers of the liver.[4] Although a British weightlifter, Shaw, died in 1990 from liver tumours at the age of 25, the evidence is circumstantial rather than direct. There is also a series of side-effects that affect women. There are reports of a number of masculinising effects including a deepening of the voice, male pattern baldness, acne, growth of facial hair, changes or cessation of the menstrual function, decreased breast size and enlargement of the clitoris.[5]

Where use occurs among youths who have not yet fully matured, the effects can be to accelerate the maturation process but to prevent the individual reaching his potential adult height.[6] However, the emergence of a scientific consensus on this particular side-effect has been hampered by studies which suggest that some steroids can indeed be taken by boys to speed up growth without also accelerating skeletal maturation.[7]

In addition to the physiological side-effects, there are also a number of psychological side-effects including increased aggressiveness, sometimes referred to as "roid rages", and mood swings.[1] In one study, 22% of the

---

1. Ljungqvist, A., "Health Risks of Steroid Use" in Shipe, J.R. & Savory, J. (eds.), *Drugs in Competitive Athletics*, Oxford: Blackwell Scientific Publications, 1991, p. 94.
2. Laseler, J.T. & Russell, J.A., "Anabolic Steroid Induced Tendon Pathology: A Review of the Literature, *Medical Scientific Sports Executive*, 23, 1991, pp. 1-3.
3. Mottram & George, 2000, op. cit., p. 63.
4. Vesselinovitch, S.D., Mihailovich, N. & Rao, K.V.N., "Potential Role of Synthetic Sex Steroids in Hepatocarcinogenesis" in Shipe, J.R. & Savory, J. (eds.), *Drugs in Competitive Athletics*, Oxford: Blackwell Scientific Publications, 1991.
5. Ibid.; and Strauss, 1984, op. cit., p. 483.
6. Daniel, W.A. & Bennett, D.L., "The Use of Anabolic-Androgenic Steroids in Childhood and Adolescence" in Kochakian, C.D. (ed.), *Anabolic-Androgenic Steroids*, New York: Springer Verlag, 1976; and Lamb, D.R., "Anabolic Steroids in Athletics: How Well Do They Work and How Dangerous Are They?", *American Journal of Sports Medicine*, Vol. 12, 1984, pp. 31-8.
7. Millar, A.P., "Licit Steroid Use – Hope for the Future", *British Journal of Sports Medicine*, Vol. 28.2, 1994, pp. 79-83.

sample of 41 steroid users exhibited manic or depressive episodes at some time during their use of steroids,[2] while a more recent study of chronic steroid users found that 83% of the sample (n=12) exhibited signs of at least one personality disorder.[3] Choi and Pope found noticeably higher levels of severe aggression towards female partners among steroid users than among non-steroid users.[4] Although these symptoms are serious, they seem to disappear once the use of steroids has been discontinued.[5] However, not all psychological effects are negative as a number of users report feeling more relaxed, powerful and confident and more content with their body image as a result of steroid use.

As regards discontinuation of use, there is a debate about the extent to which steroid use results in dependence. According to the *Diagnostic Statistical Manual IV*, steroids have the potential to produce dependence whereas the *International Classification of Diseases* (Volume 10) codes steroids as non-dependence producing substances, a conclusion generally supported by recent research which suggested that adopting the conventional criteria for determining dependence, such as the use of increasing quantities of a drug, are not so readily applicable to steroids as increasing use (or cycling) is an integral part of steroid use.[6] However, there is also some contrary evidence which suggests that prolonged use of steroids does indeed lead to addiction, especially among adolescent users.[7] It has also been suggested that depression has followed the cessation of steroid use.[8] Yet few of these conclusions can be seen as more than indicative due to the fact that most are based on a very small sample or are individual histories, often of the more dramatic cases. As a result, it is not possible to use the existing evidence as a basis for generalisation. "Although anabolic steroid dependency may be a problem, its prevalence and symptomology is difficult to reliably establish based upon the existing literature".[9] Bahrke et al., also note that given the widespread use of

---

1. Ljungqvist, 1991, op. cit.
2. Pope, H.G. & Katz, D.L., "Affective and Psychotic Symptoms Associated with Anabolic Steroid Use", *American Journal of Psychiatry*, Vol. 145, 1988, pp. 487-90.
3. Cooper, C.J., Noakes, T.D., Dunne, T., Lambert, M.I. & Rochford, K., "A High Prevalence of Abnormal Personality Traits in Chronic Users of Anabolic-Androgenic Steroids", *British Journal of Sports Medicine*, 30, 1996, pp. 246-50.
4. Choi, P.Y.L. & Pope, H.G., "Violence Toward Women and Illicit Androgenic Anabolic Steroid Use", *Annals of Clinical Psychiatry*, 6, 1994, pp. 22-5.
5. Bahrke, M.S., Yesalis, C.E. & Wright, J.E., "Psychological and Behavioral Effects of Endogenous Testosterone Levels and Anabolic-Androgenic Steroids Among Males", *Sports Medicine*, Vol. 10 1990, pp. 303-37.
6. Midgley, S.J., Heather, N. & Davies, J.B., "Dependence-Producing Potential of Anabolic-Androgenic Steroids", *Addiction Research*, 7.6, 1999, pp. 539-50.
7. Middleman, A.B. & DuRant, R.H., "Anabolic Steroid Use and Associated Health Risk Behaviours", *Sports Medicine*, Vol. 21.4, 1996, pp. 251-5.
8. Burkett, L.N. & Faldulto, M.T., "Steroid Use by Athletes in a Metropolitan Area", *Physician and Sports Medicine*, Vol. 12.8, 1984, pp. 69-74.
9. Bahrke, M.S., Yesalis, C.E. & Wright, J.E., "Psychological and Behavioral Effects of Endogenous Testosterone and Anabolic-Androgenic Steroids: An Update", *Sports Medicine*, 1996, Vol. 22.6, p. 384.

steroids there seem to be a comparatively small number of cases of psychological conditions requiring treatment.

Despite the widespread assumption of a preoccupation among steroid users with their appearance and fitness, there is evidence of an association between steroid use and the abuse of other substances including cocaine and marijuana. Anabolic steroid use by young people has also been associated with other high-risk behaviour including driving while drunk, unprotected sex and carrying a weapon.[1] In one of the most recent and comprehensive surveys of published data on the association between steroid use and a range of negative psychological effects, it was found that apart from a small minority most of the thirty-two studies confirmed the association.[2]

Testosterone

All that has been written about anabolic androgenic steroids also applies to any discussion of testosterone. However, testosterone requires a brief separate discussion because of the recent increase in its abuse by athletes. Testosterone has been added to the IOC list of banned substances and practices only comparatively recently due to its increasing substitution for other anabolic steroids and because of the difficulties that doping agencies face in distinguishing exogenous from endogenous testosterone. The need to address the problem of testosterone abuse was highlighted at the 1980 Olympic Games where it was found that as many as two-thirds of all random urine samples contained abnormal levels of testosterone. As testosterone is produced within the body so too is a smaller amount of epitestosterone, its isomer. Because of differential rates of excretion, the ratio of testosterone to epitestosterone is normally approximately 1:1. It is variation from this norm that provides the basis for identifying the presence of exogenous testosterone.

Testosterone is present in the bodies of both men and women. In pre-pubertal boys and women, the level of daily production is less than 0.25 micrograms per day, while for men the level increases to between 2.5 and 11 micrograms per day with the surge in production taking place during puberty. In women, testosterone is produced in the adrenal cortex and the ovaries; for men, production is by the testes and also the adrenal cortex. Testosterone achieves its effects through a complex series of receptors distributed throughout the body.

The assumed value of testosterone to the athlete is similar to that of anabolic androgenic steroids, namely having the physiological effect of promoting muscle growth and strength, and the psychological effect of enhancing

---

1. Middleman, A.B., Faulkner, A.H., Woods, E.R. et al., "High Risk Behaviours Among High School Students in Massachusetts Who Use Anabolic Steroids", *Pediatrics*, Vol. 96, 1995, pp. 268-72.
2. Bahrke et al., 1996, op. cit.

aggression. As the use of exogenous testosterone is comparatively recent, there are few studies which test its effectiveness in relation to sport. One of the few studies that have been carried out examined the effect of testosterone administered in weekly doses of 600 mg over a ten-week period to males with experience of weight training.[1] The men were divided into four groups, the first received a placebo and took no exercise; the second group received doses of testosterone and took no exercise; the third were given a placebo coupled with resistance training; while the fourth group were given doses of testosterone coupled with resistance training. Both groups to whom testosterone was administered showed increases in muscle size and strength, but the greatest increase was evident among the group which was undertaking resistance training as well as receiving testosterone. There have also been some studies of the relationship between endogenous testosterone levels and mood and behaviour, one of which found a positive correlation between the level of aggressive behaviour in a sample of college students and levels of testosterone.[2] In one study, it was found that "men producing more testosterone are less likely to marry: once married, they are more likely to leave home because of troubled marital relations, extra-marital sex, hitting or throwing things at their spouses ..."[3] Although there are some studies that question the link between aggression and testosterone levels, the balance of opinion is supportive of such a link and is one of the reasons for the choice of testosterone by drug abusers in sport. The psychological benefit in competition sought by abusers of testosterone is also one of the drug's main side-effects; for although athletes hope to focus their enhanced levels of aggression on the competition, it is impossible to prevent it spilling over into their non-sporting relationships.

Nandrolone

Although it is a member of the steroid family, Nandrolone also requires a separate discussion because of the attention it has attracted in recent years and the number of high-profile athletes who have tested positive for the drug, including the footballers Frank de Boer, Edgar Davids, Japp Stam and Fernando Cuoto, track athletes including Linford Christie, Dougie Walker and Merlene Ottey, and the tennis player Petr Korda. Such is its current popularity that there were 343 positive results for the drug in 1999. However, the steady rise in the number of positive tests for nandrolone needs to be placed in the context of the increase in the number of tests conducted. Globally, the proportion of total tests that show positive for nandrolone has remained virtually unchanged over the last eight years at about 0.25%.

---

1. Bhasin, S., Storer, T.W., Berman, N. et al., "The Effects of Supra-Physiologic Doses of Testosterone on Muscle Size and Strength in Normal Men", *New England Journal of Medicine*, Vol. 335, 1996, pp. 1-7.
2. Gladue, B., "Qualitative and Quantitative Sex Differences in Self-Reported Aggressive Behavioural Characteristics", *Psychological Reports*, Vol. 68, 1991, pp. 675-84.
3. Referred to in Bahrke et al., 1996, op. cit., p. 372.

However, over the same period within the UK the figure has shown a marked increase, rising from between 0.07% and 0.13% to 0.29% in 1999.[1]

Nandrolone occurs naturally in small amounts in all animals including humans and acts as an intermediary in the synthesis of estrogens from androgens. Synthetic nandrolone was developed in the 1970s and has a limited range of therapeutic uses including the treatment of breast cancer and anaemia. In addition to its therapeutic uses, it also exhibited certain properties that soon made it attractive to drug-abusing athletes, including its suitability for injection into muscle, its slow pace of release into the blood and its reduced androgenic effects. Following administration, nandrolone is metabolised (modified by the body) into a number of different metabolites (substances) which are then excreted in urine. One of the most significant metabolites of nandrolone, 19-norandrosterone, is also produced by the nandrolone that occurs naturally. Although the IOC list of banned substances does not seek to be exhaustive, newly identified specific metabolites of steroids will be added when identified. A number of metabolites of nandrolone were added in the late 1990s, for example, androstenedione in January 1998 and 19-norandrostenedione in January 1999.

The spate of positive tests for nandrolone that occurred worldwide, but which were particularly numerous and high profile in the UK, led UK Sport (a UK Government agency) to establish an expert committee to review the current procedures for testing for nandrolone.[2] The review took place at a time of considerable speculation that the increased incidence of nandrolone positives might be due variously to the continued illicit use of the drug, its unlisted presence within nutritional supplements, its ingestion from the flesh of animals given the drug and synthesis of small amounts in females from androstenedione during pregnancy.[3] The suggestion that nandrolone might be produced endogenously as a result of an athlete taking nutritional supplements, such as acetyl carnitine, was firmly rejected. The committee was more inclined to support the argument that inadequate labelling or indeed the deliberate mislabelling of some nutritional supplements might account for some of the positive results for steroids such as nandrolone. The committee also rejected the possibility that nandrolone positives might be due to the consumption of meat from animals, such as boar and horse, which produce nandrolone naturally but, due to the lack of extensive research evidence, did suggest that it would be wise for athletes to avoid offal from boar and horse. The broad conclusions of the review committee were substantially endorsed by a French study which concluded that the very small levels of endogenous

---

1. In 1999 there were some minor changes to the regulations regarding the reporting of low levels of steroids which might account for part of the increase.
2. Nandrolone Review Committee, *Nandrolone Review*: Report to UK Sport, London: UK Sport, 2000.
3. Mottram & George, 2000, op. cit.

nandrolone found in humans "have nothing in common with the high levels reported in doping controls in 1997-98".[1]

Insulin

Insulin has been in common use for the management of diabetes since the 1920s, but it was only from the 1980s that it became widely used by athletes who were attracted to the drug because of its capacity to promote anabolic processes and inhibit catabolic processes. In sport, insulin is often used in conjunction with steroids and is especially popular with body builders who use the drug after "loading" with carbohydrates as it helps increase the amount of water retained in the muscles thus giving the muscles a sharper definition. While there is only limited evidence regarding the performance enhancing properties of insulin, there is a broad consensus regarding the side-effects. "Self-administering insulin is fraught with danger with hypogly-caemia being the most obvious and greatest risk ... Complications include tremors, sweating, nausea, tachycardia, weakness and shortness of breath, with more serious symptoms due to neuroglycopaenia with drowsiness, dis-orientation, convulsions, coma and death".[2]

Herbal and nutritional supplements

Herbal and nutritional supplements have become increasingly popular with athletes over the last five years or so and there is now a substantial industry marketing supplements to the sporting community. In a study of the use of supplements in 1994, it was found that 59% of élite athletes took some form of nutritional supplement (by comparison to a figure of 35-40% among the general population).[3] In a more recent study of élite Norwegian athletes, it was found that 84% used one or more micronutrient supplements. Norwegian power athletes (boxers, weightlifters and field athletes) were found to have the highest level of usage with creatine (45%) being the most commonly used supplement.[4] The range of products and preparations is extensive and varied, and includes vitamins, ginseng, bicarbonate, carnitine, chromium picolinate, amino acids and creatine. The problems that arise for athletes in using these substances is that many are manufactured outside the strict regulatory framework that operates in relation to the production of medicines. There is consequently a greater risk of the consumption of products that have been deliberately contaminated (with steroids for example) so

1. Wright, F., Bricout, V., Doukani, A. & Bongini, M., "Nandrolone et norstéroïdes: substances endogènes ou xénoboitiques?", *Science et Sport*, 15, 2000, pp. 111-24.
2. Corrigan, B., "Drugs and Nutrition", *Journal of Science and Medicine in Sport*, 3.4, 2000, pp. 339-59.
3. Sobal, J. & Marquart, L.F., "Vitamin/Mineral Supplement Use Among Athletes: A Review of the Literature", *International Journal of Sports Nutrition*, 4, 1994, pp. 320-34.
4. Ronsen, O., Sundgot-Borgen, J. & Maehlum, S., "Supplement Use and Nutritional Habits in Norwegian Elite Athletes", *Scandanavian Journal of Medicine and Science in Sports*, 9, 1999, pp. 28-35.

as to increase the attractiveness to the sports/body-building market, or the consumption of products that contain prohibited substances and which are simply not indicated on the packaging.[1] Some of the commonly used supplements are reviewed below.[2]

Ginseng root has been in common use for some 5 000 years. The active ingredients are saponin glycosides, usually referred to as ginsenosides, and are found in over twenty different plants each with slightly different effects. Some ginseng is used to prevent fatigue while other forms are used due to claims that they are able to improve concentration and strengthen immunity from infection. There is no recognised medical use for ginseng and little evidence of beneficial effects for athletes.[3] However, the substance is heavily promoted among athletes for its capacity to increase stamina and reduce stress. A study by Cui et al. of fifty ginseng products found no ginsenosides in six and traces of ephedrine in others.[4] Further evidence of the temptation to add ephedrine to ginseng products comes from the series of positive test results for ephedrine in athletes, including Linford Christie and Antoinette Bevilacqua, who claimed that they had been taking ginseng.

Guarana, which is a form of caffeine, is another substance which has gained some popularity among athletes and is frequently found in composite nutritional products. Whereas coffee and tea contain levels of caffeine between 1% and 4%, the level in guarana is up to 5%. While caffeine is a controlled, rather than a banned, substance athletes need to be clear and cautious about the quantities of guarana they consume.

Chromium picolinate is thought to enhance the effects of insulin and, in sport, to increase the body's capacity for muscle gain. There is little scientific evidence regarding the performance enhancing effects of the substance although the evidence that does exist suggests that chromium has no identifiable effect on body composition or strength.[5] Evidence regarding the side-effects is scant and relates to isolated cases although there is some evidence of gastric intolerance. According to Corrigan, chromium picolinate is unlikely to produce any marked benefit to athletes unless they were chromium deficient.[6]

Carbohydrate supplementation is a well-established practice among athletes, especially in endurance events such as long-distance running and cycling and

---

1. UK Sport, "Drugs and Sport: Herbal and Nutritional Supplements", London: UK Sport, 1998.
2. See Maughan, R.J., "Nutritional Ergogenic Aids and Exercise Performance", *Nutrition Research Reviews*, 12, 1999, pp. 255-80; Kreider, R.B., "Dietary Supplements and the Promotion of Muscle Growth with Resistance Exercise", *Sports Medicine*, February 1999, pp. 97-110; and Corrigan, 2000, op. cit., for fuller discussions of the range and effects of supplements.
3. Corrigan, 2000, op. cit.
4. Cui, J.F. et al., "What Do Commercial Ginseng Products Contain?", *Lancet*, 344, 1994, p. 134.
5. Corrigan, 2000, op. cit.
6. Ibid.

also in tennis. There is a substantial body of evidence which indicates that the administration of carbohydrates markedly improves endurance exercise capacity and, in the case of tennis, increases stroke quality in the final stages of prolonged play.[1] There is little evidence of any harmful side-effects associated with carbohydrate supplementation.

Creatine monohydrate is perhaps the most controversial supplement to be used by athletes. Creatine is an amino acid found in fish and meat and also stored in the human body as creatine phosphate, which is used in the production of energy for high-intensity activity. Athletes have been attracted to creatine supplementation in the hope that its use will increase their store of creatine phosphate and thus their energy levels or else act as a buffer against the production of lactic acid (a source of muscle fatigue). Creatine use has been most popular in those sports that require repeated bursts of high-intensity activity such as football, handball and rugby.

There is a growing body of research which confirms the capacity of creatine to enhance muscle power with one study of handball players concluding that "short-term Cr [creatine] supplementation leads to significant improvements in lower body maximal strength, maximal repetitive high power exercise bouts and total repetitions performed to fatigue".[2] Similar results were produced in studies of "moderately resistance trained men"[3] and experienced male sprinters who improved their sprint time over 60 m by up to 0.11 seconds.[4] However, another study of sprinters reached contrary conclusions as the research team found no improvement.[5] When tennis players were given creatine, the study found that there was no improvement in "stroke performance or sprint power in match-like conditions".[6] As regards the side-effects of creatine use, the evidence is mixed with some claims that use leads to renal dysfunction[7] countered by a greater weight of research that concludes that "neither short-term, medium-term, nor long-term oral creatine supplements

1. Vergauwen, L. et al., "Carbohydrate Supplementation Improves Stroke Performance in Tennis", *Medicine and Science in Sport and Exercise*, 1998, pp. 1289-94; see also Sugiura, K. & Kobayashi, K., "Effects of Carbohydrate Ingestion on Sprint Performance Following Continuous and Intermittent Exercise", *Medicine and Science in Sport and Exercise*, 1998, pp. 1 624-30.
2. Izquierdo, M., Ibanez, J., González-Badillo, J. & Gorostiaga, E., "Creatine Supplementation and Muscle Power Output in Handball Players", paper, 6th annual congress of the European College of Sport Science, Cologne, 24-28 July 2001.
3. Volek, J.S. et al., "Performance and Muscle Fiber Adaptations to Creatine Supplementation and Heavy Resistance Training", *Medicine and Science in Sports and Exercise*, 1999, pp. 1147-56.
4. Skare, O.-C., Skadberg, O. & Wisnes, A.R., "Creatine Supplementation Improves Sprint Performances in Male Sprinters", *Scandanavian Journal of Medicine and Science in Sport*, 11, pp. 96-102, 2001.
5. Javierre, C. et al., "Creatine Supplementation Does Not Improve Physical Performance in a 150 m Race", *Journal of Physiological Biochemistry*, 53, 1997, pp. 343-8.
6. Op., B. et al., "Creatine Loading Does Not Impact on Stroke Performance in Tennis", *International Journal of Sports Medicine*, 22, 2001, pp. 76-80.
7. Pritchard, N.R. & Kalra, P.A., "Renal Dysfunction Accompanying Oral Creatine Supplementation", *Lancet*, 351, 1998, pp. 1 252-3.

induce detrimental effects on the kidney of healthy individuals".[1] Maughan, in a review of twenty-six separate studies of creatine use, concluded that "there are no documented adverse effects resulting from the ingestion of creatine".[2]

Diuretics

Diuretics affect the rate at which urine is formed and directly affect the kidneys. Diuretics are used therapeutically to treat high blood pressure and excessive fluid retention. In sport, the drugs in this class have been used either to help achieve weight loss in weight-regulated sports such as wrestling and horse-racing, and also to conceal the presence of other drugs by affecting the rate at which they are excreted in the urine. There is also evidence that body builders are using diuretics in combination with steroids in order to counteract the water-retention properties of the latter and, especially, to produce sharper muscle definition by reducing the level of water retention. As regards the effectiveness of diuretics, it has been claimed that they can lead to an average weight loss of 4.1% within a 24-hour period.[3] It is also claimed that the diuretic acetazolamide has the capacity to improve performance at high altitudes.[4]

The side-effects of diuretic use are frequently difficult to isolate as the athlete is often either using other drugs which the diuretic is designed to help conceal or the athlete might be using other methods in addition to the diuretic to lose weight. The most obvious effect of diuretic use is dehydration which might not affect the athlete's performance in the early stages of competition but will usually affect performance in any sport which requires endurance. Because many diuretics also result in the excretion of potassium, there is a consequent risk of muscle cramps and general fatigue. In addition, "a stable level of potassium ... is very important for muscular contractions, for the regularity and efficiency of the heartbeat".[5] The American College of Sports

1. Poortmans, J.R. & Francaux, M., "Long-Term Oral Creatine Supplementation Does Not Impair Renal Function in Healthy Athletes", *Medicine and Science in Sports and Exercise*, 1999, pp. 1108-10; Kamber, M. et al., "Creatine Supplementation – Part 1: Performance, Clinical Chemistry, and Muscle Volume", *Medicine and Science in Sports and Exercise*, pp. 1 763-9; Schilling, B.K. et al., "Creatine Supplementation and Health Variables: A Retrospective Study", *Medicine and Science in Sports and Exercise*, 2001, pp. 183-6; Robinson, T.M. et al., "Dietary Creatine Supplementation Does Not Affect some Haematological Indices, or Indices of Muscle Damage and Hepatic and Renal Function", *British Journal of Sports Medicine*, 34, 2000, pp. 284-8.
2. Maughan, 1999, op. cit.
3. Caldwell, J.E., Ahonen, E. & Nousiainen, U., "Differential Effects of Sauna-, Diuretic-, and Exercise-Induced Hypohydration", *Journal of Applied Physiology*, Vol. 57, 1984, pp. 1 018-23.
4. Bradwell, A.R., Dykes, P.W., Coote, J.H. et al., "Effects of Acetazolamideon Exercise Performance and Muscle Mass at High Altitude", *Lancet*, 1.2, 1986, pp. 1001-5, quoted in Verroken, M., "Drug Use and Abuse in Sport" in Mottram, 1996, op. cit.
5. Comment from Dr Andrew Pipe giving evidence to the Dubin Inquiry, 1990, op. cit., p. 117.

Medicine, in a position paper on the effects on wrestlers of attempting to "make weight", identify a series of side-effects including the following:

> *"a reduction in muscle strength, ... a decrease in work performance times, ... lower plasma and blood volumes... a lower aerobic capacity... impairment of body temperature regulation [and] ... a decrease in blood flow to the kidney and in the volume of fluid being filtered by the kidney".*[1]

Peptide and glycoprotein hormones and analogues

Human Chorionic Gonadotrophin (hCG)

Human Chorionic Gonadotrophin (hCG) is produced in the placenta and in turn stimulates the production of the hormone progesterone during pregnancy. When hCG is injected into males it has the effect of stimulating cells within the testes to produce testosterone and epitestosterone. The effect of hCG is rapid with one study reporting that the production of plasma testosterone can be increased by 50% within two hours of injection.[2]

The attraction of hCG to drug abusers is that it possesses similar properties to steroids and, more importantly, is impossible to detect. The advantage of hCG over both steroid abuse and testosterone abuse is that it stimulates the natural production of both testosterone and epitestosterone thus keeping the ratio of testosterone to epitestosterone below the IOC threshold of 6:1.[3] The side-effects of the drug are similar to those of steroids although one study has suggested that its use will prompt nausea and vomiting[4] and another noted that the incidence of the development of breast tissue may be greater due to the effect of the drug in stimulating the production of the oestradiol.[5]

Adrenocorticotrophic Hormone

Adrenocorticotrophic Hormone (ACTH) is produced by the anterior pituitary and has the effect of stimulating the production of corticosteroids which have anti-inflammatory properties, and may also affect mood. However, the interest in ACTH among drug abusers in sport is focused on one of its derivatives, tetracosactrin, which "stimulates a rise in blood cortisol and corticosterone concentration within 2 hours" and is used "in an attempt to reduce lethargy and produce 'positive' effects on mood during training and competition".[6] It is claimed that the drug is used by cyclists to "produce feelings of

---

1. American College of Sports Medicine, "Position Stand: Weight Loss in Wrestlers", Indianapolis: American College of Sports Medicine, 1976.
2. Kicman, A.T., Brooks, R.V. & Cowan, D.A., "Human Chorionic Gonadotrophin and Sport", *British Journal of Sports Medicine*, Vol. 25, 1991, pp. 73-80.
3. Ibid.
4. Goldman, 1992, op. cit.
5. George, A., "The Anabolic Steroids and Peptide Hormones" in Mottram, 1996, op. cit.
6. Ibid.

well-being or even euphoria".[1] However, the effects are not only short lived but have the serious side-effect of leading to wasting of the muscle if used over a long period. Because the use of synthetic ACTH suppresses the natural secretion of ACTH, there is a risk that a sharp reduction in drug use will result in an insufficiency of corticosteroids due to degeneration of the adrenal glands thus making the athlete more vulnerable to infection.

Human Growth Hormone (hGH)

The increasing success of the doping agencies in detecting steroid abuse has encouraged some athletes to explore the potential benefits of hGH. Released from the pituitary gland, hGH controls the natural growth of almost every body system. The main therapeutic use of hGH is to help growth hormone deficient children reach normal height, but it has also been successfully used to stimulate growth in children who are not deficient in endogenous growth hormone and also in the treatment of severe burns.[2] Among the most important effects of hGH are to stimulate nitrogen retention (an important element in anabolic effects), to help break down fat and convert it to energy, and to stimulate the production of somatomedins, which are the molecules that facilitate growth. These findings have led to "the spurious thinking by some that providing human growth hormone to otherwise healthy athletes could result in considerable improvement in muscular strength ... despite the fact that no scientific evidence exists that could document this effect in healthy individuals".[3]

Up until 1985, pituitary hGH extracted from cadavers was used, but was replaced by synthetic hGH when a number of children receiving treatment contracted Creutzfeldt-Jakob disease and subsequently died. The development of synthetic (genetically engineered) hGH coincided with an increase in its abuse by athletes who believed that, in addition to fulfilling the same role as anabolic steroids in producing muscle bulk and strength, it would also help to "prevent the breakdown of muscles after [A]AS use has been discontinued".[4] There was also a belief that hGH was able to strengthen tendons and ligaments thus reducing the likelihood of muscle damage during intensive training and competition.[5] Additional motives for using hGH included the assumption that it would enhance muscle growth but depress fat accumulation; it was also thought that some parents were supporting their children's

---

1. Donohoe & Johnson, 1986, op. cit., p. 97.
2. Van Vliet, G. et al., "Growth Hormone Treatment for Short Stature", *New England Law Journal of Medicine*, Vol. 309, 1983, pp. 277-82; and Wilmore, D.W., Moylan, J.A., Bristow, B.F. et al., "Anabolic Effects of Human Growth Hormone and High Caloric Feedings Following Thermal Injury", *Surgery Gynecology and Obstetrics*, 138, 1974, pp. 875-84.
3. Puffer, 1986, op. cit., p. 82; see also Cowart, V.S., "Human Growth Hormone: The Latest Ergogenic Aid?", *Physician and Sports Medicine*, Vol. 16, 1988, pp. 175-85.
4. Rickert, V.I., Pawlak-Morello, C., Sheppard, V. & Jay, M.S., "Human Growth Hormone: A New Substance of Abuse Among Adolescents?", *Clinical Pediatrics*, Vol. 31, 1992, p. 724.
5. Ibid.

use of hGH in order to ensure that they reached the "approved or optimal" height for particular sports.[1] Female athletes are thought to be attracted to hGH because of the absence of risk of developing the androgenic side-effects associated with steroids.[2]

The paucity of experimental data makes confident generalisations about the effects of hGH impossible. Experiments on rats seem to indicate that hGH does enhance muscle bulk, especially in atrophied muscle. There is also some evidence that when hGH has been administered for therapeutic purposes to humans, muscle bulk has increased but not muscle strength. Wadler and Hainline support Puffer's conclusion by emphasising that, "No improved performance effect has ever been demonstrated from the use of this hormone".[3] This conclusion was further reinforced by a series of double-blind placebo controlled studies.[4] As the controlled studies involved quantities of hGH far below the reported levels of use by athletes, firm conclusions about the lack of benefit of the drug need to be conditional. However, evidence that athletes tend to use hGH in combination with a steroid would seem to confirm that confidence in the ergogenic potential of hGH alone is limited. Nevertheless, the combination of enthusiasm for the drug among athletes and a lack of evidence of any proven ergogenic value should come as no surprise as so much drug taking by athletes is based more on rumour and desperation than evidence.

Just as there is little research into the ergogenic effects of hGH, whether natural or synthetic, there is also little research evidence regarding the possible side-effects of the abuse of the synthetic hGH. The evidence that exists is based on the side-effects of naturally occurring over-secretion of growth hormone and include the over-growth of bones (particularly of the jaw, forehead and fingers) and soft tissue, fluid retention and coronary artery disease. In addition, as hGH must be injected there is the risk of infections, such as Aids and hepatitis B, from dirty needles.

At present, there is no reliable test for the detection of hGH. Measurement of total hGH itself is of limited value partly because exogenous rhGH and endogenous hGH have identical amino acid sequences thus making chemical

1. Wadler & Hainline, 1989, op. cit.
2. Ehronberg, C., Bengtsson, B.-A. & Rosen, T., "Growth Hormone Abuse", *Baillière's Best Practice and Research: Clinical Endocrinology and Metabolism*, 14.1, 2000, pp. 71-8.
3. Ibid., p. 73. Very small reductions in fat and equally small increases in lean tissue have been suggested in a study by Crist, D.M., Peake, G.T., Egan, P.A. & Waters, D.L., "Body Composition Response to Exogenous GH During Training in Highly Conditioned Adults", *Journal of Applied Physiology*, Vol. 65, 1988, pp. 579-84.
4. Deyssig, R., Frisch, H., Blum, W.F. et al., "Effects of Growth Hormone Treatment on Hormonal Parameters, Body Composition and Strength in Athletes", *Acta Endocrinologica*, No. 128, 1993, pp. 313-8; Tarasheki, K.E., Campbell, J.A., Smith, K., Rennie, M.J., Holloway, J.O. & Bier, D.M., "Effect of Growth Hormone and Resistance Exercise on Muscle Growth in Young Men", *American Journal of Physiology, Endocrinology and Metabolism*, Vol. 262, 1992, E261-7.

or immunological distinction difficult and partly because normal levels of hGH vary widely. There is continuing research into the development of suitable markers for the detection of hGH use, but a reliable test still seems some way in the future.[1]

Doping methods

Blood doping: transfusion and rEPO

Blood doping by transfusion involves the removal of blood (approximately one litre) from the athlete whereupon the red blood cells are separated from the plasma and preserved. Following the removal of the blood, the athlete's red blood cell count will return to normal. Once this has been achieved (four to six weeks later), the preserved red blood cells are reintroduced into the athlete. Because the amount of oxygen that an athlete can make available to muscle tissue is limited by the number of red blood cells the overall effect of blood doping by transfusion is to increase the red blood cell count and thereby increase the amount of oxygen available to the muscles. The same effect can also be achieved by the introduction of blood from another person with a compatible blood type. The use of another's blood is by far the most common form of blood doping by transfusion as the cost of an athlete using his or her own blood is higher due to the more sophisticated laboratory requirements.

The transfusion of half a litre of blood can provide the athlete with about an additional half litre of oxygen to the muscle per minute.[2] In addition, there is evidence that not only does blood doping by transfusion increase the flow of oxygen to the muscle but it also has the effect of increasing the volume of oxygen actually used during intense exercise.[3] The practice of blood doping by transfusion is attractive because the ergogenic effects are evident almost immediately and are of especial value in endurance events such as cycling and running. The effect of blood doping by transfusion is similar to that achieved naturally through high-altitude training.

Initially, there was some scepticism about the ergogenic value of blood doping by transfusion. The explanation for the failure of early experiments to produce quantifiable gains was due to the weaknesses in technique which, once sufficiently refined, was able to demonstrate verifiable ergogenic advantage. According to evidence given to the Dubin Inquiry, blood doping by transfusion has the potential to increase the maximal capacity to use

---

1. See, for example, Wallace, J. et al., "Responses to the Growth Hormone (GH) and Insulin-Like Growth Factoraxis to Exercise, GH Administration, and GH Withdrawal in Trained Adult Males: A Potential Test for GH Abuse in Sport", *The Journal of Clinical Endocrinology and Metabolism*, 84.10, 1999, pp. 3 591-601; Kicman, A.T. et al., "Serum IGF-I and IGF Binding Proteins 2 and 3 as Potential Markers of Doping with Human GH", *Clinical Endocrinology*, 47, 1997, pp. 43-50.
2. Wadler & Hainline, 1989, op. cit.
3. Robertson, R.J. et al., "Haemoglobin Concentration and Aerobic Work Capacity in Women Following Induced Erythrocythemia", *Journal of Applied Physiology*, Vol. 57, 1984.

oxygen by 5%.[1] Other studies have confirmed the benefits of blood doping by transfusion with one reporting that athletes participating in a 10 km run were able to sustain greater speed during the later stages of races and could therefore improve their times by over one minute.[2] However, the benefit from blood doping by transfusion is greater for those athletes that have a high level of initial fitness.

There are a number of potential side-effects associated with blood doping by transfusion that arise from the use of blood which is not the athlete's own including infections, such as Aids, and reactions to incompatible blood. In addition, the increase in the volume of blood in the body may cause a dangerous increase in blood pressure.

As mentioned above, training at altitude can have a similar effect to blood doping by transfusion. The effect of altitude training is to prompt an increase in the natural synthesis of erythropoietin due to the reduction of oxygen at greater altitudes and the body's consequent need to adjust in order to maintain its effectiveness. The recognition of the process of acclimatisation has encouraged experimentation with synthetic erythropoietin (rEPO). Synthetic erythropoietin's availability dates from 1984 when the American pharmaceutical company Amgen was granted a patent for its production. Its main medical use is to help patients suffering from a range of serious illnesses including renal disease, some cancers and anaemia. rEPO was added to the IOC list of banned substances in 1990 even though a secure method for its detection was not then available. As regards the effects of the drug on sportspeople, "The administration of rEPO has a pronounced effect on the aerobic performance of endurance athletes, once time is allowed for the over-stimulation of the bone marrow to have its effect".[3]

Although the broad effect of the administration of rEPO is the same as that found for blood doping by transfusion, it is far more difficult to predict the consequences of the use of the drug. In particular, prediction of the scale of increase in the production of red blood cells is much less accurate. As a result, there is a heightened risk of dangerously elevated levels of blood pressure and blood viscosity with the increased risk of thrombosis and stroke.[4]

---

1. Dubin Inquiry, 1990, op. cit., p. 121; Gledhill, N., "Blood Doping and Related Issues: A Brief Review", *Medical Science and Sports Exercise,* Vol. 14.3, 1983. See also Buick et al., who demonstrated that the practice can lead to significant improvements in maximal oxygen consumption and total exercise time among élite runners: Buick, F.J., Gledhill, N. & Froese, A.B. et al., "Effect of Induced Erythrocythemia on Aerobic Work Capacity", *Journal of Applied Physiology,* Vol. 48, 1980, pp. 636-42.
2. Brien, T. & Simon, T.L., "The Effects of Red Blood Cell Infusion on 10 km Race Time", *Journal of the American Medical Association,* Vol. 257, 1987, pp. 2 761-5.
3. Armstrong, D.J. & Reilly, T., "Blood Boosting and Sport" in Mottram, 1996, op. cit.; for an estimate of the value of rEPO see also Eachbach, J.W. et al., "Correction of the Anemia of End-stage Renal Disease with Recombinant Human Erythropoietin: Results of a Combined Phase I and II Clinical Trial", *New England Journal of Medicine,* Vol. 316, 1987.
4. Ibid.; see also Ekblom, B.T., "Blood Boosting and Sport", *Baillière's Best Practice and Research: Clinical Endocrinology and Metabolism,* 14.1, pp. 89-98.

Pharmacological, chemical and physical manipulation

The ingenuity and effort that some athletes and their coaches put into attempts to obtain an unfair advantage through the use of drugs is matched only by their equal investment in seeking ways of disguising the fact that doping has taken place. Therefore, in 1985, the IOC Medical Commission introduced regulations to cover attempts to deceive testing authorities. The most common examples of deception are urine substitution and the inhibition of renal excretion.

There are a number of ways in which urine manipulation and substitution can take place. Athletes may, for example, store sufficient urine taken at a time when they were not taking drugs and use a catheter to reintroduce it into their bladder prior to a drug test. Perhaps the best-known example of urine manipulation concerned three German athletes, Grit Breuer, Katrin Krabbe and Silke Müller, who were tested while in South Africa for training. The urine samples they provided were so similar that it was alleged that they had come from the same person, possibly as a result of catheterisation.

Attempts to inhibit renal excretion often involve the use of the drug probenecid, normally used for the treatment of gout as a means of delaying the excretion of antibiotics and thereby prolonging their therapeutic effectiveness. The effect of probenecid and other similar drugs (such as carinamide) is to prevent the excretion of certain other drugs, particularly steroids, so that a "clean" urine sample can be given.

Classes of drugs subject to certain restrictions

Alcohol

Alcohol is one of the most common and socially acceptable drugs. Its use is a cause for concern in some sports such as motor racing, downhill skiing and ski jumping, not because of any claimed advantage that it confers but because of the threat to the athlete's safety or the safety of other participants. There is also an awareness in some higher risk sports to protect the public image of the sport which would be tarnished by accidents and particularly alcohol-related accidents. More widely, the link between sport and alcohol is a cause of concern due to its association with poor standards of crowd behaviour or with patterns of social behaviour that have developed in some sports. In general, alcohol is of value in only a limited number of sports. In the 1970s, there were some claims that some alcoholic products, beers in particular, were good sources of carbohydrates and were also useful ways of replenishing lost body fluid caused by training for competition. But beer is an inefficient source of carbohydrate and also, due to alcohol's diuretic effect, an equally inefficient source of replacement fluid.[1]

---

1. O'Brien, C.P., "Alcohol and Sport", *Sports Medicine,* Vol. 15.2, 1993, pp. 71-7.

It is common knowledge that the impact of alcohol on the body varies dramatically according to the amount consumed. Because even moderate amounts impair most sports-related functions, research into the potential value of alcohol consumption in sport has focused on the effects of relatively small amounts. Alcohol affects the body primarily through the central nervous system and reduces tension felt by athletes in stressful situations. Alcohol can also produce feelings of mild euphoria, but also depression (normally as a result of the consumption of moderate to large amounts). The effect of alcohol use in sport is limited. Although one study demonstrated that moderate amounts of alcohol could lead to an increase in strength, there is considerable scepticism at this finding which has proved difficult to replicate.[1] There is little recent evidence that alcohol, even in moderate to low amounts, has any value in improving strength or endurance.

It is generally considered that the main value of alcohol is in those sports that require a steady aim, such as shooting, snooker, darts and archery.[2] In a detailed study of the effect of alcohol on accuracy in archery, arm steadiness, isometric strength, muscular endurance and reaction time were measured among nine archers when sober, when receiving a placebo and when receiving two different doses of alcohol. The results showed no effect on either isometric strength or muscular endurance, and a worsening of both reaction time and arm steadiness. Although the authors accepted that the results might have been different if the study had been conducted under competition conditions, the results provide an important challenge to the assumed benefits of low to moderate level alcohol use.[3] The study adds weight to the summary of available research provided by Wadler and Hainline which concluded that alcohol impaired all the following skills: balance and steadiness, reaction time, fine and complex motor co-ordination, visual tracking and information processing.[4]

Marijuana

Marijuana is similar to alcohol in that the main concern of anti-doping authorities is its association with sport, and especially the consequences for the image of sport of its recreational use by athletes, rather than its ergogenic value in sport. Marijuana is also similar to alcohol in so far as it is a depressant that operates through the central nervous system.

If alcohol's value as an ergogenic drug is, at best, limited it is difficult to identify any significant ergogenic properties for marijuana. The main

---

1. Ikai, M. & Steinhaus, A.H., "Some Factors Modifying the Expression of Human Strength", *Journal of Applied Physiology*, Vol. 16, 1961.
2. Koller, W.C. & Biary, N., "Effect of Alcohol on Tremors: Comparison with Propanolol", *Neurology*, Vol. 34, 1984, pp. 221-2.
3. Reilly, T. & Halliday, F., "Influence of Alcohol Ingestion on Tasks Related to Archery", *Journal of Human Ergology*, Vol. 14 pp252 - 8 (1985)
4. Wadler & Hainline, 1989, op. cit., p. 128.

physiological effects of the drug are to increase blood pressure and the resting heart rate without any beneficial effect on sports-related capacities, such as strength, fine motor co-ordination, alertness or endurance.[1] There is anecdotal evidence that some athletes value marijuana for its capacity to reduce tension prior to and during competition.[2]

At low doses, it causes sedation and euphoria while at high doses there is a risk of hallucinations and psychosis. Chronic use of the drug has been associated with a decline in motivation and also decreased testosterone levels.[3]

Corticosteroids

Corticosteroids are quite distinct from anabolic steroids. Synthetic corticosteroids are powerful anti-inflammatory drugs which mimic the effects of the corticosteroids produced naturally by the adrenal gland at times of stress. The primary medical use of corticosteroids is as analgesics (particularly in treatment of rheumatoid arthritis) and for the treatment of asthma.

The main use of corticosteroids in sport is to treat localised injury and pain. Used as a short-term treatment for injury, the corticosteroids can be very effective. However, where they are used over the longer term there are a number of side-effects: among the most serious is osteoporosis and weakening of muscles.[4]

Beta blockers

Beta blockers are drugs which are designed to affect the body's beta adrenergic receptors of which there are two types: beta-1 receptors mediate cardiac effects while beta-2 receptors mediate bronchodilatation and the dilation of the blood vessels. There are also two types of beta blocker: those which are non-selective and which therefore affect beta-1 and beta-2 receptors, and selective beta blockers which affect beta-1 receptors. Beta blockers are used in the treatment of a variety of conditions including angina, cardiac arrhythmias, migraine, tremor and a variety of anxiety-related symptoms. The drugs function by decreasing the heart rate, the degree of contraction of blood vessels around the heart and systemic arterial blood pressure.

The main use of beta blockers in sport is in those events where steadiness of the hand or arm is required such as shooting, golf, archery and snooker. The selective beta blocker metoprolol has been shown, in one study, to improve accuracy in shooting, with the benefit being greatest among the better

---

1. Steadward, R.D. & Singh, M., "The Effects of Smoking Marijuana on Physical Performance", *Medicine and Science in Sport*, Vol. 7, 1975, pp. 309-11.
2. Wagner, J.C., "Abuse of Drugs Used to Enhance Athletic Performance", *American Journal of Hospital Pharmacy*, Vol. 8, 1989, pp. 832-4.
3. Schwenk, 1997, op. cit., p. 37.
4. Elliot, P., "Drug Treatment of Inflammation in Sports Injuries" in Mottram, 1996, op. cit.
5. Schwenk, 1997, op. cit., p. 40.

91

shots,[5] and in a second study to have improved the shooting scores in twenty-two out of thirty-three participants.[1] Beta blockers seem of value in only a narrow range of sports as the drugs also have the effect of adversely affecting both aerobic and anaerobic endurance, partly as a result of the reduction in the maximal oxygen uptake. For example, the time taken to run 5 000 m was increased by 33% following the use of metoprolol.[2] Although endurance is affected, other capacities including muscle strength and power remain unaffected.[3] However, some athletes have tried to counter this by taking beta blockers that had a shorter life and would be metabolised before the endurance element or event commenced. In addition, there is a risk that the capacity of the drug to result in peripheral constriction of the blood vessels may cause poor blood supply to the fingers which, particularly in winter, can cause considerable pain.

The side-effects of beta blockers can be serious especially in those with existing cardiac problems for whom beta blockers may cause heart failure. Other side-effects include the precipitation of breathing problems and impotence. Some of the non-selective beta blockers, especially those that are able to relieve anxiety most rapidly, are also those that tend to cause insomnia, nightmares and depression. There is also concern at the possible withdrawal symptoms "which can manifest as anxiety, palpitations, angina, excessive sweating and headaches".[4]

Genetic "doping"

The mapping of the human genetic code through the Human Genome Project has created the possibility of major advances in the treatment and prevention of many serious diseases. Although the development of therapeutic applications of genetic engineering are still clearly in their infancy there is already a broad range of potential applications including the treatment of obesity through the inhibition of a particular gene which would cause "white fat", which leads to weight gain, to turn to the more easily burned "brown fat". Research is also well advanced into the use of genetic engineering to grow new veins and blood vessels thus raising the possibility of treating some heart conditions without the need for major surgery. Other, more speculative, medical research suggests that it may be possible to identify the genes associated with particular behaviour such as suicide or attention deficit disorder. Not surprisingly, discussion of the potential of genetic engineering in a

---

1. Kaiser, P., "Physical Performance and Muscle Metabolism During Beta-Adrenergic Blockade in Man", *Acta Physiologica Scandinavica,* Vol. 536 (Supplement), 1984, pp. 1-53.
2. Armstrong, D.J., "Sympathomimetic Amines and their Antagonists" in Mottram, 1996, op. cit.
3. Tesch, P.A., "Exercise Performance and Beta-Blockade", *Sports Medicine,* Vol. 2, 1985, pp. 389-412.
4. Goldman, 1992, op. cit., p. 179.

therapeutic context has not been ignored by those seeking to treat sports injuries and enhance sports performance.

According to Munthe, there are four ways in which the knowledge of the human genome might be used in sport.[1] The first is the capacity to fine-tune the chemical composition of a drug to suit better the athlete's genetic make-up or to use knowledge of an athlete's genetic make-up to optimise his or her programme of training and nutrition. The second is the capacity to modify the genome in specific ways including the use of genetically modified red blood cells or the production of various hormones. Third, interventions may be made very early in the life of the human organism to the germ-line cells of the newly fertilised egg. The breakthrough in genetic engineering marked by the production of the cloned sheep "Dolly" indicated the scientific capacity for this level of engineering although "Dolly the heptathlete" is probably some time away. Finally, there is currently the capability to select individuals on the basis of their genetic make up. Young athletes whose genome suggests they are unlikely to reach the highest levels of performance could be identified before a governing body or sponsor invests too much money in them.[2]

As regards the use of gene therapy in the treatment of sports injuries, it is suggested that "gene therapy will be particularly useful in initiating and accelerating the repair of cartilage, meniscus, tendon, and ligament".[3] For those with an interest in the doping potential of gene therapy, attention has tended to focus on research into the use of genetic therapies to counteract anaemia and to help restore withered muscle, through the stimulation of IGF-1 (insulin-like growth factor-1) production, both of which have potential applications similar to EPO and steroids respectively. At present, experiments in increasing muscle mass have been limited to mice but results indicate a 20% increase in muscle over a two-week period. According to Professor Goldspink, the increase is likely to be substantially lower in humans but to an élite athlete an increase in muscle bulk of just a few per cent may be sufficient to transform a top-twenty ranked athlete into a potential medal winner. In addition to increases in bulk, genetic therapy offers the prospect of inserting genes into a cell to create a faster "twitch" muscle in sprinters or a stronger take-off leg for high-jumpers.

Andersen and colleagues have reported on the potential to provide a genetic advantage to sprinters by altering the proportion of "fast-type" muscles in

---

1. Munthe, C., "Selected Champions" in Tännsjö, T. & Tamburrini, C.M. (eds.), *Values in Sport*, London: E & FN Spon, 2000.
2. A crude form of genetic selection already exists in some sports, such as skating, where athletes need to start training very young. One national skating coach always asks to meet the parents of promising young skaters to see how big the parents are and thus to estimate whether the youngster will be too big to be an élite skater when they have reached adulthood.
3. Lamsam, C. et al., "Gene Therapy in Sports Medicine", *Sports Medicine*, 26.2, pp. 73-7.
4. Andersen, J.L., Schjerling, P. & Saltin, B., "Muscle, Genes and Athletic Performance", *Scientific American*, September 2000, pp. 30-7.

an athlete's legs.[4] The different contraction speeds of muscle fibre results in variation in the way in which the chemicals that create energy and power are broken down. "Slow fibres" are required in endurance events while "fast fibres" are important in sprints and also in power events such as weightlifting. The average adult has roughly equal levels of fast and slow muscle fibre. Scientists have been experimenting since the 1960s with ways to alter the ratio between fast and slow muscle fibre usually by using different training regimes. More recently, scientists have begun to consider how genetic therapy might be used to convert slow to fast fibre.

Identifying the genes that will have the desired effect is only one of a series of problems that needs to be overcome. A second major problem is identifying a safe delivery system for the gene. Although there are some potential non-viral means of gene delivery, including direct micro-injection, the efficiency of non-viral methods is considered to be low and attention has consequently turned to the use of benign viral vectors to transport the gene to the identified location. A benign viral vector is one that is able to transfer the gene to the cell without replicating or causing disease. However, the main problem facing scientists at the moment is not the transport of the gene to a particular location but controlling the effect of the gene once it has begun to work. Referring to the use of genetic therapy, Professor Saltin, a member of the World Anti-Doping Agency's committee on gene doping, commented:

> "The only thing keeping it [genetic doping] from happening today is the control problem. For example, you can insert a gene to increase EPO production ... but you can't shut [production] off when you want to."[1]

Other possible problems with gene therapy include the risk of genetic mutation and instability.

With medical research into gene therapy being at such an early stage, any discussion of potential side-effects and ease of detection is even more speculative than a discussion of applications of genetic research in sport. Until genetic therapy techniques have been refined to the extent that their impact can be precisely calibrated and controlled, and until clinical trials have been conducted, it is not possible to identify side-effects. However, there is a view that the virus used to transport the gene and the DNA within the gene will leave a "footprint" that will make detection possible, but that it will not be identifiable from a urine or blood sample and only from a tissue sample which raises substantial problems for effective doping control.

Conclusion

This brief review of the drugs and practices banned or restricted by the IOC and other major sports organisations indicates not only the variety of

---

1. Quoted in the *Observer Sports Magazine*, September 2001, p. 46.

Table 3.1: Drugs in sport: a summary of their uses and side-effects

Drug	Common legal classification	Main medical uses	Extent of use in sport	Strength of evidence of ergogenic value	Side-effects
Amphetamine	controlled	relief of mild depression, treatment of narcolepsy, and control of appetite	considerable	strong	extensive and moderately serious
Cocaine	controlled	very slight; some use as a topical anaesthetic	moderate	negligible	extensive and extremely serious
Ephedrine	controlled, except when used in OTC preparations	element in many OTC cold and cough remedies; also used in some asthma and hay fever preparations	considerable	strong	moderate
Caffeine	legal	very slight; some use in the treatment of migraine; also present in some OTC analgesic preparations	slight to moderate	debatable, though the balance of opinion suggests some value in endurance sports	serious
Morphine	controlled	relief of severe pain; some use in the treatment of diarrhoea	slight	strong	extensive and extremely serious
Anabolic androgenic steroids	controlled	treatment of anaemia, growth problems, renal failure	considerable	moderate to strong	extensive and moderately serious
Diuretics	controlled	treatment of high blood pressure and excessive fluid retention	slight	no ergogenic value, but evidence of value as a "weight reducing" agent	varied and moderately severe
hCG	controlled	testosterone deficiency	considerable	strong	moderate to severe
hGH	controlled	treatment of human growth deficiency, osteoporosis and potentially obesity	slight to moderate	weak	severe
ACTH	controlled	anti-inflammatory treatment	largely unknown, but probably slight	weak	severe
Blood doping	legal	none	considerable	strong	moderate to severe
Alcohol	legal	none	slight during competition	weak	only significant with heavy and/or long-term use
Marijuana	controlled	negligible	considerable	almost none, use is primarily recreational	only significant with heavy and/or long- term use
Betablockers	controlled	treatment of angina, migraine and tremor	slight to moderate	moderate to strong	in general only severe if pre-existing cardiac problem

OTC = over-the-counter

substances and activities that the anti-doping authorities seek to control but also the scale of the problem they face. The development of policy and arrangements would be much more straightforward if the problem to be tackled was static; if the number of drugs and the ways in which they were administered remained constant. Unfortunately, as with many other social problems, doping in sport is dynamic and complex. Its dynamism arises from the steady development of new drugs, the constant exploration of the wealth of existing drugs for those with, as yet, undiscovered ergogenic properties, and the constant refinement of existing preparations. The complexity of the problem arises from issues of definition and co-ordination between agencies as much as from problems of detection and prosecution.

Table 3.1 provides an overview of the problem of doping in sport and highlights a number of issues that will be considered in subsequent chapters. The second column in the table is significant in that it makes clear the extent to which the drugs of abuse are not those that are easily available. Apart from alcohol and caffeine, the other common drugs of abuse are, in most countries, controlled by the state. Some drugs, such as hGH, are controlled very tightly by both the state and the producers: others, such as cocaine and heroin, are at the centre of multi-million dollar police campaigns to reduce supply, with the imposition of substantial punishments for those caught possessing, and especially, supplying the drugs. The picture is more varied for the ingredients of common medical drugs such as steroids and beta blockers, but even these are usually subject to some restrictions. While it is clear that some drugs can be purchased openly, many require a high degree of collusion between producers, chemists, doctors and coaches in order for them to be available to the athlete.

The last three columns provide some evidence of the impact of research evidence on the extent of use. In general, and as one would expect, there is a reasonably close relationship between the extent of use and the strength of scientific evidence of ergogenic value. However, there is a far looser relationship between the extent of use and the seriousness of the possible side-effects confirming the frequently made point that athletes have a limited regard for their own long-term health and are willing to take considerable risks to achieve success. In the chapters that follow, the focus will turn to the problems of devising and implementing an anti-doping policy which has to be sensitive to a wide range of factors including the differing legal status of the drugs on the IOC list, the active collusion of a broad range of professionals, and the paradoxical willingness of athletes who depend on good health for sporting success to risk their medium to long-term well-being.

Chapter 4
Doping and anti-doping policy beyond sport

In the first chapter it was emphasised that the practice of sport and the men and women involved were as much a part of society as those involved in any other social pastime or occupation. This is not to suggest that the expectation that sportspeople should aspire to higher moral standards is misplaced, but rather to recognise that sport is not insulated from broader social values. However, simply to state the truism that there is a relationship between the culture of drug use in sport and that found in society does little to explain the nature of that interrelationship. Figure 4.1 is an attempt to illustrate the character of that relationship and provide a context for the discussion of policy issues that follows in this and later chapters.

Figure 4.1 : A variety of contexts for drug use in sport

Sport: competitive ; formal ; élite-led ; career oriented ; commercial
Many Olympic sports particularly in track and field
Major international sports (Olympic Games a less central focus): e.g. soccer, cricket, golf, squash
Non-Olympic commercial sports: motor racing, American football, snooker, body building
Non-Olympic and substantially non-commercial sports: e.g. lacrosse, fishing and hunting
Competitive, commercial, non-sports: e.g. professional wrestling, "Gladiators", and strength competitions
Loosely organised, non-competitive sports-related activities: e.g. keep-fit, jogging clubs, aerobics, callisthenics
Unorgan-ised, individual, non-sports-oriented activities: e.g. vanity body building
Sport: non-competitive ; informal ; mass ; non-career oriented ; non-commercial

Dividing sport from non-sport or sport from society is far from easy. There have been many attempts to define sport and particularly to distinguish it from spectacle, entertainment, pastime and games with most attempts highlighting the extent to which sport as an activity is blurred at the boundary. The purpose of this chapter is not to reopen this definitional debate but to explore the boundary of anti-doping policy for sport and also to explore the relationship between anti-doping policy for sport and that for drug abuse in wider society. More particularly, the chapter will draw upon experience in the development and operation of policies adopted to reduce the social and recreational use of drugs in order to identify the lessons that might be learnt by those responsible for the implementation of anti-doping policy in sport.

Figure 4.1 presents a continuum of sporting contexts for drug use which, for heuristic purposes, presents a view of sport which at one extreme emphasises a competitive, formal and élite-centred activity, but also one which provides the élite at least with an income-earning career within an increasingly commercial context. At the other extreme are those drug-using activities, at best with only tangential associations with sport, which are non-competitive, informal, mass, non-career oriented, and often take place in a non-commercial context. Two further characteristics that overlay the continuum are first the characteristics of the organisational context within which the activity takes place and which ranges from formal domestic sports organisations and international federations towards the left-hand side of the continuum moving through progressively looser and less formal bodies such as professional associations, short-term event organising bodies to informal and local organisations and finally to personal initiative at the other extreme. The second characteristic concerns the range of motives that lead to drug use. Although it is acknowledged that motives for involvement in different types of sport will be multiple and shifting, it is suggested that for those participating in the more formal and commercial sports, primary motives for drug use are likely to include the desire to improve the quality of performance and the chances of victory linked to a concern to retain employment/participation. For those involved in informal and individualised "sporting" activities significant motives are likely to include the enhancement of self-esteem or social success.

Current anti-doping policy in sport is derived from two sources: one from among a range of sports organisations and the other from among governments. Not surprisingly, the focus of sports organisation has been on formal competitive sport typified by participation in the Olympic Games or in one of the major international team sports. The IOC and the major international federations affiliated to GAISF (the General Association of International Sports Federations) have been the lead bodies in policy development supported by a range of governments and governmental organisations including the Council of Europe. Understandably, the sports organisations have focused narrowly on the problem of doping within their own particular sports or within the major multi-sport competitions, such as the Olympics, in which their athletes take part. Less attention has been paid to the broad range of sports on the fringe of Olympic and major team sports, such as competitive body building, power-lifting and strongman/woman competitions. Less attention still has been paid to the informal fringe sports-like activities such as keep fit, aerobics and vanity body building where the motive is more likely to be social or psychological (to enhance self-esteem or sexual attraction). The use of "sports" drugs for social and psychological motives has as much in common with the broader issue of the recreational use of drugs as it has with doping in sport and it is at this end of the spectrum of drug use that governments have their primary interest, focus their resources and have the greatest accumulation of experience. Consequently, where the focus of government concern is broad, that of the sports federations and the IOC is narrow; where government experience is of the control of illegal drugs, that of the sports organisations is with legal, controlled and illegal drugs; and where governments deploy a variety of resources including the law and extensive police, welfare and medical services, the sports organisations rely on regulation and limited regulatory, educational, medical and scientific services.

Although one can appreciate the narrowness of focus of the IOC and the international federations, the boundary between what might be referred to as mainstream sport (Olympic and major team sport) and fringe sport (such as body building, and exhibition/novelty sports events) is frequently indistinct with athletes often crossing the boundary more than once in their lives. Attitudes and policy towards drug use are not neatly compartmentalised and it is therefore important to understand the extent and character of drug use on the fringes of mainstream sport and beyond. Just as athletes will move between sporting activities they also move, even when concentrating on élite competition, between the focused activities of intense training and competition and the social milieu that élite and frequently wealthy athletes inhabit. Both these patterns of movement, represented in Figure 4.2, bring athletes into contact with a variety of work and social situations that have different drug cultures which are not discrete but overlap and influence each other, each varying in terms of the preferred drugs, range of drugs used, sophistication and intensity of use. Consequently the policy response of sports authorities and governments must, on the one hand, recognise the particular characteristics and environment of a series of drug-abusing communities while also, on the other hand, acknowledge the extent to which they overlap and drug abusers may move from one community to another.

Figure 4.2 : Drug abusing communities

A further complication is the extent to which drug-dependent cultures have become established in the richer industrial countries. While the particular drug sub-cultures associated with participation in élite sport or body building may be seen as embedded in a broader sub-culture of illegal drug use, that sub-culture is itself embedded in a wider culture which has become, over the last thirty years or so, increasingly drug tolerant, dependant and obsessed. Speaking about the United States, but in terms equally valid in much of the rest of the industrialised world, Goldman and Klatz argue that we are an increasingly drug obsessed society where pharmaceutical solutions are sought not simply for medical complaints, but also for situations and activities that are a normal part of social life. Those who want to lose weight look to drugs rather than to dietary control and increased exercise; those seeking to avoid "jet-lag" take drugs; and those women who want to control their fertility take drugs. As Goldman and Klatz powerfully argue, how can we expect potential drug abusers in sport to reconcile the contradictory messages that drugs should be shunned while also telling them that drugs are increasingly the primary and preferred solution to a range of medical and social conditions? Goldman and Klatz quote Dr Andrew Pipe who suggested that "In years gone by, men used to mistake magic for medicine, now men mistake medicine for magic".[1]

The change in social attitudes to medicine and the products of pharmaceutical companies is simply the outcome of a process which has been termed "the medicalisation of life" which has progressively blurred the distinction between health and illness.[2] Over recent years, there has been a steady broadening of the range of human conditions that have been defined as medical problems. Zola gives four examples of this process: ageing, pregnancy, alcoholism and, interestingly, drug addiction. Both ageing and pregnancy are examples of normal processes that have become problems that require medical expertise and treatment while the last two were seen, until very recently, as eccentricities that required care rather than illnesses that required cure. An increasing proportion of life events and conditions have become diagnosable making the phrases that we use to describe them, such as "healthy pregnancy", "normal puberty", and "growing old gracefully" appear oxymora. Waddington argues that this process of medicalisation has embraced sport and quotes the author of one of the first medical texts to focus on sports medicine as suggesting that, "Just as extreme youth and senility produce peculiar medical problems, so too does extreme physical fitness".[3] Once it is accepted that "extreme physical fitness" makes an athlete by definition a patient, then there is already in existence a culture, professionally supported and promoted, that encourages the treatment of healthy athletes with drugs. Even if the "drugs" are simply those which are legally available (in terms defined by both the state and the IOC) such as vitamins and food supplements, the athlete is already developing the expectations and patterns of behaviour that might initially

---

1. Goldman, B. & Klatz, R., *Death in the Locker Room II*, Chicago: Elite Sports Medicine Publications, 1992, p. 18.
2. This section draws on an excellent article by Ivan Waddington, "The Development of Sports Medicine", *Sociology of Sport Journal*, Vol. 13, 1996, pp. 176-96.
3. Ibid., p. 179. The quote is from Williams, J.G.P., *Sports Medicine*, London: Edward Arnold, 1962.

100

parallel illegal drug use, but which are to most athletes part of a common culture. Robert Voy, ex-chief medical officer for the US Olympic Committee, illustrates this point very clearly when he recorded the daily intake of legal drugs that a "national track star" was taking, "vitamin E, 160 mg; B-complex capsules, four times per day; vitamin C, 2 000 mg; vitamin B6, 150 mg; calcium tablets, four times per day; magnesium tablets, twice a day; zinc tablets, three times a day; royal jelly capsules; garlic tablets; cayenne tablets; eight aminos; Gamma-Oryzanol; Mega Vit Pack; supercharge herbs; Dibencozide; glandular tissue complex; natural steroid complex; Inosine; Orchic testicle extract; Pyridium; Ampicillin; and hair rejuvenation formula with Boitin".[1]

One must also remember that a further source of ambiguity arises from the intimate involvement of the medical and scientific professions in the development, and refinement in the use, of drugs. Mention has already been made in Chapter 2 of the central role of Dr Zeigler in identifying and disseminating information on the use of steroids among weightlifters, and of the Ciba Pharmaceutical Company in producing steroids. However, by far the clearest example of medical and scientific involvement in doping concerns the former German Democratic Republic (GDR). Writing in a confidential report in 1977, the Deputy Director of the Sports Medical Service,[2] Manfred Höppner, commented that "At present anabolic steroids are applied in all Olympic sporting events, with the exception of sailing and gymnastics (female) ...".[3] The total number of élite athletes treated each year exceeded 2 000, a number augmented by the large number of second-rank athletes and juniors who were also treated. Clearly, such an extensive doping programme could not have been carried out without the close involvement of the state and also of the medical and scientific communities. The Government of the GDR successfully shrouded the experimentation and administration of steroids under the cloak of state security and thereby maintained a remarkable level of secrecy. Scientists and doctors at the three research centres in Saxony, Leipzig and Kreischa worked closely with scientists at the state-owned pharmaceutical company, VEB Jenapharm, which developed the most widely used androgenic anabolic steroid Oral-Turinabol in the mid-1960s. In the early 1980s, it was also VEB Jenapharm which developed and produced preparations of epitestosterone propionate, "a biologically inactive compound that had no commercial value but was prepared exclusively for the governmental doping system" and whose function was to bring the testosterone-epitestosterone ratio back to the norm.[4] Such was the scale of

1. Voy, R., Drugs, Sport and Politics: The Inside Story about Drug Abuse in Sport and its Political Cover-up, Champaign, Ill: Leisure Press, 1991, p. 99.
2. Sportmedizinscher Dienst (SMD).
3. Quoted in Franke, W.W. & Berendonk, B., "Hormonal Doping and Androgenization of Athletes: A Secret Program of the German Democratic Republic Government", Clinical Chemistry, Vol. 43.7, 1997, pp. 1 262-79. Franke & Berendonk note that the exclusion of female gymnasts from the anabolic steroid programme was reversed in 1979 when female gymnasts were systematically treated with mestanlone.
4. Franke & Berendonk, 1997, op. cit., p. 1 272.

involvement of doctors and scientists in the GDR doping programme that Franke and Berendonk were prompted to observe that the "role that scientists and physicians have played in this clandestine system is particularly sad, not only because these professionals actively contributed to worldwide cheating, but also because they violated scientific and medical ethics".[1]

In addition to those doctors and scientists who were involved directly in doping programmes, there are also those medical professionals who appear, at best, ambivalent about the use of drugs in sport. The comment of Dr R.H. Nicholson, Deputy Director of the Institute of Medical Ethics and a life member of the National Rifle Association in Britain, is not unique: "there are no overriding ethical reasons that force one to conclude that drug taking by an individual sportsman is necessarily unethical, or that the governing bodies of sport must have rules to prevent and punish drug taking".[2]

The development of the medical profession and the steady expansion of its sphere of competence in society coupled with the increasing pressures, from governments and commerce, on athletes to succeed has consequently led to a deepening relationship between the athlete and the doctor (and other sports scientists) and, for most athletes, a growing dependence. Thus, the complaint voiced by an American runner who finished second that "I need a better doctor" may well represent a typical attitude among élite athletes.[3]

Body building and drug use

One activity which can be found in a variety of forms at various points across the continuum in Figure 4.1 is body building. At one extreme body building can be seen as closely linked to the Olympic sport of weightlifting, if not in terms of goals and skills then certainly in terms of similarity of many training techniques, equipment and facilities. Body building has many of the attributes of mainstream sport and, in some countries, has an elaborate and well-organised and tightly regulated competition circuit. At the less structured end of the continuum, body building shades into a more generalised weight-training activity directed at the development and maintenance of general fitness. Less structured still is the participation in body-building activities for motives not associated with sport or even fitness and health, but more with vanity and narcissism, a pre-occupation with appearance and peer-group esteem.

Within mainstream sport, weightlifting has suffered a number of drug-related scandals, probably best illustrated by the evidence given during the Dubin Inquiry in Canada. It should therefore come as no surprise that drug abuse is substantial within competitive, fitness and vanity body building. In a survey of 138 male body builders, Lindstrom found that 38% had used

---

1. Ibid., p. 1 263.
2. Nicholson, R.H., "Drugs in Sport", *National Rifle Association Journal*, Vol. LXVI.3, 1987.
3. Quoted in Mangi, R.J. & Jokl, P., "Drugs and Sport", *Connecticut Medicine*, Vol. 45, 1981, pp. 637-41.

anabolic steroids.[1] Similar results have been found in surveys of steroid use among body builders in Wales, where 50% reported steroid use and in Kansas and Missouri where the total was 54%.[2] A study of 386 steroid users in Liverpool found 58% were competitive body builders.[3] Delbeke et al. refer to "the widespread doping plague in body builders" in their review of doping amongst body builders in the Flanders region of Belgium.[4] Doping control became the responsibility of the Flemish Ministry of Health in 1988 and in the subsequent five years it carried out 379 tests of which 159 (42%) were positive (see Table 4.3). The proportion of positives found among body builders is put into perspective when the figures are compared with the proportion of positives for all sports in the same region which were 6.1%, 6.3% and 5.7% respectively for the years 1990, 1991 and 1992 when a total of approximately 1 700 tests were conducted each year.

Table 4.3: Doping results among Flemish body builders 1988-93

Date	Number of tests	Number of positives	% positives
1988	32	7	22
1989	16	2	13
1990	42	29	69
1991	99	35	35
1992	82	41	50
1993	108	45	42
Totals	379	159	42

Source: adapted from Delbeke et al. (1995)

The analysis of the Flemish results also indicated the high level of steroids being taken (sometimes over twenty times the therapeutic dose), and the tendency towards multiple drug use. Abusers often took a number of different steroids at the same time, with stimulants and diuretics also found in some samples: the former probably for their appetite-suppressing properties and the latter in order to achieve the "sculpted" look desired for competition.

Among body builders, there is a clear association between the use of anabolic steroids and psychological disorders associated with distorted body images.[5] Pope et al., for example, found cases of two types of body image

---

1. Lindstrom, M., Nilsson, A., Katzman, P. et al., "Use of Anabolic Androgenic Steroids Among Body Builders – Frequency and Attitudes", *Journal of Internal Medicine*, Vol. 227, 1990, pp. 407-11.
2. Perry, H.M., Wright, D. & Littlepage, B.N.C., "Dying to be Big: A Review of Anabolic Steroid Use", *British Journal of Sports Medicine*, Vol. 26, 1992, pp. 259-62; Tricker, R., O'Neill, M.R. & Cook, D., "The Incidence of Anabolic Steroid Use Among Competitive Body Builders", *Journal of Drug Education*, Vol. 19, 1989, pp. 313-25.
3. Lenehan, P., "Epidemiological data", paper to the Sprint Seminar on the Non-Sport Use of Banned Substances, June 1999, Lisbon, CDDS, Council of Europe.
4. Delbeke, F.T., Desmet, M. & Debackere, M., "The Abuse of Doping Agents in Competing Body Builders in Flanders (1988-1993)", *International Journal of Sports Medicine*, Vol 16, 1995, pp. 66-70.
5. This section draws on the review of recent research into steroid use by Bahrke, M.S., Yesalis, C.E. & Wright, J.E., "Psychological and Behavioural Effects of Endogenous Testosterone and Anabolic-Androgenic Steroids: An Update", *Sports Medicine*, Vol. 22.6, 1996, pp. 367-90.

disorders in a study of 108 body builders (55 steroid users and 53 non-users). Of the total sampled, 2.8% reported a history of anorexia nervosa (the norm for American males is 0.02%) and 8.3%, including two of those who had reported a history of anorexia nervosa, reported reverse anorexia, a condition in which they perceive themselves to be weak and small even though they were large and muscular. All the reverse anorexia cases were found among the steroid users and according to the responses to the structured interviews contributed to their decision to start taking steroids.[1] Support for the findings of Pope et al., came from the research of Blouin and Goldfield who also examined the relationship between steroid use and self-perception of the body.[2] In their study, they compared a group of body builders with groups of runners and martial artists and found that the body builders had the highest levels of self-reported steroid use and also the strongest expressions of dis-satisfaction with their bodies. With the caveat that the evidence of steroid use is based on self-reporting, Blouin and Goldfield found that 44.2% of body builders used steroids, but only 2.1% of runners and no martial artists used the drugs. Not only did body builders provide stronger expressions of body dissatisfaction, but they also possessed lower levels of self-esteem and personal effectiveness. Their conclusions provided additional evidence to support earlier studies that suggested that men who perceive themselves as underweight may become involved in body building and the use of anabolic steroids in order to achieve an exaggerated "hypermorphic" look. Porcerelli and Sandler measured the degree of narcissism among a group of weightlifters and body builders, some of whom used steroids and found that the steroid-using group scored much higher on a scale measuring pathologi-cal narcissism.[3] The diagnostic criteria for narcissistic personality disorder include a "grandiose sense of self-importance; pre-occupation with fantasies of omnipotence and omniscience; susceptibility to feelings of rage, shame, humiliation and emptiness; a sense of entitlement; exploitativeness; and a lack of empathy".[4] Whether it is immersion in the culture of body building that predisposes participants to develop low self-esteem and take steroids or whether those with low self-esteem are predisposed to participate in body building and take steroids is unclear.

Drugs and leisure sports

The theme of low self-esteem is also part of the discussion surrounding drug use, over-training and obsessive behaviour among those who participate in activities which are on the fringe of competitive sport such as aerobics and

1. Pope, H., Katz, D. & Hudson, J., "Anorexia Nervosa and 'Reverse Anorexia' Among 108 Male Bodybuilders", *Comprehensive Psychiatry*, Vol. 34.6, 1993, pp. 406-9.
2. Blouin, A. & Goldfield, G., "Body Image and Steroid Use in Male Bodybuilders", *International-al Journal of Eating Disorders*, Vol. 18.2, 1995, pp. 159-65.
3. Porcerelli, J. & Sandler, B., "Narcissism and Empathy in Steroid Users", *American Journal of Psychiatry*, Vol. 152.11, 1995. pp. 1 672-4.
4. Ibid., p. 1 672.

keep fit. In an analysis of a series of surveys of steroid use in the United States it was found that over one million people were spending collectively more than $100 million per year on steroids with almost half the total number of users being under 25 years old. In addition, it is estimated that between 4% and 11% of male adolescents and 0.5% and 2.9% of female adolescents had taken steroids at some time.[1] While many of those using steroids were involved in competitive sport, a substantial proportion were not and did not aspire to participate in competitive sport. Support for this conclusion is provided by Blouin and Goldfield who reported that 20% of recreational body builders admitted using steroids.

The use of anabolic steroids by the young

Clearly there is a range of motives prompting the use of steroids and other ergogenic drugs among those involved in fringe sports activities. Among the young there is some evidence of strong pressure to conform to peer group expectations and thus steroids, for example, are simply added to the list of currently fashionable recreational drugs such as ecstasy, marijuana and amphetamines. In addition, there are clear pressures arising from low self-esteem and the assumption that self-esteem can be enhanced if one's physique is closer to some ideal of masculinity or femininity. Whereas in the past it was assumed that the patriarchal character of society put intense pressure on women to attempt to shape their bodies to conform to male expectations there is evidence that an increasing number of males feel under much the same pressure to shape their bodies to fit a socially constructed ideal. However, it is still difficult to distinguish between sports-related and non-sports-related drug use by the young, but such evidence as exists provides a basis for considerable concern.

In 1993, 16 000 Canadians between the ages of 11 and 18 were surveyed of whom 2.8% had used steroids in the previous twelve months. From these data it was estimated that 83 000 young Canadians were anabolic steroid users. More significantly, the survey revealed that almost half (48%) were taking steroids for purposes unrelated to competitive sport: "their use related to ... a concern about body image".[2] A similar large-scale national survey of 8877 12- to 20-year-olds was undertaken in Norway in 1992 where a lifetime use of steroids of 0.8% was found with 0.3% admitting use in the previous twelve months. Steroid use was associated with other "problem behaviour" including cannabis use, aggression and disordered eating.[3] A United States study of Denver high school students found that 2.7% (4% boys and

1. Middleman, A.B. & DuRant, R.H., "Anabolic Steroid Use and Associated Health Risk Behaviours", *Sports Medicine*, Vol. 21.4, 1996.
2. Pipe, A. & Melia, P., "Non-Sport Use of Anabolic Steroids in Youth", paper, Sprint Seminar on the Non-Sport Use of Banned Substances, June 1999, Lisbon, CDDS, Council of Europe.
3. Wichstrom, L. & Pedersen, W., "Use of Anabolic Steroids in Adolescence: Winning, Looking Good or Being Bad?", *Journal of Studies on Alcohol*, January 2001.

1.3% girls) had used steroids during their lifetime. The most common motive for steroid use among sports participants was enhanced performance (50%), but 16% used the drugs to improve their appearance: among sports non-participants, the dominant motive for steroid use was to improve appearance (45%).[1]

Drug abuse beyond sport

As indicated in Figure 4.2 the various drug-taking communities both within sport and outside overlap, with athletes moving between élite competitive and non-élite competitive sport and between sport and non-sport communities. It is therefore not possible to treat drug abuse by athletes as a discrete phenomenon when one is examining policy options. Consequently, it is important to review, if only briefly, the attempts that have been made to control drug abuse in wider society in order to identify policy options that might inform the development of the anti-doping effort in sport.

The section that follows provides a discussion of the way in which the issue of drug abuse has been defined and the range of policies proposed in response to the problem of the social and recreational use of drugs. The intention of this discussion is partly to create a sensitivity to the difficulties of determining a successful sports anti-doping policy and partly to generate a series of questions central to the refinement of current sports anti-doping policy.

Any attempt to outline and analyse a policy issue as complex as that concerned with drug abuse is beset with problems, not least of which is the enormous number of organisations with a direct or indirect interest in the issue and the dynamic nature of both problems and policies. In order to identify the key issues and factors that will be relevant to the discussion of current anti-doping policy in sport it is necessary to adopt some fairly drastic simplifying measures. It is undeniable that some of the detail and nuances of the issue will be blurred but the reward is a sharper focus on the key aspects of the course of problem definition and policy response. One useful way of organising a discussion of the issue is to see it as progressing through a series of stages which include problem recognition, problem investigation, identification of policy options, policy evaluation, followed by policy implementation and review. It is readily acknowledged that even apparently straightforward problems do not lend themselves to such neat compartmentalisation and progression. However, there is a value in adopting such an approach as long as it is accepted that the model of policy-making as involving a series of easily identifiable stages does not always conform to experience and is best seen as an ideal type against which the actual process may be compared. In the following examination of the policy response to social or recreational drug abuse, the following stages will be discussed: how the problem has

---

1.Tanner, S. et al., "Anabolic Steroid Use by Adolescents: Prevalence, Motives, and Knowledge of Risks", *Clinical Journal of Sport Medicine*, 5, 1995, pp. 108-115.

been defined, how targets and objectives for dealing with the problem have been set, how the particular policy instruments and agencies were selected, how the policy was implemented and how success or performance was measured and, finally, how the policy was evaluated and refined. As each stage is examined, it is important to reflect on the implications for the continuing development and refinement of anti-doping policy in sport: how does the experience and practice of anti-doping policy in sport differ from that related to social anti-drugs policy and what are the lessons to be learned and the pitfalls to be avoided.

Drug use – Whose problem?

Problems are rarely if ever self-evident. What might appear to one person as a pressing public problem demanding urgent intervention might appear to someone else as a private matter which governments should avoid getting involved with. At different times and in different societies issues as diverse as domestic violence, poverty, diet and youth homelessness were all considered to be private and personal issues rather than public problems. The same is true of the history of social and recreational drug use. In almost all countries over the last hundred years or so, there has been a shift in perception of drug use from a matter of personal choice and consequence to, on occasion, a matter of urgent governmental priority. Even today there is, in a number of countries, a recurring debate about whether drug use should be a matter for such intense government policy concern.

In many countries it is only a comparatively short time ago that opiates and cocaine were deemed to be relatively harmless and were routinely present in many medicines and tonics for both adults and children. Even well into the twentieth century, there were frequent calls for the decriminalisation of cocaine and heroin. Yet, today the opiates and cocaine are perceived as dangerous "hard" drugs with few if any positive features. The history of the definition of drug use as a public problem obviously varies from one country to another both in terms of the substances considered to be problematic and also in terms of the groups and organisations that were involved in the debate over drug use. In most industrialised and many developing countries there is currently a broad agreement that the opiates, marijuana, cocaine and hallucinogens should be illegal, while alcohol and tobacco should not. One of the problems encountered in the policy response to contemporary drug use is the practice of grouping a wide and varied range of substances under the heading of "drugs", "a catch-all simplification that encourages misplaced efforts to devise uniform policies for a broad array of diverse problems".[1]

In explaining how decisions are made on which drugs to target, it is important to take account of the variety of ways in which the problem of drug

1. Smith, P.H., "The Political Economy of Drugs: Conceptual Issues and Policy Options" in Smith, P.H., *Drug Policy in the Americas*, Boulder, Col: Westview Press, 1992.

abuse can be framed. In some countries the debate on drug abuse has been stimulated and subsequently dominated by health care professionals, and in other countries the motivation for policy-making has come from groups, such as churches and political parties, concerned with moral standards in society. Other definitions of the problem of drug use have come from those with a primary focus on the law and order aspects of the issue, or a concern with the impact of the drugs trade on international relations and political stability. Perceptions of the issue are crucial in determining the organisations that become involved in selecting policy solutions. However, it is not simply the case that perceptions of drug use vary between countries they also differ over time in the same country. In Britain, for example, Lart charts how the perception of heroin addiction changed over the forty-year period between the mid-1920s and the mid-1960s from "an individualised pathology affecting unfortunates, to a socially infectious condition, needing to be controlled"[1] with influence over policy moving from doctors, who were able to use their professional judgment to decide whether to prescribe heroin to addicts, to politicians, police and the courts, who ushered in a more punitive policy which saw the drug user ceasing to be a victim and becoming a villain.

A similar inconsistency in attitudes and policy can be found in the United States, where attitudes towards drug use have changed radically more than once over the last hundred years. Hailed as a wonder drug in the late nineteenth century, cocaine, for example, was rapidly demonised in the early years of the twentieth century as a threat to the fabric of society and a danger to personal morality. Although the emphasis remained on care and cure, limitations were gradually placed on the freedom of doctors to prescribe cocaine or heroin. Gradually, during the 1920s, care and cure and the broadly welfare-based definition of the problem was replaced by criminalisation and ostracism. But even this redefinition was temporary as the cycle of liberalism followed by intolerance was repeated in the 1960s. The position on drug use adopted by most European communist governments was simply denial that a problem existed. Given the prevalence of rhetoric which portrayed drug use as a product of capitalist societies and symptomatic of their decadence it was extremely difficult for these countries to acknowledge that they too had a drug-abuse problem.[2]

Even within Europe in recent years, there is considerable variation in attitudes to drug users, the classification of drugs and the possession of drugs. In a survey conducted by the European Commission it was found that some countries (Spain, Ireland and Italy) made no distinction between "hard" and "soft" drugs. In Germany, Denmark and Portugal drug use was not specifically banned although there were laws on acquisition. Table 4.4 highlights some of the variation in relation to the law on acquisition, possession and use.

---

1. Lart, R., "British Medical Perception from Rolleston to Brain: Changing Images of the Addict and Addiction", *International Journal on Drug Policy*, Vol. 3, 1992, p. 19.
2. Inciardi, J., "Drug Abuse in the Georgian SSR", *Journal of Psychoactive Drugs*, Vol. 19.4, 1987, pp. 329-34.

Table 4.4: Comparison of legislation on acquisition, possession and use[1]

Country	Acquisition	Possession	Use
Germany	Offence, as for trafficking	Specific offence	Not an offence
Spain	Not an offence	Not an offence	Not an offence
Belgium	Offence, as for trafficking	Offence, as for trafficking	Punishable offence (but only for collective use)
Greece	Specific offence (but not if the user is an addict)	Offence, as for trafficking	Not an offence
Netherlands	Not an offence	Specific offence	Not an offence
Sweden	Offence	Offence	Offence if use in Sweden

The report reflected two profoundly different attitudes towards drug use in society. On the one hand there are those countries that considered that there is no legal basis for limiting the individual's freedom with regard to their own body, and, on the other hand, there are those governments who consider that the underlying social consequences of an individual's drug use overrides the individual's rights. Those countries subscribing to the former position also tend to consider drug use and addiction as a disease rather than a crime and thus favour treatment rather than punishment as the policy response.

Doping in sport: athletes as victims or villains

Many of the dilemmas faced by those engaged in attempting to reduce recreational drug use have parallels in the development of anti-doping policy in sport. As with recreational anti-drugs policy the anti-doping policy in sport has been variously conceptualised as a moral issue (one of cheating) and a health issue. There has also been considerable debate as to whether the issue is a private matter to be left to sports organisations or a matter of public policy which consequently involves governments. Finally, the definition of the problem takes place at both the international level and at the level of individual countries. As will be shown in the following chapters, there is still considerable tension between sports organisations, particularly the IOC and the major federations, over the issue of policy leadership and issue definition, and also tension between governmental and sports bodies over their respective roles and responsibilities in anti-doping policy.

The dominant definition of the issue of doping in sport remains, not surprisingly, that it is cheating. Underpinning this definition is a perception of the

---

1. Leroy, B., *The Community of Twelve and Drug Demand: Comparative Study of Legislation and Judicial Practice*, Commission of the European Community, 1991.

athlete as a rational person who is capable of making informed choices and who is aware of the unethical nature of doping. The decision to take drugs consequently makes the athlete a villain. Such a view, as will be shown below, led to policies that stressed detection and punishment. More recently, greater stress has been placed on the definition of doping as a serious health risk with athletes being, at least, partly ignorant of the medium and long-term consequences of their actions for their own health. The broadening of the definition of the problem is due, in part, to the increasing role of scientists, doctors and psychologists within sport and the different perspectives they bring to the problem. Although health concerns are still of secondary importance to ethics as the basis for current policy there has been a growing emphasis placed on education and information.

The mix of definitions of the problem of doping is reflected in the list of banned substances and practices produced by the IOC. The evolution of the list has been shaped by the various interested parties concerned with doping, such as doctors, sports administrators, scientists and, more recently, lawyers. Although each party will refer to a mix of criteria in attempting to shape the content of the IOC list, each will have, or at least should have, slightly different priorities. For sports doctors, a prominent criterion should be the likelihood of damage to the athlete's health; for scientists, the existence of a reliable test for a particular drug should be a central criterion; for sports administrators the ergogenic potential will be crucial, but there will also be a concern to protect the public image of sport; while for lawyers the reliability of testing methods and the probity of the testing process will be their main concerns.

The composition of the IOC list is the product of the interplay of the various interests concerned with anti-doping policy and, as such, is a regularly negotiated compromise. Where scientists might apply a strict interpretation of ergogenic effect in order to determine inclusion others, such as sports administrators concerned with the public image of sport, have pressed for the retention of drugs such as marijuana which have a negative public image but have, at best, a doubtful ergogenic value. A similar compromise exists between those who support a ban on narcotic analgesics such as cocaine, but who also support the permissibility of the administration of local anaesthetics, and those who consider that the latter should be banned because they too confer an advantage through the alteration of the athlete's natural state. In summary, the IOC list mirrors the balance of influence among those with an involvement in anti-doping policy at a particular time and is a compromise that reflects the current mix of science, morality and administrative pragmatism.

Setting objectives

The lack of a stable consensus in defining the problem of recreational drug use is complemented by a similar lack of consensus over the objectives to be achieved through the anti-drugs policy. Acknowledging that objectives will vary according to the type of drug being considered, there is still significant variation in objectives even for the same class of drug. At differing times, the objectives have been set in terms of management, containment, control and elimination with there being a subsidiary set of objectives relating to harm reduction or use reduction. In general, most countries give priority to the reduction in use and thus pursue policies designed to limit supply or to decrease demand. It is also important to note that in some countries the "drug problem" has been subsumed by a concern with the levels of crime associated with the use of "hard drugs". As a result, the primary emphasis has been placed on the elimination or, at least, the reduction of drug-related crime with the reduction in drug use itself relegated to a secondary outcome.

In the United States, for example, the emphasis has generally been on the development of policies designed to reduce supply rather than decrease demand on the assumption that without a steady supply the demand for drugs will wither. Where and when the emphasis has been placed on addressing the demand for drugs, objectives have ranged from complete elimination through containment or management to tolerance. Sweden is an example of a country seeking to achieve elimination and consequently where "no distinction [is] made between soft and hard drugs, criminal law is invoked punitively, prevention, treatment and rehabilitation are emphasised and compulsory care can be imposed".[1] A similar set of objectives was dominant in Germany until recently and was reflected in a rejection of methadone-maintenance programmes in preference for policies that sought to cut drug users off from their supply. By contrast, Switzerland, Denmark and Holland have tended to favour policies described as "harm minimisation" or "problem management".

There has been much discussion concerning what would constitute clear and realistic aims for drug policy and, given the complexity of the issue, it is not surprising that the debate seems to have made little progress with countries oscillating between elimination and containment with tolerance being introduced as a possible objective but one which is rarely adopted. Part of the difficulty lies in specifying clearly what "use reduction" and "harm reduction" mean. Some advocates of use reduction argue that there is no difference between the two objectives because if use is reduced so too will harm, but if it is accepted that a drug-free society is as impossible as a crime-free society then one must acknowledge the varied levels of risk arising from different patterns of drug use. The level of risk for those who inject is far greater than for those who take drugs orally and it is quite possible that a reduction in use may increase the level of risk especially among heavy/addicted users who become more susceptible to overdose. More significantly, for the purposes of

1. Ruggiero, V & South, N. 1995, *Eurodrugs: drug use, markets and trafficking in Europe*, London: UCL Press, p. 36.

framing policy both use reduction and harm reduction can be defined in a number of ways as Table 4.5 illustrates.

Table 4.5: Policy objectives and strategy: use reduction and harm reduction[1]

Policy definitions	Strategic implications
Use reduction – as a reduction in the number of users	Focus on light users, potential users and users at the start of their drug-using behaviour
Use reduction – as a reduction in the total volume of drugs consumed	Target heavy users, suppliers and producers.
Use reduction – as a reduction in the money spent on drugs	Target heavy users and expensive drugs (or reduce attempts to interdict supply so that prices fall!)
Harm reduction – as a reduction in net harm (that is, accepting that there are benefits of drug use to some users)	Ignore (or even promote!) use where it is deemed to generate greater benefits than costs
Harm reduction – as a reduction in total harm	Emphasis on treatment, incentives and education
Harm reduction – as a reduction in harm done to non-users (as victims of theft and violence)	Focus on criminalisation and enforcement, though possibly combined with treatment

Given the ambiguity and variability over time of the policy objectives related to recreational drug use, are those for doping in sport any clearer? Bearing in mind the involvement of governments, the IOC, sports federations and domestic governing bodies of sport, is there a consensus regarding policy objectives? With only marginal exceptions, the primary objective of current policy has been to reduce demand rather than attempt to reduce supply. In many respects, this is a pragmatic objective because of the fact that many banned substances are legal and relatively easily available, and also have multiple sources of supply. However, there are some substances, such as synthetic hGH and EPO, both of which are tightly controlled, that have only a small number of suppliers and which therefore lend themselves to policies designed to achieve an attenuation of supply. Similarly, there are some substances, such as insulin, whose successful administration is extremely difficult, if not hazardous, without professional assistance. Although restricting supply to athletes is difficult there appears to have been little consideration of this as a possible objective.

There is also a high level of ambiguity regarding the scope of anti-doping policy. The IOC is concerned with the elimination of doping at competitions organised under the auspices of the Olympic movement in order to be able

---

1. Adapted from Caulkins, J.P. & Reuter, P., "Setting Goals for Drug Policy", *Addiction*, 92.9, 1997, pp. 1 143-50.

to ensure the probity of results. The international federations vary considerably in the application of anti-doping policy with some limiting testing to established élite athletes, others to élite and near élite, and still others extending coverage to include juniors and veterans. While some governments see doping in sport as part of a broader anti-drugs policy others tend to treat doping in sport as a minor problem best left to sports authorities. Thus doping in fringe sports such as body building is often ignored as it falls outside the mainstream concerns of sports organisations and the government. Overall there is little evidence of consistency and stability regarding objectives of sports anti-doping policy although the level of dissension is far lower than in previous years and, as will be explored in Chapter 7, there is at least the basis for discussions about closer policy harmonisation.

Despite the progress that has been made in recent years towards harmonisation of objectives, it must be borne in mind that over the last thirty years or so governments have demonstrated a wide variety of motives and levels of commitment to anti-doping. Despite public statements condemning doping, it is accepted that the governments of a number of the most prominent sporting countries were systematically undermining anti-doping efforts, while a further group of countries were allowing policy momentum to dissipate through lack of support.

The drive for anti-doping policy harmonisation currently being led by the Council of Europe and WADA has sharpened many of the concerns regarding objectives. Among the objectives that need to be clarified are those relating to the boundary between ergogenic and recreational drug use, between treating the drug-using athlete as a villain who requires punishment or treating him/her as a victim who requires support, counselling and medical help, and between the burden of responsibility shouldered by the athlete and by members of his/her entourage. In addition, it must be asked whether the ultimate objective is the complete elimination of drug use in all sport, in certain sports, or only in sport at certain levels. One might also ask whether the objective is elimination or simply the containment of the extent of drug use. If, however, the objective is complete elimination then one must ask what level of commitment and resource allocation would be required for its achievement and whether the necessary commitment and resources are likely to be made available and where they would come from.

Selecting policy instruments

At some stage in the process of making policy, decisions have to be made about the most appropriate instruments (solution) to achieve the desired objectives. Although logically the setting of objectives should precede the identification of policy instruments, this is not always the case as in practice solutions currently being applied to other problems may be applied to new problems. There are many examples of this practice in relation to drugs policy, indeed in most countries anti-drug strategies are typified by a high degree of uniformity in policy response with there being, for example, few significant illustrations of countries seeking to tailor policies to particular categories of drug user or particular drugs.

Over the years, a wide range of policy solutions have been developed and applied to aspects of the recreational drug problem. Policy solutions may be categorised in a number of ways such as according to the objective, but it is frequently the case that the same solution may be used to achieve a variety of objectives. It is more useful to categorise policy solutions in terms of the extent to which they rely on extrinsic or intrinsic instruments with incentives or penalties being examples of the former and changes in attitudes being an example of the latter. Table 4.6 provides a simple schematic presentation of combinations of policy instrument with particular causes of non-compliance. In essence, it is suggested that, first of all, judgments have to be made about the causes of non-compliance with objectives. For some, the cause of non-compliance might be ignorance or inability to comply, while for others the cause may lie in a conscious decision not to comply. Each of these causes could be sub-divided: for example, an inability to comply may be due to the level of intelligence of the individual, or the lack of a particular skill, such as speaking the language of the country in which he or she is resident, or it may be due to constraints imposed by others who consequently prevent compliance.

Table 4.6: Recreational drug use: the causes of non-compliance and the effectiveness of various policy instruments

Policy instruments				
	Inducements		Constraints	
Cause of non-compliance	Rewards	Education/ information	Erection of barriers	Deterrents
Ignorance or incompetence	Negligible effect	Substantial effect	Moderate effect	Moderate effect
Inability to comply (lack of free will)	Negligible effect	Negligible effect	Negligible effect	Negligible effect
Conscious decision not to comply	Moderate effect	Negligible effect	Moderate effect	Moderate effect

Table 4.7 lists three main causes of non-compliance and suggests that these may be analysed in relation to the main distinctive types of policy instrument available to governments and to other authoritative bodies, such as sports federations and the IOC. As mentioned above the use of incentives or threats are among the most common instruments adopted by governments to attempt to ensure compliance, but the use of rewards (access to government resources such as finance, medical treatment, welfare services, etc.) is also common in anti-drugs policy. However, the limits of rewards are evident

when related to the three causes of non-compliance identified in the table. Rewards are unlikely to be of much value where the impediments to compliance are the result of ignorance or some other barrier to compliance such as literacy, an ability to communicate in the language of the host country or doubts over security of residence. By contrast, rewards might be successful where the source of non-compliance lies in choice.

A policy solution that relies on education and information may be more successful than simple rewards in overcoming the causes of non-compliance and it is very common for the two to be used in combination. One would hope that ignorance can be overcome through the provision of information (such as the health warning provided on cigarette packets or clearer information regarding the side-effects of steroids). Information coupled with rewards might also undermine the resolve of those who consciously resist compliance. However, information is unlikely to be of much value where the cause of non-compliance is a lack of free will.

It is possible to refine the analysis presented in Table 4.6 by further analysis of the causes of non-compliance and particularly whether the basic cause is seen as the consequence of personality, understanding/cognition or situation (Table 4.7).

Table 4.7 : Problem perception and policy implications[1]

Problem location	Assumptions	Implied policy focus
Personality	1. The individual has a propensity to take risks 2. The individual has a misperception of risk	The user: counselling and psychological therapy
Understanding/ cognition	Drug use (addiction) interferes with perception of risk	The drug: control access
Situational	Environment of potential user is one where drugs are more likely to be available: for example, fitness/body building gyms	The environment: modify gym culture and/or more strict inspection and policing

Policy instruments actually deployed reflect differing perceptions of the primary location of the problem and are often combinations of instruments, for example coupling rewards with information/education. It is also the case that policy instruments that are based on inducements are frequently combined with threats or constraints. For example, barriers may be erected to make the targeted behaviour more difficult to undertake. Barriers may be of various types including physical (fences or trenches at football grounds to prevent

1. Adapted from: Leigh, B., "Peril, Chance, Adventure: Concpts of Risk, Alcohol Use and Risky Behavior in Young Adults", *Addiction*, 94.3, 1999, pp. 371-83.

pitch invasions), psychological (street cameras in "red light" areas), and bureaucratic (high levels of tax on tobacco). Stronger constraints may come in the form of deterrents such as threats of exclusion, imprisonment or fines. The success of policy instruments derived from constraints is also affected by the cause of non-compliance. Constraints are not going to be of much value where the basis of non-compliance is ignorance or a lack of choice or free will. Threats and other constraints may, however, be more successful where non-compliance is the result of a conscious decision to break a regulation or law.

At the domestic level, policy instruments designed to reduce demand frequently rely on combinations of inducements and constraints. In the past, the emphasis has tended to be on increasing the cost to the drug user of obtaining drugs by, for example, an intensive arrest and prosecution policy which imposes on the user the cost of punishment. More recently, there has been a trend away from a reliance on constraints and a more sympathetic attitude towards policy instruments aimed at reducing demand by the treatment of existing users, for example with heroin substitute, and education of potential users to avoid drugs.[1] The policy instrument is partly an inducement, as care and a steady supply of the heroin substitute are offered as a reward for compliance.

In addition to strategies targeted at established drug users, there are also examples of strategies aimed at preventing the non-user or occasional user becoming an established user. Where the policy objective is drug prevention (in other words, a reduction in demand) the policy instrument is usually focused on the provision of information and education about the dangers of drug misuse and may be targeted at a variety of target groups, including potential users, their peer group and their parents and teachers.[2] Policy instruments may consequently need to be varied and subtle and tailored to the particular circumstances of the non-user (both the never-exposed and the exposed), the experimental user, the non-dependent regular user, the addicted user and the vulnerable ex-user.

The possible combinations of policy instruments is vast and the examples given above are designed to illustrate current policy and, more importantly, to provide a point of comparison when considering current anti-doping policy in sport. Table 4.8 adopts the same framework as used in Table 4.6 for exploring the relationship between causes of non-compliance with anti-doping regulations and policy instruments. The most obvious cause of non-compliance is a conscious decision to seek a competitive advantage through the use of drugs, but it is not the only cause. For example, there are plenty of

---

1. Hough, M., "Problem Drug Use and Criminal Justice", London: Home Office Drug Prevention Initiative, 1996.
2. Duke, K., MacGregor, S. & Smith, L., "Activating Local Networks: A Comparison of Two Community Development Approaches to Drug Prevention", London: Home Office Drug Prevention Initiative, 1996.

examples of athletes who would claim that they had little option but to take drugs due to the character of the political regime under which they lived. However, the debate about the limits imposed by others on an athlete's free will is a highly controversial basis for non-compliance and one that is examined in detail in the next chapter. In contrast, ignorance or lack of competence is a more plausible basis for non-compliance. There are many examples of athletes claiming ignorance of the chemical properties of medicines and given the complexity of the current IOC list it is probably unrealistic to expect every athlete to be familiar with the full list and its interpretation.

As regards the variety of instruments available to anti-doping authorities, the most commonly applied is the deterrent. Deterrents range from a life ban from competition at one extreme through fixed-term bans to public warnings at the lenient end of the scale. Where drug users have broken the criminal law, it is also possible that prison sentences might be imposed, although there are few examples of custodial sentences. Deterrents are unlikely to be successful where the cause of non-compliance is either ignorance or incompetence. Deterrents are also likely to be of only limited value where athletes' choices regarding drug use are constrained, especially when the constraint is being imposed by the state. This policy instrument is therefore only likely to be effective when sports authorities are supported by the domestic government and where there is relatively easy access to athletes to conduct tests: in other words, where the athlete is acting in an individual capacity (or with the support of only one or two others) in a country where both the governing bodies and government are supportive of the anti-doping policy.

The erection of barriers to inhibit drug use is an alternative policy instrument, but one that relies heavily on the co-operation of other groups or organisations that might not always share the same objectives as the supporters of anti-doping. For example, one could seek tighter control of the supply of drugs prepared by the pharmaceutical industry, especially those that are produced in relatively small quantities and which are mainly distributed through hospitals. However, how realistic is it to expect pharmaceutical companies to forego the opportunity to expand the market for a particular drug: ethics and profit are not always complementary. One might also expect doctors to constitute an effective barrier to the abuse of drugs, but such an expectation needs to be moderated by the knowledge that there are significant examples of doctors prescribing ergogenic drugs for athletes. For effective barriers to be erected it would probably require government intervention to force greater control over supply on the part of the pharmaceutical companies and a greater willingness on the part of professional associations to interfere with the traditional autonomy of doctors to prescribe as they see fit. If barriers could be effectively established they would undoubtedly have a significant impact on the athlete's access to drugs, but the problems of erecting effective barriers are formidable and there are few examples, if any, of their success as policy instruments with regard to either recreational or sports drugs.

In many countries with an established anti-doping strategy, education is an increasingly important policy instrument. Targeted at both the junior and the adult athlete, educational programmes often seek to raise awareness of the health risks and the career risks associated with drug use, as well as promoting an appreciation of the ethical issues raised by doping. Where ignorance is the cause of drug use, then obviously an educational programme is likely to be effective, but it is unlikely to have an impact on the other two causes of non-compliance.

Rewards have considerable potential to promote compliance. Many governments have rewarded athletes whom they consider models for their citizens, with national honours, and sports organisations have inducted athletes in "Halls of Fame". Although a clean record on drugs is not the sole criterion for a reward, it is often taken into account and may be effective with those athletes attracted by the long-term status that honours confer.

Table 4.8: Doping in sport among adult athletes: causes of non-compliance and the potential effectiveness of policy instruments

	Policy instruments			
	Inducements		Constraints	
Cause of non-compliance	Rewards	Education/ information	Erection of barriers	Deterrents
Ignorance or incompetence	Negligible effect	Substantial potential effect	Modest effect	Negligible effect
Inability to comply (lack of free will)	Negligible effect	Negligible effect	Moderate effect	Negligible effect
Conscious decision not to comply	Moderate effect	Moderate effect	Moderate effect	Moderate effect

The IOC and most of the major international federations have, not surprisingly, relied on policy instruments which directly parallel those developed to combat recreational drug use. Among the most common instruments are the use of threats of loss of eligibility to compete, often combined with programmes of education and information. But there are also examples, resulting from co-operation with governments, of attempts to restrict supply either through the tightening of control over access to drugs currently available "over-the-counter" in pharmacies or through attempts to limit the leakage of controlled drugs such as hGH onto the black market. However, many questions remain including whether the balance of policy instruments is appropriate, and whether the mix of policy instruments varies to suit the type of drug use or drug user being targeted. In addition, there have been debates recently about whether the athlete is the proper target for anti-doping policy or whether members of the athlete's entourage, or indeed his/her national governing body, should be the proper focus for achieving compliance.

Monitoring implementation and measuring success

There is a frequent temptation to consider that once agreement on objectives has been reached and policy instruments and implementing organisations have been identified the bulk of the work involved in policy-making is complete. This is, unfortunately, far from being an accurate picture of the policy process. For a variety of reasons, it is essential that ways are devised to measure the success of the selected policy instruments and agencies in achieving the desired objectives. However, what makes this task at times extremely problematic is that policy objectives are frequently unclear and they are also subject to relatively rapid alteration.

One of the unavoidable dangers of using performance indicators is that frequently they are designed to measure outputs rather than outcomes. For example, in the campaign against social and recreational drug use claims of "success" are often based on increases in the volume of drugs intercepted at ports and borders, the arrest and successful prosecution of leading drug wholesalers, increases in the number of arrests of drug users and the ratification of anti-drugs conventions promoted by international organisations. At best, these measures are indirect and suggestive of progress but are highly unreliable as a guide to progress towards the central objective of reducing drug consumption and the number of drug users. For example, success in intercepting imported drugs might simply result in drug users switching to domestically produced alternatives, and increased arrest rates for drug users might simply transfer drug users from the streets to prisons where drug use is often extensive. In the context of the anti-doping campaign in sport, techniques for measuring progress towards policy objectives are poor, relying mainly on trends in the number of positive test results.

Overall, it would seem that the development of reliable performance measures for the assessment of the success of current anti-doping remains elusive and generally a low priority. One of the key problems is the reliability of the data currently collected. The numbers of positive results will be affected by a number of factors including the number of tests carried out, their distribution between sports, and the balance between in-competition and out-of-competition tests. Further, not all positive test results are deemed to be doping infractions. A second difficulty with the interpretation of doping records is that the decline in the number of positives for one type of drug might indicate success in anti-doping policy implementation but might, more plausibly, indicate an evolution in the drug culture, for example, away from amphetamines to steroids and, more recently, from steroids to testosterone, or greater sophistication among users in avoiding detection or, indeed, a shift to other less easily detected drugs. Finally, it remains difficult to identify reliable time-series indicators of progress due to the rapidity with which the nature of the problem evolves. Not only does the range of available and preferred drugs continue to expand, but so too does the range, and application, of testing procedures. As a result, it is not possible to draw firm conclusions about the

119

current level of policy success. Consequently, the repeated claims to be "winning the war on doping in sport" will continue to prompt scepticism rather than congratulations until a set of agreed benchmarks are established. Ironically, probably the best indicator of success is the decline in performance in some events at recent Olympic Games. For example, Franke and Berendonk draw attention to the decline in performance in women's javelin, discus and shot-put following the introduction of out-of-competition testing in 1989.[1] Not only did the best performance of the year decline but so too did the average performance of the best ten athletes. In the shot, for example, the best performance in 1987 was over 22.5 m, but between 1989 and 1993 no female athlete put the shot further than 22 m and in 1996 no athlete exceeded 21m. A similar pattern is found in the javelin where no one has got within 4 m of the 1988 world record, and in 1996 the best throw was some 10.5 m short of the record.

Policy review and modification

There are three developments that prompt a review of policy instruments: first, the failure of the policy to produce improvements in the selected measures of performance; second, the emergence of new dimensions to the target problem; and third, a redefinition of the problem. Given that problems are, at best, moving targets it is only to be expected that policy instruments will need to be regularly reviewed to ensure that they are still appropriate. In practice, however, it is common for policy to become fixed and to get progressively out of step with the problem is was intended to address. It is also common for policy instruments to be subject to political competition as different interests attempt to affect the way in which the instrument is interpreted and applied. It is when examining the way in which policies are reviewed that the weaknesses of attempts to explain the policy process as a series of stages are most apparent.

Where debate is relatively open, the process of policy review may result in the decision to maintain the current policy. It may, however, result in the decision to replace the existing policy with one thought more suitable, that is policy succession. Alternative outcomes include the decision to modify the existing policy or indeed to terminate the policy.[2] The most common result is the decision to reconfigure the "ingredients" in the existing policy, for example, by altering the balance between constraints and inducements. In general, radical alterations to existing policy are infrequent often because interested bodies have too much credibility invested in particular policies. Within anti-drugs policy this is amply illustrated by the determination of many countries to resist the introduction of policies based on treatment, decriminalisation and reward to replace policies based on punishment of users and the

---

1. Franke & Berendonk, 1997, op. cit.
2. See Hogwood, B. & Peters, B.G., *Policy Dynamics,* Brighton: Wheatsheaf Books, 1983.

interdiction of supply. With regard to current anti-doping policy, it might seem premature to discuss policy review and modification when many would argue that the policy is still being established. However, one feature of drug abuse in sport is the pace at which the problem evolves, largely due to the advent of new drugs but also due to the emergence of new problems such as the increasing frequency of legal challenges to federation decisions. As will be seen in Chapter 7, the current concern with policy harmonisation is providing an important opportunity for policy review and refinement.

Conclusion

Although doping in sport has a number of distinctive features, the key conclusion of this chapter is that it is not possible to isolate the problem of doping in sport from the wider series of related drug-abuse issues in society, no more than it is possible to isolate sportspeople from drug abuse in wider society. In relation to the development of policy towards recreational drug abuse, the chapter has also highlighted the deep interconnection between domestic and international policy-making and the wide range of organisations that are active in the policy process. A similar range of organisations are involved in combating drug abuse in sport and it is also the case that successful policy implementation relies on a co-ordinated strategy functioning at both the international and the domestic levels. Where drug abuse in sport differs from recreational drug abuse is that the organisational source of policy momentum in sport lies more securely at the international level with the IOC, WADA and the IAAF in particular. Nevertheless, the sport anti-doping policy is just as vulnerable as recreational drug abuse policy to being undermined by weak support at the domestic level.

Sport also shares similarities with recreational drug abuse in so far as the character of the problem being addressed is not static. The evolution of the issue has been marked by change, not only in terms of the drugs considered to be the most serious challenge to the integrity of competitive sport, but also in terms of the sports most at risk from corruption through drug use. It is not surprising that the sports and governmental bodies at the heart of the anti-doping strategy have utilised a range of policy instruments over the last twenty years: however, most of them have been adaptations of existing instruments used to tackle problems of recreational drug abuse. This brief review of the way in which the issue of drug abuse has been defined and redefined illustrates not only the shifting nature of the definition of social problems, but also the variety of organisations and interests involved in attempting to influence the process of definition. Doctors, welfare professionals, politicians, courts and the police are only some of the more prominent interests involved in shaping policy at the domestic level. Although it is possible to characterise drug abuse as a personal or community problem, it is increasingly accepted that it is located within a global context of production and supply. When account is taken of the international dimension of problem definition, it would be necessary to examine the contribution of individual governments, international police networks and international governmental organisations such as the United Nations and the European Union.

In the chapters that follows current anti-doping policy objectives and instruments will be examined as will be the organisations involved in policy implementation. The analysis of current policy begins with an exploration of the way in which the problem of doping in sport has been defined.

Chapter 5
Defining the problem: the ethics of doping

Doping, it is often argued, is anathema in sport because it is unfair. If further defence is required then it may also be argued that doping in sport is "cheating, plain and simple",[1] is dangerous to the health of the athlete, is harmful to the image of the activity and may deter sponsors, or is a poor example to set to younger, aspiring athletes. If these justifications fail to impress then the circular argument is relied upon that doping is a breach of governing body rules. As will be shown below all these arguments have a certain plausibility but none is, by itself, capable of providing a sufficiently strong underpinning for the enormous investment of resources currently devoted to the anti-doping strategy.

Until a satisfactory answer can be given to the question "Why oppose doping?", it is not possible to define with sufficient clarity the problem that the sporting and governmental authorities are trying to tackle nor is it possible to defend anti-doping policy with confidence. Moreover, the policy instruments selected will, to a very large extent, be determined by the formulation of the basis on which doping is opposed. Quite simply if the primary objection is that doping damages the health of athletes the policy instruments selected will be very different from those chosen if the problem is formulated solely as a breach of sporting ethics.

The central focus of this chapter is an examination of the basis on which doping in sport may be opposed. A second aspect of the issue of doping in sport, namely how sporting and other organisations define the problem they are addressing, forms the basis of Chapter 6, which examines current anti-doping policy.

In most recent discussions of doping, there are a limited number of recurring justifications for opposing doping. In the concluding chapter of his report into drug abuse by athletes in Canada, Justice Dubin quoted from the Olympic Charter, which states that "They [the Olympic Games] unite Olympic competitors of all countries in fair and equal competition". He then proceeded to castigate Canadian athletes who have not lived up to this ideal and who "resorted to performance-enhancing drugs and other banned practices, thereby gaining an unfair advantage over those who did not do so... Those who have cheated have threatened the very future of sport and tarnished its reputation ... They have also unfairly cast a cloud of suspicion over the majority of athletes, who abide by the rules, and have threatened their future financial support from governments, corporations, and the general public".[2] A similar view is expressed by members of the Australian Senate

---

1. Voy, 1991, op. cit., p. xvi.
2. Dubin Inquiry, 1990, op. cit., p. 517.

Committee investigation into drugs in sport. Following an extensive discussion of the possible reasons for opposing drug use the committee concludes:

> *"The Committee takes the view that performance-enhancing drugs should be banned because they can potentially damage the health of those taking them, whether they are élite athletes who stand the risk of being detected using them, or the recreational sportsperson who is unlikely ever to be tested. They should be banned also because anyone using them is trying to gain an unfair advantage over those athletes who wish to maintain normal health. They are cheating, because their use is against the rules of the sporting federations".* [1]

These three reflections on the rationale for opposing doping in sport have much in common. For the IOC, the essential reason for attempting to ban doping is a wish to protect fair and equal competition. That doping should be opposed because it introduces inequality and unfairness into sport is a view shared by Justice Dubin who refers to the desire to seek an unfair advantage as cheating, but also adds that doping should be opposed for the additional reason that doping might undermine the financial viability of sport due to the withdrawal of governmental and corporate support. Not only is doping cheating, it is also inimical to the security of the resource base of the activity. The Australian Senate Committee, like Dubin and the IOC, bases its condemnation of doping on the grounds that it is cheating, but also adds that the potential health risks provide a further justification for banning drugs. In summary, the rationale for the investment of extensive resources in developing an anti-doping strategy is, first, that it is potentially injurious to the athlete's health, second that doping is unfair and, third, that it might undermine the credibility of sport in the eyes of external bodies or interests including government, corporations and the general public. It is important to note not only the variety of possible justifications but the specific focus of each justification. The first, harm to the athlete, takes the individual as its focus, the second, unfairness, directs attention to the sports community or co-competitors of the drug-user, while the third is framed in terms of abstract notions of the ideals of sport.

Athlete's rights and responsibilities

It is worth emphasising at this stage in the discussion the importance of the tension between these three justifications and particularly the potential for conflict between a rationale built upon the rights (and occasionally the obligations) of the individual and the interests of the sporting community. For many, sport represents an embodiment of the virtues of individualism and a profound metaphor for the political value of liberal individualism where the rights of the individual are seen as prior to the interests of society or community. Sportspeople, through their hard work, risk-taking and dedication, seek

---

1. Government of Australia, 1989, op. cit., p. 60.

to achieve success in competition. Such a strong liberal tradition, especially in the United States, makes many wary of sanctioning any further intrusion upon the rights of individual athletes. The current growth in commercialism in sport provides further justification for those critical of current anti-doping policy who argue that athletes' rights to earn a living must be protected. However, the contrary view stresses the obligations of the sportsperson to other athletes arguing that sporting competition is not an isolated activity and is not possible without a community of athletes to compete against.

Many of the arguments about anti-doping policy share a common concern to see the athlete as part of a sports community, a view which recognises their rights but also accepts that they have responsibilities as well. The tension between the right of the individual to pursue his/her own interests as long as they do not interfere with the freedom of others taps deeply held values in many countries. Opponents of current anti-doping policy frequently justify, or at least strengthen, their opposition by emphasising the importance of limiting infringements of the rights of the individual athlete while the proponents of current policy emphasise that athletic activity, by its very nature, is a community enterprise. As will become clear, the contemporary debate on the justification for an anti-doping policy is sharply focused around questions of individual rights, community interests and ascribed ideals of sport, and is a key theme that will be returned to more explicitly in the concluding discussion.

When the issue of drug use by athletes is being considered, it is understandable that the focus tends to be on exemplar drugs, most commonly anabolic steroids which, using Lavin's terminology, may be described as additive in so far as they "let users reach performance levels exceeding what they might otherwise reach when healthy".[1] The central focus of this chapter is on the use of additive drugs but it is important to bear in mind that other categories of drug exist which cannot always be treated in the same way. Apart from additive drugs, there are those which are restorative in character and which are either designed or intended to restore an injured athlete to "normal" functioning. In addition, there are also drugs that have been taken by athletes but which have no proven ergogenic properties and which are primarily recreational.

Doping is unfair

Although there are other justifications for the current anti-doping policy, it is appropriate that the discussion should begin with an evaluation of the most commonly offered rationale, namely that doping is unfair. While unfairness is the most common justification, it is also one of the most problematic. Simply to assert that doping confers an advantage is an insufficient justification for

---

1. Lavin, M., "Sports and Drugs: Are the Current Bans Justified?", *Journal of the Philosophy of Sport*, Vol. XIV, 1987, pp. 34-43.

banning doping as it can be powerfully argued that sport is all about seeking an advantage over other competitors. Much of the strength of this argument hinges on the distinction between a fair and an unfair advantage. Sportspeople will spend much of their time seeking an advantage over others through the development of improved training techniques, diet and equipment. As Black and Pape argue: "athletes turn to every possible device to improve their performance, including coaching, high-altitude training, videos, amino acids, special diets, vitamins, and drugs".[1] In addition, athletes start with differing physiological and psychological attributes and profiles which will give some an advantage over others. As a result it is not a cause of adverse comment when we find that one boxer has more stamina or a longer reach than his opponent or when one footballer has a better sense of balance than another, or when one netball player is taller than her opponent. In general, advantages conferred by nature do not lead to accusations of unfairness. The only exception, and then only partial, is where the disparity in natural endowments is so marked that the quality of the contest is devalued or undermined.

In some sports, therefore, such as boxing, wrestling, judo and weightlifting, the international federations segregate competition by weight. There are also many sports that segregate by sex or age for similar reasons. However, the rationale for the creation of weight divisions, for example, is not based on a perception of a weight advantage as a form of cheating but due to a desire to preserve what they consider to be the essential nature of the contest; in the case of boxing, the balance of strength, stamina and skill that prevents a one-sided contest. Yet, even this response to unevenness in natural abilities and endowments between athletes is not consistently applied. In tennis, for example, there is no complaint when the number one seed is drawn against an opponent 100 or so places below him/her in the ranking table. Leaving aside the degree of inconsistency in the application of the practice of segregation in sporting contest, it does raise the intriguing prospect that one solution to the problem of drug use is to segregate according to drug use. Some weightlifting and body-building contests already offer drug-free competitions alongside "open" competitions. Natural advantage is not considered to be an unfair advantage although rules might be adjusted to take account of natural endowments. However, it is not sufficient to argue that the dividing line between what is ethical and what is not can be drawn between natural and unnatural advantages for, as will be shown, not all unnatural advantages are considered to be in the same category as doping. It is also the case that the current generation of new drugs contain a number which are natural (or naturally occurring if not naturally achieved) such as blood doping and enhanced levels of testosterone.

---

1. Black, T. & Pape, A., "The Ban on Drugs in Sport: The Solution or the Problem?", *Journal of Sport and Social Issues*, Vol. 21.1, pp. 83-92, 1997.

Seeking "the edge"

It has already been suggested that sport is predicated on the search for an advantage or an "edge" over one's rivals and that exploiting one's natural advantages, for example, through more effective or rigorous training is applauded rather than frowned upon. As Fost observes, "The mere seeking of an advantage is not implicitly unfair, nor is the gaining of an advantage implicitly unfair".[1] The question of the boundary between what is fair and what is unfair is blurred, albeit slightly, when account is taken of advantages whose source is external to the athlete. For example, while most people would consider the pursuit of an intensive and rigorous training schedule as reflecting many of the virtues of sport such as dedication and application, would the same response be generated if the improvement in performance had been due to the outcome of an elaborate and expensive computer analysis of the athlete's technique? In this situation, one might argue that the advantage accruing to the athlete is still the product of his/her effort and dedication. But supposing the advantage was the result of a swimmer wearing swimwear with ultra-low water resistance, a cyclist riding a cycle that incorporated state of the art design and materials, a pole-vaulter using a pole with additional spring and strength, or a Formula One racing driver whose car has the best engine and best engineers. In all these cases, the source of the advantage is, like anabolic steroids for example, external to the athlete, but, unlike anabolic steroids, the response of sports authorities is less clear cut. Perry in his discussion of the ethics of blood doping suggests a test for the permissibility of an external, or in his words supplementary, advantage.[2] He suggests that if an enhanced performance due to supplementation is to be accepted it must fulfil at least one of two key functions: to eliminate a deleterious effect (for example, a new shoe design may reduce the risk of ankle injury), or to remove a barrier to improved performance (allowing the use of synthetic running surfaces or the use of running spikes). In addition, one might add a third criterion namely that advantages gained through supplementation must also be generally available. Applying Perry's criteria it would not be possible to argue that drugs such as steroids or hGH "eliminate a deleterious effect" as most agree that they may cause deleterious side-effects (to the user if not to the quality of the sporting spectacle). It is doubtful whether it is possible to sustain the argument that any drugs eliminate a deleterious effect although there may be a case to be made with regard to restorative as opposed to additive drugs. Perry's second criterion, along with the third, would both provide a justification for drug use if it is accepted that some drugs do indeed provide an ergogenic advantage and that drugs are generally available.

---

1. Fost, N.C., "Ethical and Social Issues in Anti-Doping Strategies in Sport", in Landry et al., 1991, op. cit.
2. Perry, C., "Blood Doping and Athletic Competition", *The International Journal of Applied Philosophy*, Vol. 1.3, 1983, pp. 39-45.

Differential access

When the American pole-vaulter Bob Seagren sought to use a fibreglass pole at the 1972 Olympic Games, its use was prohibited until the new pole became more widely available. However, the rationale for the prohibition was that differential access to the new pole was unfair not that the pole itself was illegitimate. Similarly, when the Németh javelin with its improved aerodynamics was introduced it provided a distinct advantage over the more conventional Sandvik javelin until the former was banned in late 1991.[1] Yet there are many examples of advances in equipment that have not led to bans, either temporary or permanent. The use by American swimmers of low-friction swimsuits, the Lotus-designed cycle and the use of aerodynamically designed helmets, skis and ski-sticks have all, at various times, conferred a generally acknowledged advantage upon those able to gain initial access. The response by sports authorities to unnatural advantages which are clearly similar in their effect in competition is far too inconsistent for a case against the use of drugs to be sustained simply on the basis of differential access. Moreover, there is a plausible case to be made that access to drugs is far from differential and that, at the élite level at least, access to drugs is reasonably uniform. Indeed one could go much further and suggest that if the concern with the use of anabolic steroids and other ergogenic drugs is differential access then the balance of the argument favours removing the prohibition rather than attempting to enforce it. Black and Pape argue that the most appropriate response to the problem of differential access to the regularly produced advances in training, diet etc., that give an athlete an edge over his or her competitors is to seek ways of speeding the process of diffusion. Policy therefore needs to be designed to ensure that the competitive edge conferred by a particular advance is reduced as rapidly as possible by making the advance available as widely as possible and as quickly as possible. As Black and Pape argue "After the advantages gained by artificial devices are competed away, the most naturally gifted sportsperson will win".[2] The logic of this argument is that far from maintaining fair competition the (flawed) attempted imposition of a ban on drugs creates and magnifies unfairness in sport as only some athletes abide by the rules.

Black and Pape's argument has close parallels to the prohibition against "insider trading" on the stock market where traders seek an advantage over competitors through accessing information likely to affect share values before others and keeping such inside information secret until they secure their advantage. The response of regulators and legislators has not been to attempt to prohibit access to certain types of advantageous information (the equivalent of banned drugs in sport), but rather to ensure that information is

---

1. The main motive for banning the Németh javelin was the risk that the distances being achieved were outgrowing many arenas and becoming a danger to other athletes and also to the public.
2. Black & Pape, 1997, op. cit., p. 85.

made available as quickly as possible to all "players" in the market so as to "compete away" the advantage of selective access.[1]

One problem with the logic employed by Black and Pape is the assumption that the effect of free access to drugs would be to equalise advantage. As Gardner suggests if unrestricted access to drugs were to be permitted "inequalities would exist not just between users and non-users but among users".[2] Because athletes are unlikely to respond to drug use in the same way and to the same degree, inequalities would still remain. However, the inequalities arising from differential reactions to drugs would not necessarily give cause for complaint because it may be argued that the degree of benefit achieved is the result of natural differences in athletes' physiology and biochemistry. But a further problem would also remain, namely the fact that no matter how swiftly new drugs were made available someone would gain access first (possibly due to the possession of sufficient wealth to purchase increasingly costly drugs such as hGH) and be able to benefit first. If access by the first user coincided with a major tournament, this might be sufficient to secure a very significant sporting and financial advantage. It would appear that each avenue that is taken in the pursuit of a secure basis for banning drugs on the grounds of fairness turns into a cul-de-sac of ambiguity or inconsistency, or worse still rebounds against the proponents of anti-doping policy and is used to challenge current policy.

One response to the ambivalence arising out of the discussion of differential access is to argue that rather than basing one's objection to an advantage which is external to the athlete on the extent of differential access, one should rather ask whether the intention of the athlete was to keep the advantage secret. However, this is no more viable as a rationale for the banning of drugs than differential access as it is not possible to avoid the charge of inconsistency. Not only do many athletes closely guard the secrets of their training or dietary regimes but there are also examples of athletes who do not need to maintain the secrecy of their advantage because there are sufficient alternative and equally effective barriers to access such as cost and expertise. Hence, there are important advantages, such as training and dietary regimes, that are acknowledged to confer significant advantages but which do not prompt significant ethical challenge although they do raise ethical concerns.

All a matter of perception?

It is possible that the acceptability of an advantage depends not on whether it is natural or unnatural, or whether it is differentially available but rather on a perception of how the advantage is acquired. Advantages that accrue from

---

1. For a fuller examination of the ethics of "insider trading" see Barry, N., *The Morality of Business Enterprise*, Aberdeen: Aberdeen University Press, 1991.
2. Gardner, R., "On Performance-Enhancing Substances and the Unfair Advantage Argument", *Journal of the Philosophy of Sport*, Vol. XVI, 1989, pp. 59-73.

location (it is an advantage to be a competitive skier living in Austria rather than in Holland), natural endowment (in soccer, Luis Figo's balance and determination or in boxing, Lennox Lewis' reach), technical innovation (Dick Fosbury's high-jump techniques) or practice (in cricket, Shane Warne's bowling action) are all significant but considered fair and indeed encouraged. A useful illustration of the importance of considering the process by which an advantage is gained is provided by attempts by bowlers in cricket to increase the variability of the flight of the ball. It is common, permissible and acceptable for bowlers to polish one half of the ball so as to create conditions where the ball is more likely to spin due to the differential movement of air over the polished as opposed to the unpolished side. The existence of a polished and unpolished side also makes the bounce of the ball slightly more difficult to predict. An alternative way of creating the same effect is to score the unpolished side with the fingernail or even to attempt to lift the leather from the seam. While the former method is acceptable, the latter is not and is considered to be ball tampering and treated as a serious breach of the rules of cricket by the governing body.

A second illustration of the importance of process is the methods used to improve the capacity of the blood to transport greater quantities of oxygen to the muscles. There are two common ways of making this improvement, the first is through blood doping and the second is through a prolonged period of high-altitude training. While the former is condemned, the latter technique is acceptable. Interestingly it does not seem to matter to the general public or those involved in sport if an advantage such as prolonged high-altitude training is the result of greater wealth. It would appear that even if an advantage can be described as unfair, such as an unequal distribution of wealth, it does not mean that it will be perceived as being unacceptable. To take an exaggerated, but not implausible example, we might have a competition between two runners one of whom is born with an optimal physique, has wealthy supportive parents, benefits from the best coaches, trains in the relaxed atmosphere of a well-equipped university athletics club, the other is born with a physique that has potential to develop the necessary attributes, has an unsupportive family, works full time and trains part time at the local YMCA. If the two were to meet in competition and the former won it is unlikely that there would be any accusations of unfairness, although if the latter were victorious there might be some expressions of delight that the underdog had won through.

It is possible that acceptability depends on whether the advantage is either a natural endowment or has been earned through hard work and training. But the weaknesses of this suggestion are easily made apparent. How much effort is required to justify an advantage? Some athletes have to work much harder to secure their advantage than others: do the former have a stronger moral entitlement to the advantage than those who acquire the same advantage through a less onerous training regime? The inconsistencies in this argument do little to help in the search for a watertight basis for anti-doping policy.

Is the use of restorative drugs also unfair?

The preceding discussion has focused on the use of drugs with an additive function, designed to give an athlete an advantage, rather than on those with a restorative function. It is possible to argue that where an athlete is below his/her normal level of fitness, whether through illness or recovery from injury, the use of drugs simply to restore normal performance should not be subject to the same prohibition as the use of additive drugs. The argument is, at first sight, a powerful one. Athletes who have trained for a particular competition and then receive an injury whose effects can be nullified by the use of a drug can argue that they are not increasing their chances of success but simply maintaining their normal level of competitiveness. Leaving aside the complex problem of determining the athlete's "normal level of fitness", it is possible to treat restorative and additive drugs in the same way. At the heart of the issue is the way in which the concept of normality is being used. One way of defining an athlete's normal level of fitness is simply to say that it is that level of fitness possessed by the athlete at any particular time and if they are ill the level of fitness they possess during their illness is their "normal" level. In other words, it cannot be accepted that an athlete is able to select their level of fitness at a particular time and claim that as their normal level of fitness. If this view is rejected then it would be possible, for example, for athletes who had sustained an injury which permanently reduced their capabilities to justify the use of drugs for the rest of their career as a way of restoring their pre-injury level of fitness.

If it is not possible to justify drug use where the objective is to restore an injured athlete to his/her normal level of fitness then it should be even less acceptable to allow drug use where the athlete's "ill health" is due to decisions about training or diet. Hyland provides a good illustration of the dilemma by recounting the example of the American middle-distance runner Mary Decker Slaney. Due to her intensive training regime, Slaney's leg muscles had outgrown the sheath which contained them causing considerable pain. The problem was resolved by an operation that cut the muscle sheaths thereby relieving the pressure in her legs. At first glance the operation appears restorative in that it relieved the pain. On reflection one could argue that the pain she had been experiencing was a signal from her body that she had reached her limit of normal muscle growth and that the operation allowed abnormal growth and was therefore additive in character. As Hyland observes, Slaney could have "dealt with the problem just as well by slackening off on her training".[1]

---

1. Hyland, D.A., *Philosophy of Sport*, 1990. New York: Paragon House, p. 52.

Doping is a danger to the athlete's health

If a rationale for banning drugs constructed around fairness fails to provide the desired watertight basis for policy, an alternative is frequently sought in arguments framed in terms of the health of the athlete. As was made clear in the discussion of the effects and particularly the side-effects of the variety of drugs banned by the IOC, there are some drugs where the weight of scientific opinion confirms that there are indeed clear deleterious effects arising from drug use but that there are also many banned substances where few if any significant side-effects have (as yet) been identified. As a result, relying upon health-related arguments to provide a basis for anti-doping policy which is capable of covering all the drugs included on the IOC list is not possible. Nevertheless, it is worth exploring the health arguments in relation to those drugs, including steroids, amphetamines and hGH, where scientific opinion warns of significant negative side-effects. If it is assumed that the taking of some drugs poses substantial health risks to the athlete the question remains as to whether this would provide a sufficient basis for prohibition.

For the purposes of the present discussion, we will assume that we are considering drug use by adult athletes who are capable of making rational decisions. In relation to competent adults, there is a general reluctance, especially in liberal democracies, to interfere with the individual's right to make choices about lifestyle even when those choices might contain a significant element of risk. This is especially evident in relation to current debates within the field of medical ethics where there has been a determination in many European and North American countries to alter what has been characterised as an imbalance in the relationship between the doctor (professional) and the patient (client). Empowerment of the client/patient enhances the responsibility of the client for making decisions about his/her health. To impose a ban on the use of drugs in sport by competent adults would be considered an unwarranted intrusion into their lives and unjustified paternalism.

"Soft" and "hard" paternalism

Unfortunately, distinguishing between justified and unjustified paternalism is not always easy. Paternalism is not in itself an invalid basis for establishing an anti-doping policy. In some circumstances, such as where children are concerned, paternalism has a strong justification. Dworkin distinguishes between "soft" and "hard" paternalism. Soft paternalism is defined as "the view that 1. paternalism is sometimes justified, and 2. it is a necessary condition for such justification that the person for whom we are acting paternalistically is in some way not competent".[1] The crucial basis for soft paternalism is the lack of competence of the other person due, for example, to coercion, ignorance or

---

1. Dworkin, R., "Paternalism: Some Second Thoughts" in Sartorius, R. (ed.), *Paternalism*, Minneapolis: University of Minnesota Press, p. 107.

incapacity. By contrast, hard paternalism refers to situations where the person is competent and yet a basis for paternalistic intervention is claimed. The requirement in many countries that drivers and often passengers should wear seat belts in cars is an example of hard paternalism: so too is the requirement that motor cyclists wear crash helmets and that bicycles have lights if ridden at night. Hard paternalism is often strongly resisted on the grounds that it conflicts with the principles associated with individual freedom dominant in western democracies. However, the fact that hard paternalism is employed as a basis for policy in some areas indicates that although it is a source of tension in policy debates it is not deemed an inadmissible basis for government action. As will be demonstrated in the conclusion to this chapter, the balance between individualist liberalism and communitarianism is not fixed.

Protecting athletes from themselves?

With regard to sport, there are many individual sports which involve a substantial risk to the athlete's health and where, at first glance, "hard" paternalism might be supported. Even if one is reluctant to go as far as Fost does when he claims that "sport itself carries per se a substantial risk of death and permanent disability",[1] many would share the view of Lavin when he suggests that "Modern training regimens often keep players on the edge of injury".[2] Boxing is probably the clearest example of sport where the risk to health is integral to the sport, but it can also be argued that there are many other sports where the probability of injury is great. Full-contact sports such as American football, rugby union and rugby league can all provide examples of serious, and very occasionally, fatal injuries to participants. Mountaineering, and especially the current fashion for alpine-style climbing, has a long list of fatalities: for example, in May 1996 eleven climbers, using conventional mountaineering methods, lost their lives attempting to climb Everest. Even sports where the risk of fatal or serious injury is low, such as soccer and field hockey, pose a health risk to participants through repeated minor injury often resulting in chronic conditions such as arthritis. With the exception of the ban on boxing in a small number of countries and the recurring debate about its appropriateness in Olympic competition, there is little serious debate about banning high-risk sports.

A further weakness in relying on the desire to protect the health of the athlete as a justification for anti-doping policy is that there are many examples where athletes have competed with injuries without hindrance even when the risk of compounding the injury is substantial. The British runner Peter Elliot won a silver medal at the 1988 Olympics but was in such pain that he had to have five pain-killing injections to enable him to run seven races in nine days. After the Games, Elliot returned to Britain on crutches and needed

---

1. Fost, 1991, op. cit., p. 481.
2. Lavin, 1987, op. cit., p. 37.

a considerable period of physiotherapy before he was able to walk and run with ease. The use by athletes of analgesics and anti-inflammatory preparations is routine in almost all sports and, more importantly, the health of the athlete routinely comes second to the requirements of the team or squad for them to compete. There seems little difference between the athletes who risk their health by competing when injured and the athletes who risk their health through the use of additive drugs.

If intervention to ban participation on health grounds fails with regard to sports where there is clear quantitative data on injury and fatalities, a similarly paternalistic rationale will not persuade with regard to drug use. As Fost notes: "Even proving that an activity is harmful is therefore not a sufficient reason for preventing a competent person from pursuing that activity".[1] Consequently, even if the taking of anabolic steroids could be proved to be more dangerous than rugby, American football or mountaineering, the concern for the athlete's health would not provide a secure and plausible basis for supporting a ban on their use. Or put another way, if one is prepared to accept that concern for the athlete's health provides a sound basis for intervention, then one would be obliged to pursue this logic and examine the many additional aspects of sports involvement which expose participants to health risks.

Approaching the issue from a different angle, Black and Pape provide a further challenge to anti-doping policy by arguing that the current attempts to impose a ban on drug use puts athletes' health at a greater risk than if the ban were lifted. They argue that reliance on the black market for drugs heightens the risk to the athlete because, among other things, the purity of drugs cannot be guaranteed, advice about correct dosage is not available, and hygienic administration, especially of drugs taken intravenously, cannot be assured.[2] The conclusion drawn is that the ban on drug use is a greater threat to health than drug use itself. This argument has much in common with the case made against the policy of prohibition of alcohol in the United States. In other words, the policy was more damaging than the problem it was seeking to solve.

A bad example to the young

A variation on this argument is that drug use, especially by élite athletes constantly in the public gaze, establishes harmful role models for children who may aspire to emulate not only the achievements of their heroes but also their methods. While there is little reliable evidence to support this argument, there is some anecdotal evidence that use of androstenedione increased following the acknowledgement by US baseball star Mark McGwire that he used the drug during his record-breaking season. Unfortunately, this hard

---

1. Fost, 1991, op. cit., p. 482.
2. Black & Pape 1997, op. cit.

paternalistic rationale for banning doping is weakened by a number of inconsistencies. It is inconsistent because it is only considering one among many aspects of sport that might be considered dangerous. In order to be consistent it would be necessary to apply the same argument to the dangers arising from intensive training, training while injured and potentially dangerous diets. The second source of inconsistency arises from the failure to apply the same argument, or at least to apply it so rigorously, to other potential role models for the young especially from the world of music, television and cinema. The fact that many musicians, dancers and television and film stars have admitted using drugs does not lead to a condemnation of their performance in the way that Ben Johnson's Olympic run was condemned. Third, the focus on the responsibility of élite athletes to set a good example to the young neglects the greater, or at least equal, burden of responsibility on the parents, coaches and teachers of the young. Unfortunately, comparing sportspeople with these other groups is of only limited value. Within music and the arts generally there is no strong view from either performers or audiences that these forms of entertainment should be drug free, nor is there a situation where artists and performers publicly decry drug use while at the same time taking drugs in secret. There is clearly not the same sort of feeling among drug-free artists and the audience for the arts that drug abuse debases or devalues the spectacle or entertainment.

Although "hard" paternalism provides a weak basis for an anti-doping policy "soft" paternalism, particularly when applied to children, might be a more secure basis for policy intervention. As Brown notes, the soft paternalist justifies a limitation on the freedom of the individual when his/her actions "are not fully voluntary because they are not fully informed, or because one is not fully competent or is in some relevant way coerced. All these factors may plausibly be seen as present in the case of children's sport".[1] The lack of experience of young people makes them especially vulnerable to misjudgments that might have long-term consequences for their health and well-being. Drug use would clearly come into this category where a decision based on information and experience cannot be expected from the young. The same argument can also be mounted when considering the capacity of young athletes to appreciate the risks in some training regimes.

Young people are routinely subject to controls over their participation in sport that would not be applied to (or respected by) adults, such as non-swimmers wearing life preservers or identification wrist bands, or having to abide by different rules in "mini" versions of adult contact sports such as rugby. The agility and enthusiasm of young people in sport is counterbalanced by their lack of awareness "of their own limitations, their susceptibility to injury, and the long-term consequences of injuries to their development or effective

---

1. Brown, W.M., "Paternalism, Drugs, and the Nature of Sports", *Journal of the Philosophy of Sport*, Vol. XI, 1984, pp. 14-22.

participation".[1] The basis for intervention is the assumption that the paternalistic adult is making decisions that the young person would make had they been an adult. The soft paternalist position also recognises that at some arbitrary age the responsibility for decision-making transfers from the adult to the young person.

An interesting and important extension of this argument is where paternalistic intervention is justified on the basis of protecting the young person from exploitation by others. One would expect that trained youth coaches would counterbalance and restrain the overenthusiastic parent for example, who might push their child too hard in training and competition thus risking physical and psychological damage. Intervention to protect the young person from him or herself, or to protect them from the ambitions and misjudgments of others is founded on a set of values and understandings concerning the nature of youth and sport. By extension this same value base may also lead the paternalist to seek opportunities to instil positive sports values in the young person regarding, for example, fair play and respect for the decisions of officials and thus complement the paternalist's concern with the development of physical skills. Part of this value set will be attitudes towards drug use. The value set that underpins the paternalist's concern to instil supportive attitudes towards the current anti-doping policy in the young is, in most respects, no different from that which underpins the value set in relation to adults except that there is sufficient evidence to support the view that drug use by young people has potentially more serious side-effects than for adults. For example, as made clear in Chapter 3, the use of hGH by young people can lead to severely distorted growth patterns.

Arguments in support of soft paternalism in connection with children can be extended to some adult groups whose competence is clearly limited, such as those athletes with learning difficulties. The threshold between soft and hard paternalism is where one wishes to interfere with the decisions made by competent adults: one suggested basis for the justification of hard paternalism is where the adult is subject to coercion.

Doping is the result of coercion

A further basis on which doping might be opposed is the claim that athletes do not take drugs freely but are coerced into drug use. At the heart of this argument is not the assumption that athletes are physically coerced to take drugs, but rather that athletes competing at the élite level are placed under severe peer or wider social pressure to take drugs. One version of this argument emphasises the narrowness of the gap between success and failure in many sports where the difference of less than one per cent separates the winner from the athlete who comes in fourth or fifth. Athletes are consequently under intense pressure to take ever-greater risks to find that extra

---

1. Ibid., p. 16.

centimetre or tenth (or hundredth) of a second: drug taking is simply one additional risk that they are compelled to take. As the sprinter, or more especially the high diver or gymnast, is being continually required to undertake increasingly intense training regimes or ever more complex and risky dives and routines so the pressure mounts on them to take that extra step and use drugs. Central to this argument is the assumption that drug use is rife at the élite level and that it is not possible to compete effectively at the top level unless one also takes drugs. In some ways this argument is also paternalistic but intervention is justified on the basis of preventing the actions of one person (the drug user) causing harm to another (the non-drug user) rather than simply being justified on the basis of preventing injury or harm to oneself.

Two questions arise from this discussion, the first of which is whether drug use is qualitatively different from the other forms of advantage mentioned above. In other words, if a number of forms of risk-taking in sport are increasing (more intense training, drug taking, and higher risk manoeuvres, in gymnastics, Formula 1 and diving for example) why single out doping and how might the obvious inconsistency be justified?[1] One possible answer is that, unlike the other examples, doping undermines the integrity or values of sport – a response that is considered in more detail below. The second question that needs to be addressed is whether the harm to other, clean athletes justifies the restrictions on the rights of the drug user. Although it must be acknowledged that complete freedom of choice is an illusion, the weaknesses of the argument based on coercion are clear. Unless one is referring to sport within repressive political regimes athletes are always able to refuse drugs and simply to settle for fourth place or worse. Moreover, the reliance on an argument which justifies drug use on the grounds that "everyone at the top takes them" is untenable because of the lack of empirical evidence to sustain it and also because the low ethical standards of others provides no justification for lowering one's own. In addition, the same argument is not heard in relation to other similar pressures. For example, if some athletes adopt a more intensive training regime which is perceived as successful would a claim of coercion be made, let alone sustained, by the other athletes who emulated it?[2] Drug use provides no greater basis for the claim of coercion than does particular dietary regimes, warm weather training, hypnosis or any other aspect of athletic preparation. If coercion is accepted as a possible basis for intervention, a further problem arises with regard to the difficulty of defining the point at which peer or social pressure becomes coercion.

---

1. See Schneider, A.J. & Butcher, R.B., "An Ethical Analysis of Drug Testing" in Wilson, W. & Derse, E. (eds.), *Doping in Elite Sport: The Politics of Drugs in the Olympic Movement,* Champaign, Ill: Human Kinetics.
2. Tamburrini provides a useful analogy to the competition between war correspondents, arguing that if one correspondent takes risks to get news from the "front line" should she be prevented from doing so because it is coercing her colleagues to take similar risks? Tamburrini's answer is that such a suggestion would be "preposterous". Tamburrini, C.M., "What's Wrong with Doping?" in Tännsjö & Tamburrini, 2000, op. cit.

A variation on this argument suggests that coercion arises from the inability of the athlete to provide informed consent to the use of drugs. It can be argued that modern élite athletes are surrounded by an array of experienced professional advisers, coaches, physiotherapists, doctors, dieticians, psychologists, etc., and are locked into an unequal relationship of professional and client. The disempowerment of athletes is best reflected by the way they are treated in many team sports as mere commodities to be traded between team owners with only minimal consultation and little regard for their interests. Athletes are therefore expected to fulfil a passive role within sport and the development of dependent relationships with professional staff is often encouraged. The weakness of this view is the profound difficulty in identifying the point at which the individual athlete cannot be held responsible for his or her actions. Even if athletes are locked into heavily dependent relationships, there has been so much publicity surrounding the anti-doping policy that it is hardly plausible for an athlete to deny knowledge of the policy and claim that they were unable to exercise their right to walk away from drug-based sport.

Even if one is prepared to entertain the argument that the source of coercion is not external to the athlete but an inner compulsion, the argument is still weak. To suggest that those who compete successfully at the highest levels display signs of psychological disturbance is not new. It is frequently suggested that élite athletes are obsessional and are simply not capable of making rational judgments about what is in their own best interests and will consequently take risks with their health that "normal" people would not. However, even if this hypothesis were to be accepted psychological imbalance might constitute a mitigating factor in defence of drug taking but it does not provide a justification for abuse.

A variation on this argument is that athletes in many sports are from poorer sections of society and from poorer countries and that they are under significant pressure because of the importance of sport as an escape route from poverty. Their social situation of vulnerability and marginalisation, so the argument runs, coerces them into making choices and taking risks that someone from a wealthier background is able to avoid. Poverty, as is the case with psychological disorder, might (and only might) provide a basis for mitigation but it does not provide a justification for doping. This is not simply because in some sports, boxing for example, the majority of competitors are from similarly poor backgrounds, but because the individual cannot be so easily freed from taking responsibility for their own actions and the desire to "get rich quick" is one of the least plausible.

Doping undermines the integrity of sport

The argument that doping conflicts with the core values of sport is strongly expressed by Schneider and Butcher who argue that "What is required is ... a reaffirmation of the fundamental values of sport and the clarification of the mixed messages that the Olympic sports hierarchy currently sends out".[1] One presentation of this argument emphasises the extent to which sports "are held as essentially related to games in that both are rule-governed activities" and that games are defined in terms of their specific rules. If the rules of a particular game are broken then one cannot continue to claim that one is still playing that game. For example, if a soccer player picks up the ball and runs with it he/she is no longer playing soccer. In the same way, if the rules prohibit drug use and a participant takes drugs then he or she has ceased to play that game and is playing a new game. This argument is attractive as it is more convincing to see anti-doping rules as being of a similar character to the rules that define the mode and form of play.

While each sport may claim, and may well have, an identifiable essence all sports attempt to provide a mix of skills and challenges that make for a "good contest". Thus, one might argue that for each sport it is possible to describe the particular mix of characteristics that the sport is designed to test. It might therefore be argued that one criterion for deciding whether doping should be banned is whether it undermines or invalidates the essential test or challenge of the sport. Gardner illustrates this argument by referring to the development and subsequent banning of U-grooved clubs in golf. It was claimed that U-groove clubs gave players better control over the flight of the ball especially out of the rough with the poorer quality players gaining the greater advantage. The decision to outlaw the U-groove club was not because its use gave less talented golfers an advantage over the more talented but rather that it gave golfers in general an "advantage" over the sport itself, or at least an important element of it, namely the test of playing out of the rough: "what is being objected to here is not that performance enhancement will create inequality among athletes, but that it will lead to parity. In the end, U-grooves are more responsible for the performance than the golfer".[2] Extending this discussion it has been suggested strongly in Formula One motor racing that the driver's contribution to success is increasingly marginal. When the Williams team decided not to renew Damon Hill's contract, despite the fact that he had just won the world championship, it was partly explained by the alleged view within the Williams' team camp that any top class driver could win in a Williams car and that having the best driver was not a necessary condition. Side-stepping the question of whether Damon Hill was, at the time, the best Formula One driver in the world it can be argued that, in general, the preferred relationship between the athlete and any equipment that he or she might use is one where a greater contribution to success is made by the former rather than the latter.

An extension of this argument is that sport encapsulates some deeper, more profound sense of humanity to which the rules of particular sports merely

---

1. Schneider, A.J. & Butcher, R.B., "The Mesalliance of the Olympic Ideal and Doping: Why They Married and Why They Should Divorce" in Landry et al., 1991, op. cit., p. 495.
2. Gardner, 1989, op. cit., p. 69.

approximate and which drug use challenges and corrupts. Notwithstanding the difficulty of empirically verifying such an assertion, there is also the problem of responding to the equally attractive counter-claim that sport, just like religion, is a social construction and imposes no prior obligation on the individual. A similar argument, voiced by Schneider and Butcher, is that drug use undermines the essential humanity of the athlete. According to this view, "One could describe the essence of sporting competition and excellence as the drive to perfect one aspect, the physical, of what it is to be human".[1] However, this attempt to identify the essence of humanity is as weak as the previous attempt to identify the essence of sport. As discussed above, the distinction between what is essential and what is not in sport is far from easy to draw.

Simon adopts a slightly different approach suggesting that "competition in athletics is best thought of as a mutual quest for excellence ... Competitors are obliged to do their best so as to bring out the best in their opponents".[2] For Simon, the stress is on the mutual obligation of the athlete to maintain the essential aspect of sport as a competition between persons. The opponent is therefore not an obstacle to success to be overcome by whatever means but a co-worker in a joint undertaking. Simon's view is clearly at odds with the populist wisdom that winning is everything and that the cliché, that "taking part is more important than winning", is at best wistful nostalgia. Yet among sports enthusiasts there is likely to be a high level of agreement that, in track events for example, increasingly fast times are not the only criterion by which a good or enjoyable event is determined. The process by which the outcome is reached is also important: strategy, skill and stamina for example are some of the many ingredients of successful sport. "On this view, athletic competition, rather than being incompatible with respect for our opponents as persons, actually presupposes it."[3] Drug use tests merely how one body reacts to drugs in comparison to another. Any improvements in performance are due to how a person's body responds to the drug and does not reflect the person's hard work, dedication and skills and is not founded on respect for one's co-competitors. Simon acknowledges that his position rests on an ability to sustain the view that his conceptualisation of sport has a privileged moral standing. Indeed, Brown criticises Simon for basing his argument on a foundation that is "too vague to be persuasive".[4] Simon's position is further weakened by many of the criticisms of the attempts to distinguish between internal and external, and natural and unnatural advantages discussed in the earlier sections of this chapter. However, Simon's view is important in attempting to develop a plausible normative rationale for an anti-doping

---

1. See footnote 7, p. 139 *ante*. Ibid., p. 499.
2. Simon, R.L., "Good Competition and Drug-Enhanced Performance", *Journal of the Philosophy of Sport*, Vol. XI, 1984, pp. 6-13.
3. Ibid., p. 10.
4. Brown, W.M., "Comments on Simon and Fraleigh", *Journal of the Philosophy of Sport*, Vol. XI, 1985, pp. 33-5.

policy and thus moving beyond the impasse arising from current attempts to secure a logically watertight foundation for policy.

Discussion

The preceding discussion has focused on a series of overlapping justifications for the current anti-doping policy. Justification has been sought in terms of the particular properties of drugs, a set of attributes associated with the athlete and a set of attributes associated with sport. Attempts to identify a set of morally objectionable qualities inherent in the current range of banned substances and practices is probably the weakest source of a viable policy rationale. There is no secure basis for objecting to advantages gained through using substances as it is only particular substances that are objected to and there are no definitive criteria that distinguish between the acceptable and the unacceptable. As Gardner notes there have been a number of attempts to distinguish "good" from "bad" substances such as distinguishing "food from non-food, restoratives from additives, [and] drugs from non-drugs" all with little success.[1]

Discussions that focus on the athlete and the effect of drugs on his/her natural state provide a stronger basis for the anti-doping policy but one which still has too many inconsistencies to provide a secure basis for policy. Much the same may be said of justifications based on claims regarding the particular properties of sport. However, it is this area, the nature of sport and the process by which it is socially constructed, that offers the most secure basis from which to defend current policy and to support its further refinement.

At first glance, the least satisfactory basis on which to justify banning drug use is that it is simply against the rules of particular sports. Rules are obviously imposed (and modified) for a purpose. That purpose might be to make a sport more exciting and attractive to spectators, television companies and viewers: rules might also be changed to make it more attractive to participants. Whatever the purpose might be, it undoubtedly has to be one that is understood by, and is persuasive to, participants, spectators and other interested parties. Consequently, if drug use is to be banned one must be able to answer the question "Why ban drug use?" in a convincing manner. For many supporters of the anti-doping policy there appears to be a worryingly high number of opponents of the policy who argue cogently for its abandonment. The opponents of the anti-doping policy base their opposition on a mix of pragmatism and principle. The most commonly expressed pragmatic argument against current policy is to highlight the large number of inconsistencies and ambiguities in current policy. In addition, the opponents of the anti-doping policy argue that current policy implementation is inadequate and counter-productive as it creates greater inequality between the (covert)

---

1. Gardner, 1989, op. cit., p. 66.

drug user and the non-user and that a more effective way of ensuring maximum fairness would be allow free use of drugs, on the assumption that any advantage would rapidly be competed away. Finally, there are those who oppose anti-doping efforts on the principled ground that it is an unwarranted interference with individual autonomy. In other words, not only is the current attempt to implement an anti-doping policy so flawed as to be doing more harm than good but also the extensive investment in the policy is based on a disregard for the fundamental rights of the individual.

Individual athletes' rights versus community interests

The defence of individual autonomy is powerfully expressed in Mill's classic statement of the liberal position: "... the only purpose for which power can be rightfully exercised over any member of a civilised community, against his will, is to prevent harm to others. His own good, either physical or moral, is not a sufficient warrant. He cannot rightfully be compelled to do or forbear because it will be better for him to do so, because it will make him happier, because, in the opinions of others, to do so would be wise, or even right. ... Over himself, over his own body and mind, the individual is sovereign".[1] Not only does Mill provide a compelling argument for the sovereignty of the individual but it is a view that has been strongly in the ascendant over the last twenty years or so in much of the industrialised west and in Britain and the United States in particular. Burke for example argues that the "drug ban ... may be seen as an unwarranted intervention in the private practice by some athletes" and also suggests that drug use is compatible with some sporting ideals such as the pursuit of excellence and with extending the careers of top athletes.[2] Despite the arguments of philosophers such as Burke, there is considerable unease with the individualist position. Counterbalancing the respect for individual autonomy is a concern that this can easily be overemphasised to the detriment of the interests of the community and to the neglect of the individual's responsibilities towards others.

The foregoing discussion would appear to leave the supporter of anti-doping with little to cling to by way of a rationale with the possible exception of the paternalistic argument with regard to children. Schneider and Butcher, referring to the research by Voulle and Heinila, show that "whereas there was almost unanimity against doping in sport when 'youth was concerned', there was far greater laxity in the case of top level sport and competitive sport in general".[3] Only 60% of athletes and 53% of coaches agreed that doping

---

1. Mill, J.S., "On Liberty" in Warnock, M., *Utilitarianism: Essays of John Stuart Mill*, London: Fontana, 1962, p. 135.
2. Burke, M.D., "Drugs in Sport: Have They Practiced Too Hard? A Response to Schneider and Butcher", *Journal of the Philosophy of Sport*, Vol. XXIV, 1997, pp. 47-66.
3. Schneider & Butcher, 1991, op. cit., p. 495; Voulle, P., "Doping-tutkimus" in Siukonen, M. (ed.), *Doping*, Jyväskylä, 1982, pp. 69-100; Heinila, K., "Social Research on Sport in Finland", *Sportwissenschaft*, Vol. 1, 1988, pp. 9-28.

was not permissible under any circumstances compared to 82% of the general public. The concern that these figures indicate the vulnerability of the anti-doping campaign to erosion among key interest groups leads Schneider and Butcher to conclude with obvious frustration that "We nonetheless share the general conviction that steroids have no place in sport; yet, we still are actively seeking a solid justification for that conviction".[1]

Balancing individual rights and community interests: a way ahead

There are two possible arguments that the supporter of an anti-doping policy might deploy to justify current policy, one taken from the individualist standpoint and the other from the communitarian critique of individualism. Although the liberal tradition in philosophy is varied, it emphasises the rights of the individual over the interests of society and argues that it is not possible to start with a conception of the interests of society (or the interests of the sporting community) and derive individual rights and responsibilities from that conception. Primacy in any discussion of the relationship between the individual and society must be given to the individual. Banning drugs because the users might harm themselves is not sustainable as the liberal individualist position reserves the right of a person to do what they wish with their own bodies and would only consider intervention, in the form of laws for example, if the actions of the drug user caused harm to others. Thus, drinking heavily alone is not a basis for intervention but drinking heavily and driving a car would justify intervention due to the danger to others. The argument that drug users coerce others also fails because to intervene on the basis that another might be pressurised into imitation of the drug users is pre-empting the exercise of individual choice by the non-drug user. Banning drugs because it is inconsistent with the ideals or integrity of sport offers some possibility of obtaining support from the liberal individualist but only if the values of sport in general or of separate sports are a reflection or embodiment of individualist values. But to argue that sport or sports have an essence that is distinct from the individuals that participate is not persuasive and is simply seen, quite rightly, as reification. However, a rather more sympathetic response from the liberal individualist may be obtained in support of the argument that drugs should be banned because their use is unfair.

Rawls provides one of the most interesting and promising bases from which to defend a prohibition on drugs in sport and one that avoids rejection on the grounds set out by Mill and the other anti-paternalists. Rawls' device for thinking about fairness and justice is to ask what social arrangements people would make in a hypothetical situation which he terms "the original position" where they were ignorant of their particular personal circumstances and attributes. At the heart of Rawls' position is that if people are ignorant of who they are going to be and the talents, wealth and social advantages they

---

1. See footnote 3, p. 142 *ante*. Ibid., p. 500.

will possess it makes sense for them to arrive at a series of fair principles for organising society and, by implication, social activities such as sport. The question that then arises is whether in this hypothetical naive condition would individuals (athletes) suggest control over drugs in sport. If an athlete is unaware of his/her own physical endowments and physiological capacity to profit from drug use would this necessarily lead him/her to prohibit drug use? As Mulhall and Swift suggest, "One way of thinking about what happens in the 'original position' is as a kind of bargaining process, in which each person, acting rationally in her own self-interest, seeks to get as good a deal as possible for herself".[1] Unfortunately, the Rawlsian position, like many liberal individualists, adopts no particular moral imperative: it is not based on any particular conception of what is "good" in society. The primary concern of Rawls is to ensure that each individual has the greatest opportunity to choose and adhere to their particular conception of the good life, whether that involves participating in sport, studying philosophy or gardening.

The twin assumptions that people are ignorant of their talents and endowments and that they are not motivated by a desire to protect a particular conception of the "good" leads Rawls to establish two basic principles of justice or fairness, first that "each person is to have an equal right to the most extensive total system of basic liberties with a similar system of liberty for all" and second that "social and economic inequalities are to be arranged so that they are both (a) to the greatest benefit of the least advantaged, and (b) attached to offices and positions open to all under conditions of fair equality of opportunity".[2] The key question in relation to doping is whether athletes in the "original position" would choose to regulate or deny access to drugs, or put more accurately would individuals who do not know that they will choose sport as a significant pastime/career choose to deny access to drugs? Rawls assumes that individuals will behave rationally and it would therefore be logical for them to ensure that the least privileged position in society was as good or comfortable as can be just in case it is they who will be in that position. In a situation where there is maximum uncertainty about the future, it is unlikely that individuals would rationally deny themselves access to any opportunity to compensate for inequalities that they might be disadvantaged by in life. Consequently, it would not be rational for individuals who might be interested in an athletic career to deny themselves access to any of the aids to training and competition that might help to compensate for a particular disadvantage bestowed by nature.

Conclusion: playing by the rules

It would appear that attempts to argue in favour of an anti-doping policy from "first principles" derived from the interests of the individual are difficult

---

1. Mulhall, S. & Swift, A., *Liberals and Communitarians,* Oxford: Blackwell, 1992, p. 5.
2. Rawls, J., *A Theory of Justice*, Cambridge, Mass: Harvard University Press, 1971, p. 302.

to sustain. If anti-doping policy is not rejected on the grounds that no rational person would introduce anti-doping rules if there is a chance that doping might compensate for some natural inequality then it can be rejected on the grounds that the primary risks of drug use are borne by the taker and consequently are not a sound basis for limiting the individual's rights to endanger themselves. Neither of these bases are without weaknesses that the supporter of doping control might exploit but a more profitable avenue for reaching a convincing basis for current policy is to abandon the search for an a priori rationale for policy and concentrate on middle-order justifications which are derived from social experience. Such a shift of focus would bring the discussion back to the earlier theme of rules where it was suggested that doping should be rejected because it is a breach of the rules of the governing bodies of sport. In the earlier discussion it was suggested that this was a weak foundation for anti-doping policy as it was based on a circular argument, namely that the use of anabolic steroids, for example, is cheating because their use is not allowed by the rules of sport. However, if we treat doping rules in the same way as we treat other rules of sport, that is as part of the agreement entered into by individuals before they are able to participate then we are able to avoid the necessity or expectation that current rules have to be located in a set of principles that exist independently of the sport itself. There would not be any expectation that we should have to provide a rationale external to the sport of golf for the arbitrary rules that there shall be eighteen holes played rather than nineteen or that the ball shall be of a particular size. The rules depend for their survival on the extent to which they are able to command the respect and support of those who wish to play golf. This is not to argue that sport is an activity that is isolated from society and therefore does not need to take account of broader social opinion. Indeed, boxing has adjusted its rules on a number of occasions due to social concern at the risk of injury to participants.

At the heart of this position is the acceptance that sport is a socially constructed activity. The development of a satisfying sport that retains its popularity among both players and spectators is not the product of a rational calculation but rather the outcome of, an often prolonged process of, design, refinement and chance. The current rules and style of individual sports are the outcome of complex social processes which, while not unchanging, possess a considerable degree of inertia which gives them the permanence of social institutions. As such, sports reflect clusters of attitudes and values. The cluster of attitudes and values that describe and support a particular sport, and sport in general, are not limited to the rules and style of play but also cover contextual aspects of sport and include, among other things, attitudes to the taking of particular drugs, the adoption of training regimes and the financial rewards paid to athletes.

Lavin, in his examination of the ethics of drug use, proposes a similar way forward, but one which he admits is vulnerable to challenge. He suggests

145

that even though there is widespread inconsistency among the general public and significant interest groups regarding doping there is none the less a much higher level of consensus about which pharmaceutical preparations are considered acceptable and which are not and are subject to "pervasive disapproval".[1] Pervasive disapproval is the product of a democratic process which far from claiming to encapsulate timeless values in sport is a product of a particular age, but which none the less captures the current core values of sport. Such a stance is consistent with the evidence available from the previous chapter where it was shown that the social perception of particular drugs, opium for example, is far from fixed and may move dramatically from tolerance and amusement to intolerance and demonisation.

The virtue of Lavin's position is that it accepts the absence of a tightly argued and philosophically watertight foundation for the prohibition on drug use, but also, and more importantly, acknowledges the need for a more pragmatic basis for current policy. Unless a more pragmatic response to the question "Why ban drug use?" can be established and defended the inadequacies of attempts to build a rationale based on secure principle will continue to be exploited. Extending Lavin's position further, one can argue that what is required is a popular and democratically secure basis for policy rather than an unassailable philosophical position. The various rationales for anti-doping policy that have been suggested above take the policy maker only so far along the road to policy implementation: it is the addition of the notion of democratic process that enables the completion of the journey. One would also hope that the tension between the rigour of philosophical argument and democratic decision would provide a degree of security that popular democracy will not lapse into mere populism, but also that the limitations of philosophical argument about drug use will not be too readily exploited by the unethical.

Balancing principle with popular support

The tension between philosophical principle and democratic opinion may be amply illustrated in current debates about many social issues including euthanasia, abortion and capital punishment. In all three of these areas of social policy, debates can be compartmentalised in terms of principle or opinion but in practice the philosophical debates inform, sensitise and respond to popular discussion. Policy positions based solely on principle are unsustainable unless there is popular support. In sport, the clearest example of the problem of sustaining a policy based on principle without popular support is the gradual undermining of both amateurism and the exclusion of women from many sports during the twentieth century.

The search for a rationale for anti-doping policy within a democratic process is highly consonant with the current debates on communitarianism and the

---

1. Lavin, 1987, op. cit., p. 39.

communitarian critique of liberal individualism. Communitarianism rejects liberal individualism in preference for a theory which argues that the self and aspects of social reality, including sporting values, relations, culture and institutions, are the products of social construction. Communitarianism has much in common with contemporary pragmatic philosophy, which stresses the importance of seeking justifications for what we do in our daily practices rather than in the search for objective truths about the world. The dual strands in communitarian thought have substantial significance for the current debate on drugs in sport. The first strand is that it is not possible to conceive of the individual except as a member of his/her community and its practices and values. As Frazer and Lacey argue "The community constitutes the person. Social processes and institutions, the family, churches, political and educational systems, shape the infant into a social being who experiences emotion, who desires, who has understanding of and attitudes towards the social world and her place in it".[1] The implication of this view is clear for any discussion of the rules that should govern participation in sport and drug use in particular, namely that it is only possible to discuss the rights of the individual athlete to take drugs from within an understanding of the social institution of sport, that is as part of the web of human relationships that exist within sport in general and sporting competition in particular. The second strand of communitarianism concerns the development and "ownership" of values. The communitarian argument is that values are the product of, and are validated by, particular communities and do not proceed naturally from universal human nature as is commonly argued by the liberal individualist. Following from the assumption that human beings are essentially social results in an emphasis on those values that reinforce attitudes, beliefs and practices that acknowledge and reaffirm the communal and mutually supportive elements of human life. "Thus reciprocity, solidarity, fraternity and community take the place of the liberal priorities such as fulfilment of individual rights and respect for individual freedom in the sphere of political value."[2]

The applicability of these views to the sporting community is obvious and provides a powerful rationale for the current anti-doping policy. The current anti-doping policy is seen as the product of the dominant values and attitudes within the contemporary sport community rather than the product of abstract principle. Consequently, the ambiguities and inconsistencies in current policy are not necessarily weaknesses in the policy but are rather reflections of the differentiation between particular practices and substances that emerge from community experience and which reflect collective opinion. The attraction of the communitarian approach to policy justification is that it clearly roots the legitimacy of a policy in the level of popular support it

1. Frazer, E. & Lacey, N., *The Politics of Community: A Feminist Critique of the Liberal-Communitarian Debate,* Hemel Hempstead: Harvester-Wheatsheaf, 1993, p. 108.
2. Ibid., p. 110-11.

commands. From the policy maker's point of view an important aspect of successful policy implementation is the maintenance of the high level of support for the "pervasive disapproval" on which the credibility of the policy depends.

The dangers of basing anti-doping policy, or indeed any policy, solely on its capacity to generate support within a community are obvious. The confidence shown by communitarians in the common sense of democracy needs to be tempered with a reminder of how easily democratic common sense can slip towards arbitrary populism. In addition, the proponents of anti-doping would be in great difficulty if they were faced by a sports community which endorsed doping for they would have no basis on which to challenge the democratic will. Despite the attractions of communitarianism, the dangers of moral relativism are all too apparent. It is therefore important not to abandon the debate based on the more abstract notions of individual rights, fairness, harm and essence of sport as they might well be needed to provide constraints on the exercise of popular judgment. Indeed, among communitarians there are those such as Charles Taylor who moderate their defence of moral relativism by arguing strongly that community-derived values must be compatible with a set of deeper moral intuitions about the worth and dignity of other human beings, about what constitutes a good life and about what makes us worthy of the respect of others.

In conclusion, the quest for a set of universal and unassailable principles on which to base an anti-doping policy in sport is not capable of being fulfilled although reference to the intuitive values that Taylor refers to gives some external justification for policies designed to eradicate doping. Current policy is, though, capable of being strongly defended on the basis of the weight of democratic community condemnation and pervasive disapproval. In many respects, this is no different from the way that policy towards many other contemporary moral issues: abortion, divorce, treatment of prisoners in war and treatment of refugees, is determined. Of overriding importance is the fact that policy is consequently never secure but always in need of defence, support and refinement. The challenge to the sports authorities is to develop a persuasive definition of doping and a programme of policy implementation that takes account of the need to sustain popular disapproval of doping. Without strong community support for anti-doping the policy may suffer the same fate as other principled positions, such as that regarding amateurism which gradually became unsustainable due to the erosion of public support and confidence.

Chapter 6

The evolution of anti-doping policy: problems and solutions

From the local to the global

Over the last forty years, anti-doping policy has been transformed from a concern of a small group of governing bodies and countries to a global affair which has prompted the development of a series of international agreements, the establishment of new global forums, most notably the World Anti-Doping Agency (WADA), and the commitment of many millions of dollars of public and governing body funding. Up until the end of the 1980s, with the notable exception of the Council of Europe, anti-doping policy was formulated within a series of discrete and narrowly focused policy arenas. Individual international federations and individual countries tended to adopt a limited view of the nature of the problem of doping and of their responsibilities. Most federations and governments, if they were interested in combating doping in sport, were largely content to ensure the probity of their own sport or event, or to ensure that their national squad were "clean". The limited scope of much anti-doping policy up to the late 1980s was reinforced by the sharp divisions among the major sporting countries which could be seen as falling into one of three categories. The first category was a small number of countries, including France, Belgium, and the Scandinavian states, whose governments were actively pursuing an anti-doping strategy, even if limited to their own territory. The second category included the much larger number of passive countries, the governments of which, for a variety of reasons, did not treat doping as a priority for public policy. The motives for inaction included a lack of resources among the poorer countries, but also, among a few major "sports powers" such as Australia and Canada, a reluctance to investigate their own sports systems in case it jeopardised their increasing international success. The feeling was that some stones were best left unturned. This category also included a group of countries, of which the United States was the most prominent and which also included West Germany, which strongly suspected that doping was extensive in some communist countries and that this therefore justified their own ignoring of the issue. The third category of country was the most significant and included those countries, such as the former East Germany and the Soviet Union, where the government actively colluded in the systematic doping of its international athletes. The prominence of this subversive group together with the large number of passive countries made it very difficult to build momentum at an international level for the anti-doping effort.

The ending of the cold war, the trauma of scandal in Canada and Australia caused by the Ben Johnson positive test result at the Seoul Olympic Games and the extent of doping uncovered at the Australian Institute of Sport in the late 1980s, the growing litigiousness of athletes and a greater awareness of the geographical mobility of athletes encouraged renewed attempts to reinvigorate anti-doping policy and move it beyond the narrow confines of specific sports, events or national boundaries. Throughout the 1990s, steady progress was made in establishing forums for the exchange of information on doping, the sharing of experience in managing sample collection and conducting disciplinary hearings and appeals, and the establishing of a series of regional and bi-lateral agreements between national anti-doping agencies which often included agreements on testing of athletes from each other's country. Similar efforts were being made among international federations as they sought to come to terms with the increasing pressure from governments to take doping more seriously and from their athletes to ensure fair and reliable testing and tribunal procedures.

The most recent phase of policy activity was prompted by the near collapse of the 1998 Tour de France and led to one of the most significant developments in the short history of anti-doping policy, namely the formation of WADA and the much more rigorous programme of doping control that was put in place for the Sydney Olympic Games. While we should always be wary of claiming too much significance for particular developments in policy, the formation of WADA was a major development as it established an organisation which was not only global in representation and coverage, but which also brought together the three most significant sets of policy actors – the IOC, the international federations, and governments. Yet the route to the formation of WADA has been erratic and littered with false optimism and hollow claims that the "war against doping is being won".

Tracing the pattern of policy change

In any discussion of current anti-doping policy, it is important to bear in mind just how recently the issue of doping in sport has been defined as a problem and how recently drug testing and other policy solutions have been introduced. Forty years ago, there was not only no testing but little discussion of drug abuse within sport outside a small group of administrators, coaches and doctors. Thirty-five years ago, the first tentative steps were taken towards developing a definition of doping and beginning the process of policy formulation. Thirty years ago, there was only limited testing at major international and some national sports events. Twenty-five years ago, the first steps were being taken to introduce out-of-competition testing. Given the recent history of anti-doping policy, it is hardly surprising that the pace of policy development has not slowed over recent years and that sports administrators argue that anti-doping policy is still characterised by its dynamism rather than its stability.

The evolution of anti-doping policy can also be traced along four main dimensions, namely:

• clarification of policy focus;

• generation and maintenance of political commitment;

• technology development; and

• the establishment of the necessary resource infrastructure.

Clarification of the focus refers to the progressive refinement of the broad categories and particular examples of drugs and doping practices targeted by the policy makers. The second dimension concerns the stimulation of political support for policy implementation. Here the focus is not just on governments and sports authorities but also on athletes and the general public and is a continuing activity. Not only is the progressive widening and deepening of the coalition of support a benefit to the supporters of the anti-doping policy it is also a requirement for the continuance of policy momentum that each significant policy development stimulates a round of routine maintenance and reinforcement of that coalition of support. The third dimension refers to the technological demands of the policy. With regard to anti-doping, effective policy implementation depends substantially on the development of testing and analytical techniques and the continuing refinement of these techniques to match the advances in pharmacology and in the deviousness of drug-using athletes. The final dimension directs attention to the resource infrastructure which supports policy implementation and includes the provision of money, procedures (sampling and legal), laboratories, sampling officers and research.

Until the mid-1960s, concern about doping had been limited to a relatively small group of specialists within sport and the private concern had not yet become a public issue. The series of high-profile scandals in the early to mid-1960s forced the issue on to the agenda of both governments and sports bodies. A series of doping incidents in the previous years and especially the death of the Danish cyclist Knud Jensen at the Rome Olympics of 1960 prompted a convention in January 1963 of European sports governing bodies. One outcome of this meeting was the provision of a definition of doping which was later adopted by the International Olympic Committee and the International Doping Conference of the Fédération internationale de Médecine sportive in Tokyo in 1964. Doping was defined as:

> *"the administration to, or the use by, a competing athlete of any substance foreign to the body or any physiological substance taken in abnormal quantity or by an abnormal route of entry into the body, with the sole intention of increasing in an artificial and unfair manner his performance in competition".*[1]

---

1. Barnes, L., "Olympic Drug Testing: Improvement Without Progress", *Physician and Sports Medicine*, Vol. 8, 1980.

The weaknesses of this early definition are obvious given the discussion of the ethics of doping in the previous chapter. The difficulty of operationalising phrases such as "any substance foreign to the body", substances taken in "abnormal quantities", "abnormal route of entry", or "with the sole intention ..." are too obvious to require further elaboration. This early attempt at specifying the problem to be tackled marked the start of a period of intense discussion by all the key bodies interested in the definition of doping. Incidents of doping associated with cycling were again the stimulus to action, this time by the Council of Europe rather than the federations. The refusal by the five leading cyclists taking part in the 1966 World Road Race Championships to provide a urine sample and the death a year later of a professional rider in the Tour de France caused substantial public criticism and discussion, and prompted the Council of Europe to debate and pass a resolution condemning doping by athletes.

The condemnation was justified on grounds of health, poor example to the young and that doping was contrary to the spirit of fair play in sport. Included in the resolution was a definition of doping as the "administration to or use by a healthy person, in any manner whatsoever, of agents foreign to the organism, or of physiological substances in excessive quantities or introduced by an abnormal channel, with the sole purpose of affecting artificially and by unfair means the performance of such a person when taking part in a competition".[1] This definition attempts to resolve some of the ambiguities of the 1964 definition, but the additional phrases (such as the reference to the use of drugs by "a healthy person") compounded the problems and consequently shared many of the weaknesses of the 1964 attempt. Despite the continuing problems in arriving at an operational definition, the Council resolution also included a recommendation to its member governments to encourage their sports associations and federations to initiate action to condemn doping and to penalise offenders. Probably the most important statement within the resolution was the exhortation to member states to encourage their federations to apply anti-doping regulations "to any person who, in another member state, has been penalised".[2] The significance of the statement lay in its recognition of the international nature of the emerging problem and foreshadowed the current emphasis on harmonisation of policy between federations and between countries.

Drug testing

While the political momentum was growing for a policy to challenge doping, the deficiencies of current technology were becoming all too apparent. In the 1960s when testing began, the early tests were focused on cycling and were directed at the detection of amphetamines, the most widely used drug.

---

1. Council of Europe, Resolution (67) 12 on the doping of athletes, adopted 20 June 1967.
2. Ibid., paragraph 1.c.

Although there was an awareness of the increasing use of anabolic steroids, there was no reliable test for this class of drug. As regards testing for amphetamines, Verroken and Mottram note that "early testing methods were relatively unsophisticated: the technology available to analyse an athlete's urine resulted in inaccurate findings that failed to deter drug use".[1]

The intervention by the Council of Europe in the 1960s was significant not only because it responded to a wave of public concern about the issue of doping in sport but also because it was a sharp reminder to international sports organisations that governments also had an interest in the issue of doping. Paralleling the growing interest of the Council of Europe was an increasing number of individual governments that were introducing legislation or regulations aimed at drug abuse in sport. As early as 1965, the governments of France and Belgium legislated against doping followed by Turkey and Italy in 1971. Consequently, the action by the Council and the increasing threat of legislation by individual governments spurred the IOC and a number of key international federations, such as the Union Cycliste internationale and the IAAF into action. The IOC had for many years been wary of governmental interest and involvement in sport and particularly Olympic sport.[2] Although the IOC had established a Medical Commission in 1961 and passed a resolution condemning doping as early as 1962, it was not until five years later that it re-established and reinvigorated the Medical Commission with a brief to advise the IOC and to oversee the development of policy. Limited testing was introduced by international federations in mid to late 1960s, with FIFA being among the first when it announced that tests would be carried out at the 1966 World Cup in England. Two years later, tests were conducted at the Winter and Summer Olympic Games in Grenoble and Mexico City respectively, followed by testing at the 1970 Commonwealth Games and the 1974 European Athletics Championships. In these early years, very few positive results were recorded not only because there was an uncertainty about the reliability of the tests, but more importantly because there was a marked lack of clarity about where the primary responsibility for the implementation of testing lay. As is so often the case with new policy initiatives, initial enthusiasm was slowly being replaced with a growing appreciation of the organisational and financial costs of effective testing. This was particularly true for event-organising bodies, such as the IOC and the Commonwealth Games Federation and for the international federations, none of which was financially strong. Even the IOC was at that time a relatively modest body relying substantially on voluntary activity and the largesse of host countries.

The IOC, for example, clearly saw its responsibility limited to alerting national Olympic committees to the need to promote drug-free sport and to ensure

---

1. Verroken, M. & Mottram, D.R., "Doping Control in Sport" in Mottram, 1996, op. cit., p. 235.
2. See Houlihan, B., *Sport and International Politics,* Hemel Hempstead: Harvester-Wheatsheaf, 1994, for a discussion of the tensions in the relationship between the Olympic movement and international governmental bodies such as Unesco, the EU and the Council of Europe.

that local organising committees for Olympic Games made arrangements for testing. It made a point of stating that the organising of testing is "a responsibility that the International Olympic Committee is not prepared to take".[1] Despite the obvious reluctance by the IOC to adopt a central policy role, it has steadily increased its involvement in the policy area, most notably through the accreditation of laboratories for the analysis of samples and also through the maintenance of what has become the benchmark list of banned substances and practices, producing the first such list in 1971. Where the IOC has drawn the line is at extending its involvement in the administration of testing beyond IOC-sanctioned competitions.

The first Olympic Games at which there was reasonably comprehensive testing across all events was at the 1972 Munich Games when just over 2 000 tests were conducted and seven athletes disqualified. Tests were conducted for narcotic analgesics and for stimulants, but not for anabolic steroids as no reliable tests had yet been developed and the IOC was unwilling to list a substance for which there was no test. By the mid-1970s, testing for stimulants was sufficiently accurate to provide a deterrent against the use of the most common drugs in this class such as amphetamines. However, by the early 1970s it was acknowledged that the major drugs abused by athletes were no longer stimulants but steroids. Whereas tests for amphetamines and most other stimulants were easy and cheap to devise, as they merely required the adaptation of existing analytical procedures, the development of a test for steroids required original research which had to be funded. The breakthrough came early in the 1970s when a reliable test for many drugs in the steroid class was developed by Professor Raymond Brooks. The radioimmunoassay test was piloted at the 1972 Olympic Games under the direction of Dr Manfred Donike and was officially used at the 1976 Montreal Games, the drug having been added to the IOC list the previous year. Eight athletes were disqualified from the Games due to positive test results for steroids. Over the next ten years, the IOC gradually added to its list of banned substances and practices through the addition of testosterone and caffeine in the early 1980s, beta blockers and blood-doping in 1985, and diuretics in 1987.

While the IOC was reluctant to adopt a leading role in global policy development, it was forced to become more deeply involved in a number of aspects of anti-doping policy implementation, if for no other reason than to protect the integrity of the Olympic Games. The accreditation of laboratories is one such example. Some work on accrediting laboratories had been undertaken by the IAAF in the mid-1970s, which did much to inform the protocols adopted by the IOC in 1976 for initial accreditation and in 1985 for re-accreditation. Accreditation was introduced primarily in an attempt to protect the IOC and international federations from legal challenge to the procedures adopted within laboratories. Currently accredited laboratories are subject to

---

1. *IOC Newsletter*, August 1968, quoted in Verroken & Mottram, 1996, op. cit., p. 236.

re-accreditation on an annual basis and have their analytical standards tested every four months although responsibility for this process has now passed to WADA. The work undertaken by the IOC in establishing quality standards for laboratories dealing with urine samples from Olympic Games has resulted in the IOC requirements becoming the *de facto* standards for all sports drug analysis laboratories such that many non-Olympic sports send their samples to IOC-accredited laboratories. Although the IOC deserved much credit for developing quality standards for laboratories there was (and to an extent still is) some concern that there is no independent verification that laboratories have met the current standards or deserved re-accreditation. Justice Dubin during his inquiry into drug use by athletes in Canada considered that the practice of members of the IOC sub-commission who granted accreditation also being heads of IOC-accredited laboratories constituted a conflict of interest. The establishment of WADA has, to a large extent, undermined this criticism although it is possible to argue that WADA is still too close to the IOC and the international federations to be an appropriate watchdog.

Many of those closely involved in shaping IOC policy on doping were also involved in similar discussions within their own international federations. Not surprisingly given the centrality of track and field events to the Olympics, the IAAF was particularly closely involved in IOC deliberations with its policy-making keeping in close step with that of the IOC. The IAAF formed its Medical Committee in 1972 and placed both blood doping and anabolic steroids on its list of banned practices and substances even though reliable tests were not yet firmly in place. In 1976, the Federation formed a Doping Sub-Commission and a year later introduced mandatory doping control at Federation Championships. Progress towards agreeing a set of penalties for breaches of doping regulations was slower, but by 1978 the federation had introduced a minimum suspension of eighteen months for doping infractions. Eight years later, the federation began a process of refinement of penalties when it modified its policy to differentiate between unintentional use (for example, of ephedrine which is a common ingredient in many over-the-counter medicines) for which the penalty was to be a suspension of three months for a first offence, and a set of stronger penalties for the use of major drugs such as steroids where the penalty was to be a ban of two years for a first offence. A second offence concerning ephedrine or its derivatives resulted in a ban of two years with a life ban for a third offence. A life ban was to be imposed for a second offence concerning a major drug.

Gathering momentum

The late 1980s marked the start of a period of intense policy development. In 1987, the IAAF supported the first in a series of symposia on doping organised under the aegis of the International Athletic Foundation and aimed at raising the profile of the issue among athletes and also providing a forum for discussing aspects of implementation. The "Göteborg Manifesto", accepted by the IAAF in 1989, was supported by an extensive series of changes in policy including the establishment of a "flying squad" of sampling officers, the arrangement for world-recognised visas for flying squad members to prevent countries taking advantage of advance warning of their arrival, and the provision of financial support to domestic governing bodies to support testing programmes.

By the 1970s, the Council of Europe was beginning to treat doping as an aspect of a broader policy relating to the maintenance of ethical standards within sport. Consequently, references to doping were made within the context of related policy statements such as that on "Sport for All" in 1976. Within the European Sport for All Charter, itself a series of moral imperatives, Article V provides the exhortation that "methods shall be sought to safeguard sport and sportsmen from exploitation for political, commercial or financial gain, and from practices that are abusive and debasing, including the unfair use of drugs". This position was reinforced at the Second Conference of European Ministers responsible for Sport held in 1978 at which Prince Alexandre de Merode, President of the IOC Medical Commission, reported on the substantial problems in making progress in encouraging domestic sports organisations and international federations to adopt rigorous anti-doping measures.[1] The second conference adopted a resolution which again linked opposition to doping to a strong statement on the ethics of sport, but went further than the earlier statement by identifying the main agents of policy implementation and the steps that should be taken in developing an effective policy response to the problem. Although the statement was directed towards member governments, it was acknowledged that policy formulation and especially implementation would require the support and resources of domestic and international sports bodies. However, it was recognised that governments had an important role to play in the provision of specialist facilities to support drug testing, such as analytic laboratories, and also in facilitating the development of an internationally co-ordinated response. More importantly, the conference identified a series of key aspects of successful policy development many of which remain issues of continuing concern. The first aspect concerned the need to compile and publish "accurate and detailed lists of stimulating agents and means of testing for them"; the second referred to the need to identify ways of "instituting and supporting practical and regular doping tests" both "at and between events"; while the third concerned "instituting stricter sanctions for athletes found using stimulants, which should also be applied to trainers, doctors or managers who have encouraged their use" supported by a "publicity campaign directed at athletes on the dangers to health of doping". These three issues, agreeing

---

1. By the early 1970s, action was being taken by a number of national sports organisations including the Deutscher Sportbund of the Federal Republic of Germany and the Norwegian Confederation of Sport, generally taking their lead from the IOC, but in the case of the Norwegian Confederation providing a lead to other federations and to the IOC.

the list of proscribed practices and substances, the testing process, and the penalties to be applied and to whom, are recurring themes in the refinement of anti-doping policy.

During the late 1970s and early 1980s, the lead on debating and developing policy on anti-doping lay, publicly at least, with the IOC and increasingly with the IAAF. However, it should be borne in mind that the Council of Europe and a number of individual governments played a significant part in encouraging the Olympic movement to adopt a policy leadership role. The IOC's central-ity to policy-making on doping was in part through intent and partly through a concern not to lose, by default, control over a high-profile issue in sport to governments. In reality, policy-making on doping was rapidly emerging as inherently a twin-track process where the relationship between sports organ-isations, on the one hand, and governments and international governmental bodies, on the other, hovered between mutual support and reinforcement of common objectives and mutual suspicion that the other was either subvert-ing the policy or was attempting to dominate the policy arena.

Scientific advances: keeping ahead of the drug user?

Paralleling developments in the political relationship between sporting and governmental organisations was the steady progress in the refinement of sample analysis techniques. Although the breakthrough in the development of a test for anabolic steroids in the mid-1970s resulted in the apprehension of a number of drug abusers, it did little to stem the rapid increase in the pop-ularity of the drug. While radioimmunoassay was successful in identifying the presence of a number of steroids it was less successful with the more sophis-ticated drugs in the class and also less successful in identifying very small traces of the drug. As Robert Voy, former Chief Medical Officer of the Unit-ed States Olympic Committee, noted "before 1983 drug testing and detec-tion at all international competitions was very ineffective, simply because the technology was primitive and undependable".[1] Pre-1983 testing produced not only false negatives but also false positives with the result that athletes were often able to appeal against decisions on the grounds that the outcome of the test could not be guaranteed beyond reasonable doubt. Voy also pointed to the inadequacies of sampling procedures, especially the inability of anti-doping agencies to guarantee the security of the "chain of custody" and to state authoritatively that tampering or contamination of the sample could not have occurred. The deficiencies in the collection process provided "the biggest opportunity to challenge the testing system".[2] The main conse-quence of the weaknesses in procedures and the fear of legal challenge was that sports authorities would only proceed with the small number of test results that were deemed to be unchallengeable and many positive results

1. Voy, 1991, op. cit., p. 77.
2. Ibid., p. 78

were ignored. By the early 1980s, new and more sensitive detection methods were available based on gas chromatography/mass spectrometry (GC/MS) which was capable of identifying traces of steroids as small as one part per billion. In addition to enabling testing for anabolic steroids, GC/MS was also able to indicate the level of testosterone in the athlete's urine. It was the announcement that GC/MS analysis was to be used on samples from the 1983 Pan-American Games that led, allegedly, to the high number of withdrawals by athletes prior to the Games and the high number of positives at the Games. The increasing use of anabolic steroids that gave such urgency to the search for analytic methods and technology to enable their detection also led anti-doping authorities to a realisation that the deterrence value of effective competition testing was undermined by the use of steroids as training aids rather than competition aids. More importantly, it was also realised that the introduction of GC/MS technology was being used by unscrupulous athletes to determine the excretion time for different drugs in order to identify when they needed to stop taking the drug prior to competition.

The mid to late 1970s was the period when the move to introduce out-of-competition testing was made, not with the intention of replacing in-competition testing, but rather to complement it. Norway was one of the first countries to introduce out-of-competition testing. Its initial programme was introduced in 1977 with the proportion of total tests conducted out-of-competition rising to over 70% by the late 1980s. Britain was typical of the majority of countries that began to introduce out-of-competition testing during the mid-1980s. In Britain, out-of-competition testing was introduced by the British Amateur Athletic Board on a pilot basis with Sports Council funding in 1985. In 1988, the practice was adopted by a broader group of governing bodies due, in large part, to the encouragement and financial support from the Sports Council. One of the most significant lessons learnt from the early experience of out-of-competition testing was the need to develop a procedure that was adapted to the increasingly international training and competition schedules of élite athletes. If short notice, or preferably no-notice, testing were to be effective, it was essential that governing bodies knew where athletes were throughout the year. There were too many instances of athletes deliberately selecting inaccessible locations for training or "forgetting" to inform their governing body of their movements. The process of establishing a testing infrastructure appropriate to an increasingly internationalised athletic community has been slow and is not yet complete. However, there have been some moves to develop the necessary framework for implementation. In 1988, the Council of Europe adopted a recommendation on out-of-competition testing to which GAISF gave its support as did the European Sports Conference a year later. Of especial importance was the decision, in 1989, by the IAAF council to impose random testing on all international-level athletes thus by-passing any domestic governing bodies that had been dragging their feet on the issue. In May 1990, the first IAAF "flying squad" of testing officers visited the then Soviet Union, followed by visits to France and Italy.

The role of the Council of Europe

For the Council of Europe, the next notable stage in its contribution to the policy process was the formulation of a recommendation to member governments prompted by the 1978 ministerial conference. The recommendation left aside the increasingly difficult question of the definition of doping and concentrated on the more practical issues of implementation. In the recommendation the emerging issue was that of harmonisation of policy between federations. There was also some elaboration of earlier policy tools. For example, the earlier emphasis on the need to publicise to athletes the dangers of drug use was expanded to include coaches and administrators. Emphasis was also placed on the need for investment in the scientific resources, especially laboratories, necessary to support an effective testing regime. At the time of formulating the recommendation there were only three IOC-approved laboratories in the twenty-two member states of the Council of Europe.

The work of the Council was paralleled within the Olympic movement. Of particular importance was the 11th Olympic Congress in Baden-Baden in 1981 where a resolution from athletes gave legitimation and added momentum to the IOC's anti-doping activity. The Baden-Baden resolution also added to the growing interest within the Council and its advisory groups in developing a comprehensive policy statement in the form of an anti-doping charter. The significance of the European Anti-Doping Charter was primarily as a public statement of commitment by governments to the anti-doping campaign. The charter was also of value as a benchmark and focus for policy development at the national level, and as an important symbol of the elimination of doping as a joint endeavour by sports and governmental organisations. The text of the charter was drafted by an expert committee chaired by Prince Alexandre de Merode who played, and continues to play, a central role in the IOC's anti-doping efforts.

The charter was adopted in 1984 and was, at one level, an expression of political intent to tackle the issue of doping.[1] However, at a more significant level it provided a series of recommendations for the construction of an effective policy response to doping at the domestic and at the international levels in terms of the provision of resources to support the efforts of sports organisations to counter doping. Legislation was suggested to restrict the availability of drugs likely to be used in sport doping and financial support was recommended to help meet the cost of testing. Member governments were encouraged to facilitate the harmonisation of anti-doping regulations

---

1. A copy of the charter is included in *The Council of Europe's Work on Sport 1967-91. Vol. I*, Strasbourg: Council of Europe Publishing, 1992, pp. 63-6.

and procedures among governing bodies using the IOC and IAAF recom-mended regulations and procedures as the guide. The status of the charter was that of a recommendation, though it was hoped that "it would have a moral, political and practical impact higher than that of an ordinary recom-mendation".[1] Although it is always wise to be wary of ascribing too much significance to public expressions of support for statements of intent, the charter did generate considerable interest among both governmental and non-governmental organisations. Within twelve months of its publication, the General Association of International Sports Federations and the IOC had both passed resolutions endorsing the charter and, in 1985, the Association of European National Olympic Committees also expressed its support. Acknowledgements of the status of the charter came from Unesco, the European Union and the World Health Organisation. At around the same time, countries outside Europe were also showing interest in using the charter as the basis for shaping domestic policy with Canada being an early supporter. In late 1987, and with more than a trace of irony, a group of sports organisations in socialist states contacted the Council of Europe with a request for a set of internationally accepted rules and obligations on doping. The following year, in June 1988, the first Permanent World Conference on Anti-Doping was held in Ottawa and co-chaired by the IOC and Canada. Of particular importance was adoption by the conference of an International Doping Charter, later endorsed by the IOC and retitled the Olympic Anti-Doping Charter, modelled very closely on the European charter.

By the late 1980s, the issue of doping had moved from being a marginal sub-ject in sport with discussion limited to a core of experts and "insiders" to being an issue which held centre stage in a series of sporting and non-sport-ing organisations and also increasingly within the media. In addition, although in public the relationship between governmental and non-govern-mental bodies was one of mutual support it disguised an underlying tension. The basis of unease among governments and governmental organisations was not so much an explicit distrust of the commitment of either the IOC or the major federations to anti-doping but rather a more general concern with their reliance on self-regulation in preference to inviting an independent agency to take responsibility for anti-doping policy implementation. On the other hand, sports organisations were suspicious of the motives of govern-ments particularly at a time when the prestige and public relations opportu-nities afforded by the Olympic Games and other major international sports events were becoming increasingly apparent.

The decision of the Council of Europe to redesignate the charter as a con-vention to which member states would be asked to sign and to which non-member states would be invited to support was a mark of the progress that

---

1. Council of Europe, "Explanatory Report on the Anti-Doping Convention", Strasbourg: Council of Europe, 1990, p. 9.

had been made over the previous ten years in raising the profile of the issue and was also a recognition that co-ordination at the international level by both sporting and non-sporting bodies was essential for effective implementation (see Appendix B for the text of the convention). The focus of the convention was on harmonisation of policy between countries and between sports. As in the charter, the emphasis in the convention was on implementation through sports organisations although it was clearly acknowledged that the resources of the state, whether legislative or financial, were essential for successful policy implementation. The early concern to provide a comprehensive definition of doping was replaced by a less problematic statement that "'doping in sport' means the administration to sportsmen or sportswomen, or the use by them, of pharmacological classes of doping agents or doping methods".[1] Pharmacological classes of doping agents or doping methods were simply defined as those "classes of doping agents or doping methods banned by the relevant international sports organisation".[2]

Table 6.1: Incorporation of countries of central and eastern Europe into the Council of Europe, in chronological order

Country	Ratification of Accession to ECC	Ratification of Accession to ADC	Membership of CE
Hungary	Nov. 1989	Jan. 1990	Nov. 1990
Poland	Nov. 1989	Sept. 1990	Nov. 1991
Czech Republic	May 1990	April 1995	June 1993*
Slovakia	May 1990	May 1993	June 1993*
Russian Federation**	Feb. 1991	Feb. 1991	Feb. 1996
Bulgaria	Sep. 1991	June 1992	May 1992
Romania	Dec. 1991	Dec. 1998	Oct. 1993
Estonia	May 1992	Nov. 1997	May 1993
Latvia	May 1992	Jan. 1997	Feb. 1995
Lithuania	May 1992	May 1996	May 1993
Albania	June 1992		July 1995
Slovenia	July 1992	July 1992	May 1993
Croatia	Jan. 1993	Jan. 1993	Nov.1996
Moldova	May 1994		July 1995
Ukraine	June 1994	Nov. 2001	Nov.1995
Bosnia and Herzegovina	Dec. 1994	Dec. 1994	
"The former Yugoslav Republic of Macedonia"	Nov. 1995	Mar. 1994	Nov. 1995
Armenia	April 1997		Jan. 2001
Azerbaijan	April 1997		Jan. 2001
Georgia	April 1997		April 1999
Non-member states			
Belarus	Oct. 1993		
Bosnia and Herzegovina	Dec. 1994	Dec. 1994	
Yugoslavia	Feb. 2001	Feb. 2001	

Notes: Source: Council of Europe
*   as Czechoslovakia
** as Soviet Union

1. Council of Europe, Anti-Doping Convention, 1989, Article 2, paragraph 1, section a.
2. Ibid., Article 2, paragraph 1, section b.

The preparation of the convention marked a watershed in the activity of the Council on anti-doping policy not just because there was a now a benchmark against which to measure the commitment of other countries but also because it coincided with the collapse of the governments and sporting infrastructures in the communist countries of central and eastern Europe. The need in these countries to rebuild sports organisations with often negligible state support gave an opportunity for the Council to provide advice and support not only on sports infrastructure but also on the importance of reaffirming a set of sports values that incorporated a strong anti-doping element. Indeed, as Table 6.1 shows, for many ex-communist countries accession to both the European Cultural Convention (ECC) and the Anti-Doping Convention (ADC) was a common precursor to an invitation from the Committee of Ministers to join the Council of Europe (CE) itself.

The late 1980s: scandal and policy review

The late 1980s marked a watershed in policy development not just for the ex-communist countries but also for some of the countries that had considered themselves to be occupying the moral high ground on the issue of doping. In Australia, the United Kingdom and Canada scandal, allegations of abuse and suspicion of collusion by sporting authorities in covering up positive results raised the public and political profile of drugs in sport. For many Australians, sporting success epitomised the character and qualities of the country giving sport a particular prominence in Australian culture.[1] Sustained international sporting success in the post-war years was complemented by innovations in sports development activity which were frequently seen as models in the non-communist world of the 1980s. The publication of allegations of systematic drug abuse at the flagship élite sports development centre, the Australian Institute of Sport (AIS), in 1987 caused such a public outcry that a Senate Committee of Inquiry was established. At the heart of the allegations was the suggestion that coaches and administrators at the AIS had colluded with athletes to circumvent doping-control procedures. The picture painted of Australian anti-doping policy was one of minimal compliance, and a culture which sought to test the boundaries of current policy. There was little harmonisation of policy among governing bodies and even less enthusiasm to give the issue priority over maximising the medal count at international sports competitions. Anti-doping policy in the mid-1980s, such as it was, was unco-ordinated and unenthusiastically implemented. Although over 500 athletes were covered by the testing programme it was, in the words of the athletics coach at the AIS "regarded as a joke by athletes. In the case of track and field the only tested meet is usually the national championships and they know when that is on, so athletes can easily organise their schedules to avoid the testing".[2]

---

1. For a more detailed discussion and analysis of the events at the AIS, see Houlihan, 1997, op. cit.
2. Government of Australia, 1989, op. cit., p. 84.

The inquiry highlighted a range of specific problems that included the lack of commitment from many athletes and coaches, the lack of confidence in the laboratories that undertook sample analysis, and the general unwillingness of governing bodies to provide a strong lead on anti-doping. In many respects, these problems with effective policy implementation highlight the problems faced by anti-doping advocates arising from the context of modern sport. The lack of enthusiasm among athletes and coaches, especially those based at the AIS was, in part, a fear that they might lose the financial support that government gave to individual athletes if the level of achievement declined. Staff at the AIS were under considerable pressure to justify public expenditure on the facility through the continued success in international competition. Similarly, there was a disincentive to governing bodies to pursue rigorously drug abusers as they too were dependent on Olympic success for the continuation of their government funding. This link between Olympic and international achievement and funding level is common in many countries and consequently poses a powerful dilemma for coaches and officials when choosing between an Olympic medal and continued or enhanced public funding, on the one hand, and challenging a successful élite athlete suspected of using drugs, on the other. The enthusiasm of the Australian Olympic Federation was, at that time, no greater than that of the AIS. The federation was deliberately slow in introducing random out-of-competition testing so as not to compromise athletes before the Olympic trials and also to enable them to ensure they were "clean" before testing commenced. Governing body and governmental determination to eradicate doping was further undermined by an acknowledgement that many other countries and, until recently, especially those in the communist bloc, had little commitment to drug-free sport. As was made clear in Chapter 2 there are currently similar concerns about the commitment of the Chinese sports authorities to anti-doping objectives.

The report of the senate inquiry was an indictment of the approach of Australian sports organisations towards anti-doping. The report criticised the testing regime because "there are major questions over the collection of urine samples, the selection of athletes for tests and the low frequency of testing".[1] Up to the time of the inquiry only 239 tests had been carried out and none had proved positive. The standard of administration of testing was also criticised on the grounds that athletes were able to provide a sample unchaperoned, and twenty athletes turned up to provide their sample up to thirty days after the forty-eight-hour deadline and incurred no penalty. The conclusions of the committee could hardly have been more damning. According to the committee, the institute's testing programme "was a response to outside pressures to be seen to be 'drug-free', rather than from any real concern for the need to strictly apply IOC guidelines to ensure the integrity of Australian sport and the health of its athletes. ... The Committee

---

1. See footnote 2, p. 164 *ante*. Ibid., p. 494.

believes that in many ways the AIS drug-testing program was worse than having no drug testing program at all. It provided the protection of appearing to do something to prevent the use of drugs, but was conducted in such a manner that it may have been possible for athletes using drugs to claim that the program showed them to be drug free".[1]

The investigations of the senate committee marked a significant turning-point in anti-doping policy in Australia. However, the reinvigoration of anti-doping policy was due to an intensification of government involvement and consequently at the cost of governing body autonomy. The main outcome of the inquiry was the establishment by law of the Australian Sports Drug Agency (ASDA) in 1990, which was given the objective of reducing "the harm associated with the use of drugs in sport in order to promote the well-being of the individual and enhance the value of sport to society".[2] ASDA's mission was supported by the role of the Australian Sports Commission, a government agency, which required any governing body receiving public funds to comply with ASDA anti-doping regulations. The impact of government intervention through ASDA has been dramatic with the number of tests rising rapidly to over 2 000 each year and covering almost fifty sports. Although tests are spread across a range of sports, those with a history of drug abuse are allocated a higher proportion of tests. Since the establishment of ASDA, there has been a steady decline in the number of doping infractions and in the number of examples of "inadvertent use" of drugs by athletes. Part of the explanation for these trends probably lies in the success of the drug-testing programme, but there is also the concern that it may reflect the increasing sophistication of drug users who have moved on to some of the newer and less easily detected drugs. In general, the senate inquiry resulted in a considerable improvement in the effectiveness of anti-doping policy implementation and placed Australia among the group of countries with a more reputable record on combating drug abuse. However, the cost of the improvement in compliance by athletes and their governing bodies has been a substantial increase in the involvement of government in the activities of voluntary bodies.

A similar pattern can be found in the United Kingdom, except that the involvement of government dates from a much earlier phase of policy development. As early as the mid-1960s, the newly established Advisory Sports Council took an interest in the emerging issue of drug abuse by athletes. However, it was from the late 1980s that government intervention became more evident. In part, the increase in government involvement was the result of frustration at the recalcitrance of a small number of governing bodies and the general lack of urgency of the sector to introduce more rigour and commitment to policy implementation and refinement. Government intervention

---

1. See footnote 2, p. 164 *ante*. Ibid., p. 495.
2. About ASDA, 1991, p. 3.

was stimulated by the increasing rumours of collusion in the undermining of drug testing by sports authorities. In general, the strategy of the government was to rely on exhortation and inducements to encourage governing bodies to take a more determined lead in the development and implementation of anti-doping measures. However, by the mid-1980s it was apparent that the pace of change was too slow for the government's liking. In 1985, the Chair of the British Sports Council criticised governing bodies for dragging their feet on drug testing despite the fact that the cost of testing was underwritten completely by the Council. At about the same time that the disquiet within government was growing, a series of allegations was published in the national newspaper *The Times* in December 1987 which claimed that coaches and officials were colluding in aiding athletes to avoid both testing and the publication of positive results. The allegations were subsequently investigated by a committee of inquiry instigated by the Amateur Athletic Association and chaired by the lawyer Peter Coni.[1] Although many of the more damaging allegations were rejected, the report created a strong impression that domestic governing bodies of sport were unprepared, if not simply unable, to respond effectively to the challenge of doping.

While the Coni report was published too late to have been a direct influence on government thinking, it certainly reinforced the conclusions that had already been drawn regarding the need to strengthen the anti-doping campaign through the adoption by the government of a more prominent role in policy implementation. A report co-authored by the sports minister, Colin Moynihan and the athlete, Sebastian Coe, in 1987 led, in 1988, to the establishment of the Doping Control Unit, as an agency within the British Sports Council. The role of the unit was to provide information and develop educational material, but also to co-ordinate and conduct testing. The unit in effect took control of the technical aspects of testing and left the governing bodies with the responsibility for identifying those to be tested and dealing with positive results. The establishment of the unit came at the same time as the introduction of out-of-competition testing. As was the case in Australia, the pattern of policy development in the UK has resulted in a very similar testing regime and a greatly enhanced role for government and its agencies.

The pattern is little different in Canada where anti-doping policy in the 1970s and early 1980s was characterised by governing-body inertia combined with governmental indifference until the dramatic positive drug test by Ben Johnson at the 1988 Olympics. The Dubin Inquiry that investigated the Johnson affair and the existing anti-doping policy was scathing in its description of a sports community at best unwilling to investigate the claims of widespread drug abuse voiced by a minority of coaches and officials and at worst, a community that actively colluded in the development of a drug-based élite sports culture.

---

1. Amateur Athletics Association, "AAA Drug Abuse Report" (Chair: Peter Coni), London: AAA, 1988.

As in Australia and the UK, the outcome of the upsurge of governmental interest in the policy issue was the establishment of an anti-doping agency, the Canadian Centre for Drug-free Sport, which co-ordinated the testing programme and technical analysis, and also gave a clear lead to sports governing bodies about other aspects of policy implementation including athlete selection and penalties to be applied to sportspeople guilty of doping infractions.

If the late 1980s can be characterised as a watershed in policy development which marked, in many countries, a substantial increase in government involvement in policy development and implementation, it is ironic that this was occurring at the same time that the elaborate state-sports structures of the communist bloc in central and eastern Europe were disintegrating. In Europe the collapse of communism ended a prolonged period of state dominated and manipulated sport best characterised by the maintenance of sham amateurism, but which touched all aspects of sport from the distortion of sporting opportunities in favour of the élite to the disadvantage of the mass of the population, on the one hand, "to the long-term state production, testing, monitoring, and administering of performance-enhancing drugs in regard to athletes as young as seven and eight", on the other.[1] 1989 brought a rapid collapse of the communist-state sports infrastructure and faced governments and sports authorities with immense problems in refashioning a sports system that benefited the mass of the population and also attempted to retain some level of élite success. In many respects, ex-communist sport faces an acute dilemma. The scaling down of the intensity of state control over sport provides an opportunity to rebuild a drug-free sports system, but the poverty of most ex-communist countries and the continuing priority among some to define rapidly a refashioned national identity makes the establishment of drug-free sport more difficult.

The pressures on sports administrators and athletes to acknowledge the legacy of the sports system of ex-communist countries is amply illustrated in reunified Germany. Despite initial declarations that the East German sports system would be totally dismantled after reunification, the German Government then became increasingly ambivalent about some aspects of the East German system. At worst, condemnation of state-sponsored doping in the east was tempered by a deeply ambiguous attitude to doping among some athletes and coaches in the Federal Republic. According to Hoberman:

> "The enormous success of East German athletes at the 1976 Montreal Olympic Games produced a traumatic effect on the West German sports establishment that ended only with the collapse of the Communist state."[2]

---

1. Riordan, J., "Communist Sports Policy: The End of an Era" in Chalip, L., Johnson, A. & Stachura, L., *National Sports Policies: An International Handbook*, Westport, Conn: Greenwood Press, 1996, p. 111.
2. Hoberman, J., *Mortal Engines: The Science of Performance and the Dehumanisation of Sport*, New York: The Free Press, p. 242.

In late 1990 following a series of highly publicised and damaging revelations of doping in the former East Germany, but also in West Germany, an Independent Doping Commission was established supported by the government, the National Olympic Committee and the DSB (the German Sports Federation). While the Commission found evidence of extensive doping in the former GDR and evidence of less extensive, but none the less significant, doping in the Federal Republic its conclusions were muted. In contrast to Australia and Canada, for example, the commission recommended leaving the resolution of the problem in the hands of sports authorities rather than advocating greater government involvement. More ambivalently, it recommended a doping amnesty thus legitimising the East German records as German national records. Finally, the commission's emphasis on the significance of élite sporting success for nation building in the new Germany provides the most likely reason for the commission's reluctance to challenge doping more forcefully. Germany's results at the Atlanta Olympic Games demonstrated the extent to which unified Germany relied on the children of the communist sports system. Of the total of 104 medals won, 48 were won by former East Germans: 12 of the 22 gold medals were also won by former East Germans. The significance of the contribution by East Germans to national success is illustrated by the fact that they account for only 21% of the total German population. However, as the evidence of systematic doping within the GDR has accumulated the attitude of the German Government has hardened considerably with a series of prosecutions and conviction of coaches alleged to have caused "bodily harm to minors" through the administration of drugs. The government also amended the statute of limitations to allow investigation of doping to continue until October 2000.

Maintaining the momentum

A central role in the development of sport in post-communist Europe has been played by the Council of Europe. Much of the responsibility for maintaining the momentum on anti-doping policy following the preparation of the convention lay with the monitoring group, which has met annually since 1989. A significant amount of the work of the group has focused on a series of technical and legal aspects of policy development and implementation but the work of the group also reflected the shift of emphasis away from treating doping as a discrete aspect of sports policy and towards seeing anti-doping policy as an integral element in a broader set of sports ethics. The work of the group complemented the increasing concern of the Council to identify and reinforce the ethical basis of sport and the positive contribution of sport to society in general and to the young in particular. In 1990, the Council, through the Committee for the Development of Sport (CDDS), published the conclusions of its debates on the responsibilities of parents and teachers in inculcating positive values towards drug-free competition. A year later, a seminar was organised that focused on sports ethics and young people, and although concerned primarily with issues of fair play more generally the debate had a deep resonance for those developing and promoting the anti-doping policy. The emphasis on ethical issues was reflected most strongly in the publication of the European Sports Charter in 1992 which took, as one of its aims, the commitment to "protect and develop the moral and ethical bases of sport ... by safeguarding sport, sportsmen and women from ... practices that are abusive or debasing, including the abuse of drugs". The Council adopted a Code of Sports Ethics in the same year, which also emphasised the centrality of drug-free sport to the broader notion of fair play.

The elaboration of the political and ethical context for sport over the last ten years or so has been matched by a continuing refinement of testing procedures and technologies. The introduction of in-competition testing in the late 1960s, the development of GC/MS analytical techniques in the 1980s, the introduction of out-of-competition testing in the late 1980s and the development of urine and blood tests to identify EPO use all represent quantum steps in testing procedures. However, it is also important to note the rapidity with which these developments have been matched by the drug abuser. As Voy notes, "The science of avoiding drug detection is probably as sophisticated today as the science of drug testing itself".[1] Voy cites two examples from 1988 when athletes, especially in field events, withdrew from competition because of the nature and timing of the testing procedures to be adopted. Competitions scheduled close to the date of the Olympic trials in the United States were especially vulnerable as drug-using athletes would still have been taking steroids. At the 1988 Pepsi Classic, scheduled a few weeks before the Olympic trials, the shot-put and discus events had to be cancelled because so few athletes accepted the invitation to participate.[2] By the late 1980s, it was apparent that the effectiveness of out-of-competition testing was under threat because of the improved knowledge among drug users of the clearance time for drugs combined with the practice of giving advance warning of an out-of-competition test. Advance notice testing which was common in many countries made a mockery of claims of rigour made by the advocates of out-of-competition testing. In some countries, advance warning of up to a month might be given and even where the period of notice was much shorter the fact that the more sophisticated steroids could be flushed out of the system in under forty-eight hours meant that the drug abuser was under little real threat of identification. In the early 1990s, a number of countries introduced no-notice testing, but the practice is far from the norm across all sports and countries. However, by the mid-1990s of those countries that had introduced out-of-competition testing, 64% of tests were conducted with no notice and no country had an advance notice period of greater than forty-eight hours.

1. Voy, 1991, op. cit., p. 93.
2. Ibid., p. 94.

The 1998 Tour de France and the establishment of WADA

Progress in anti-doping policy-making has always been erratic and episodic with periods of almost frantic activity followed by periods when the issue appeared to be slipping off the agenda of the IOC, international federations and governments. Although progress continued to be made during the 1990s, it required yet another doping scandal to recapture the momentum of the early 1990s. The near collapse of the 1998 Tour de France was significant for four reasons: first, the sheer scale of the scandal and the number of teams and élite riders involved; second, the global status of the tour as one of the five or six most important world sports events; third, the fact that the UCI, the international federation for cycling, had been prominent for so long in anti-doping efforts yet had proved so ineffective in checking the spread of doping in its own sport; and fourth, the strong intervention by the French Government. It was perhaps the last factor that caused greatest concern to the IOC and the international federations. The French Government rejected protests from the UCI that the extent of doping uncovered during the tour was a matter to be resolved through the union's processes and asserted that doping at the tour was a matter of public concern and one which would consequently be dealt with by the police and courts.

The response of the IOC was to convene a World Anti-Doping Conference in Lausanne in February 1999. The conference proved to be a watershed in anti-doping policy: first, because it marked a long overdue attempt by the IOC to recapture the initiative in policy-making from governments; and second, because it forced to the surface a series of tensions that had stymied earlier attempts at policy development. While in public sports, organisations maintained a show of common cause and unity it masked a number of deeply rooted antagonisms that had, for many years, limited co-operation in a number of areas including doping. Tensions arose from the desire of the federations, especially FIFA, but also the IAAF, to share in the success of the Olympic Games while also protecting their individual world championships. Further tensions existed between the IOC and the federations, most notably the IAAF, over the division of income from the sale of television broadcasting rights for the Olympics with the federation arguing that it was track and field events that were the main attraction for television companies and that consequently the IAAF should receive a larger proportion of income. In general, the federations were keen periodically to remind the IOC that it was they who controlled the sports stars and allowed them to compete in the Olympics. However, the international federations and the IOC were united in their collective lack of confidence in (and at worst outright distrust of) governments and in the deeply held assumption that most governments treated international élite sport as a convenient political resource rather than as an important global cultural event. For their part, an increasing number of governments perceived sports organisations as unwilling, if not unable, to put

169

their own house in order. If the Lausanne conference was to make progress, it had to overcome some deeply entrenched hostilities.

The aim set for the conference was to "discuss and adopt measures allowing the fight against doping to be intensified" and was based on the preparatory work undertaken by a series of working parties that had prepared position statements on a range of topics including finance, ethics and legal aspects. Most of the first day of the conference was given over to a succession of brief statements by sports ministers and representatives of government anti-doping agencies which, with only a few exceptions, were fiercely critical of the IOC in general and the leadership provided by Samaranch in particular. If President Samaranch expected the statements to contain a chorus of congratulations he was to be sadly disappointed as a succession of ministers and government officials used their allotted five minutes to berate the Olympic movement for its complacency and myopia towards doping, to challenge the sincerity of its stated aims for the conference and to question its moral authority to oversee the proposed international agency. The intensity of criticism was not due solely to a perceived lack of commitment to anti-doping by the IOC, but was overlain with indignation at the unfolding story of corruption among IOC members concerning the selection of Salt Lake City to host the 2002 Winter Olympics.

The intensity of criticism was lower on the second day when consideration was given to the remit, financing, location and accountability of the proposed new agency. The initial suggestion was that the agency be established "as a foundation under Swiss law, ... be headquartered in Lausanne, governed by a council presided over by the IOC President, consisting of three representatives each of the IOC, the international federations, the National Olympic Committees, athletes designated by the IOC Athletes Commission, international governmental organisations and three persons representing sponsors, the pharmaceutical industry and the sporting goods industry" (IOC, 1998). The council would direct the work of the agency and be responsible, among other things, for funding, revising the list of banned substances and practices, validating the accreditation of IOC-approved laboratories and appointing the director of the agency. As regards funding, the working group proposed the designation of an initial sum of at least $25 million to cover running costs and to commission research to develop reliable tests for the detection of natural steroids, EPO and hGH.

The strength of support for an international agency was qualified by a widespread concern that it should be completely independent of the IOC. Consequently, the declaration agreed at the conclusion of the Lausanne Conference was ambiguous about the relationship between the proposed agency and the IOC. It was agreed that an "independent International Anti-Doping Agency shall be established so as to be fully operational in time for the XXVII Olympiad in Sydney in 2000". The brief of the body was less clear as this would now be determined by a new working group convened by the IOC and with membership drawn from among athletes, governments and the Olympic movement. However, the Lausanne Declaration did indicate that part of the remit of the agency would be to give consideration to "expanding out-of-competition testing, co-ordinating research, promoting preventive and educational actions and harmonising scientific and technical standards and procedures for analyses and equipment" (IOC, 1999).

Despite the intensity of criticism from politicians, the overall outcome of the Lausanne conference was positive. When the rhetoric of the government representatives was stripped away along with the posturing designed to satisfy domestic constituencies, there was an acknowledgement that a global body similar to that proposed by the IOC was essential if progress in the anti-doping campaign was to be made. The central issue was therefore not whether there should be an international anti-doping body, but who would control it. After six months of negotiations within a working group appointed at the Lausanne Conference, a revised set of proposals was published. The focus and remit of the new agency, the World Anti-Doping Agency (WADA), did not differ greatly from the initial IOC proposals.[1]

> "The Agency's principle task will be to co-ordinate a comprehensive anti-doping program at international level, developing common, effective, minimum standards for doping control ... Among its duties, the new Agency is expected to commission unannounced out-of-competition controls in full agreement with [the] public and private bodies concerned.
>
> The Agency is expected to work with existing authorities to promote the harmonization of anti-doping policies and procedures, identify a reference laboratory to advise the accredited testing laboratories, and co-ordinate the numerous educational efforts now underway. It also is expected to publish an annual list of prohibited substances."
>
> (IOC press release, 9 September 1999).

It was acknowledged that the agency would not seek responsibility for the determination of doping infractions or for the imposition of sanctions: both these responsibilities would remain with the international federations. The most significant recommendation, strongly supported by the Council of Europe, the European Union and the United States, was that the agency would now be far more independent from the IOC. Thus, membership of the agency's board would have equal representation from sports bodies and governments (or international governmental bodies). Responsibility for funding would also be shared equally between governments and sports bodies with the IOC agreeing to fund the agency for its first two years at $4 million per

---

1. The title World Anti-Doping Agency was preferred to the original suggestion (the International Anti-Doping Agency) because of the possibility of the acronym IADA causing confusion with the International Anti-Doping Agreement, which is a multilateral agreement between a group of states.

year until the governments could finalise their funding formula. Half the total of $4 million would be used to fund about 5 000 out-of-competition tests, a total which represented a 10% increase on the number of out-of-competition tests currently undertaken globally: the remainder of the funding would be used to cover the other activities of the agency including the production of educational materials, the provision of information and administration. Research was to be funded separately. As regards location, it was agreed that WADA would be located initially in Lausanne, but after voting in August 2001 a permanent home was found for the agency in Montreal. It was also agreed that Richard Pound, IOC Vice-President, would be the first president although some, including Barry McCaffrey, considered that he had a conflict of interest by virtue of the fact that he was an IOC Vice-President and, more importantly, was responsible for the marketing of the Olympic Games – a product that can only be damaged by revelations of doping. However, following a meeting with Pound, McCaffrey felt sufficiently reassured that Pound would only act as interim president to lend him his support.

WADA was formally established on 10 November 1999 with an executive committee chaired by Richard Pound comprising five representatives of the Olympic movement and five representatives of public authorities, and board also chaired by Pound with three IOC representatives, four from the Association of National Olympic Committees, three from the Association of Summer Olympic Federations, one from the General Assembly of International Sports Federations, one from the Association of International Winter Federations plus eighteen representatives of various public authorities including individual countries but also regional bodies such as the European Union, the Council of Europe and the Supreme Council for Sport in Africa.

Although the timescale was tight, WADA made a significant and favourable impression at the Sydney Olympic Games. Not only did the agency fund some 2 500 additional tests prior to the Games, but it also acted as an independent observer evaluating the doping control procedures during the Games. The creation of the Office of Independent Observer was agreed between WADA and the IOC and "was a crucial step in demonstrating doping control transparency and accountability at Olympic Games".[1] While there was some ambiguity regarding the respective roles and relationships between the observers, the IOC Medical Commission and the Games Organising Committee, the general perception was that WADA had played an important part in raising the level of confidence in the doping-control procedures.

Following the conclusion of the Sydney Games WADA, understandably, concentrated on formalising its internal procedures and finances, and also agreeing its permanent location. By late 2001, the agency had agreed the basis on which the various regions of the world would be represented and by whom.

---

1. WADA, *International Observer Report*, Lausanne: WADA, 2000, p. 1.

Agreement had also been reached on the formula for apportioning the 50% financial contribution of the public authorities to WADA and it had been agreed that Montreal would be the agency's permanent location. In addition to finalising its organisation and finance, WADA has acted quickly to establish an agenda and work programme for the next two to three years. At its meeting in January 2000, it was agreed that there were three priorities: the first of which was agreeing with the international federations, protocols for out-of-competition testing and embarking on the first round of testing; the second was the development of an accreditation mechanism for laboratories; and the third was the design of a test-results management system. WADA had also established a series of working committees, some of which were procedural such as that for Finance and Administration, but others which reflected the extended agenda of the agency's activities and included committees for Ethics and Education, Health, Medical and Research, and Standards and Harmonisation.

That WADA has clearly developed considerable momentum since its establishment is in part a tribute to the commitment of its members and the support of the Australian Government during its early activities at the Sydney Olympic Games. However, part of the explanation for the promising start by the agency is also due to significant changes in the policy environment. There have been three changes of particular note: the increasing interest of the European Union, the active involvement of the United States, and the formation of the International Intergovernmental Consultative Group on Anti-Doping in Sport (IICGADS).

The changes made to the Lausanne proposals were a recognition by the IOC of its increased resource dependence on governments and the greater determination of the latter to tackle doping. The IOC was especially conscious of the potential influence of the EU which was confirmed by the newly appointed President of the European Commission, Romano Prodi, who as President-designate told the European Parliament that one of the issues that he intended to make a priority for the new Commission was doping "an issue where decisive, co-ordinated transnational action is clearly needed" (Prodi, 1999). The EU has only gradually developed an interest in sport in general and doping in particular, partly because there was no explicit basis in the various treaties that define the spheres of competence of the Union for its involvement in sport until the Treaty of Amsterdam. However, the EU was able to justify its interest in doping by reference to a wide range of general responsibilities. Article 152.1 of the EU Treaty deals with public health and refers to "action in reducing drugs-related health damage". Other bases for action include directives that concern the protection of young sportspeople and the protection of workers; treaty provisions on tackling drug trafficking; and, finally, the general research remit of the Commission.

While it is possible to trace EU interest back to the early 1990s when two declarations against doping in sport were made, it was not until the late

1990s that the EU became more directly involved. In December 1998, the European Council expressed its concern "at the extent and seriousness of doping in sport, which undermines the sporting ethic and endangers public health" and encouraged the involvement of the Commission in working with international sports bodies to "fight against this danger".[1] The views of the European Council were endorsed by the European Parliament later in 1999 and by a series of informal meetings of EU ministers for sport. With its deepening interest in sport in general and doping in particular, it is not surprising that the EU was closely involved in negotiating the statutes that would define the remit and govern the operation of WADA. From the perspective of the IOC, the EU has a range of existing programmes that could support the work of WADA particularly in relation to the funding of scientific research, furthering the harmonisation of laws among member states, and the funding and co-ordination of public health campaigns aimed at doping in sport.[2] But while the IOC was doubtless aware of the value of harnessing EU resources to the anti-doping campaign they were probably more acutely aware of the EU's interventionist and regulatory culture and the threat that that posed to the independence of sports organisations.

Of comparable significance to the increasing involvement of the EU was the new-found enthusiasm for action on doping within the United States, which was stimulated partly by accumulated pressure from other countries for the United States to adopt a more proactive and positive policy towards doping and partly due to the central position of America in the bribery scandal concerning the selection of host cities for the Olympic Games. It was difficult for the American Government to secure the moral high ground over the bribery issue when it had so patently failed to tackle the major ethical issue of doping within its own territory. The appointment of Barry McCaffrey as the White House "Drug Czar" and the formation of a White House task force on drug use in sport in mid-2000 ensured that the high profile of the issue would be maintained and that moves to reform anti-doping policy within the USOC would receive strong federal endorsement. In December 1999, the USOC called for the creation of an independent body to enhance the credibility and effectiveness of US efforts to tackle doping. The US Anti-Doping Agency (USADA) was duly established in 2000 with responsibility for sample collection, testing, adjudication, sanctions and research. USADA will receive enhanced funding, part of which will come from the federal government and part from the USOC enabling the agency to increase the number of tests to

1. European Commission, *Doping in Sport: The Fight Against Doping at Community Level – State of Play*, Brussels: European Commission, 1999, p. 1.
2. See the Helsinki Report on Sport (Commission of the European Communities' report from the Commission to the European Council (1999)) for an indication of the scope of EU interest in sport, its general priorities and its specific objectives in relation to doping. The EU's acknowledgement of the importance of sport and its potentially central role is in part due to the preeminent role of Europe as the focus for élite-level sport. In 1999, Europe hosted seventy-seven world championships and over one hundred European championships.

approximately 7 000 per year as well as fund research. By "putting its own house in order", the United States has substantially enhanced its credibility in relation to global anti-doping policy and enabled one of the major world "sports powers" to be fully involved in the establishment of WADA.

The final development in the context of global anti-doping policy was the formation of the International Intergovernmental Consultative Group on Anti-Doping in Sport (IICGADS). IICGADS was established as an informal and interim body because of the need for a collective voice for the public authorities in relation to the IOC proposal for a new global anti-doping agency and also because of the need for a constituency from which representatives of public authorities could be selected. The governments of Canada and Australia were instrumental in convening the International Summit on Drugs in Sport in November 1999 in Sydney that led to the formation of IICGADS, which was given a brief to co-ordinate worldwide government participation in WADA and to facilitate the process of harmonisation of policies, especially in areas of exclusive government jurisdiction or responsibility such as customs regulations and the labelling of medicines and supplements. For the first time, there now existed a global forum for governments to exchange views on doping issues and to co-ordinate their contribution to WADA.

Conclusion

The challenges that the relative novelty of the policy issue presents to policy makers is compounded by two major factors: first, the complexity of the issue and, second, its dynamic nature. The complexity can be illustrated in many ways but one could simply point to the necessity to develop a policy which is effective at both domestic and international levels, which involves approximately thirty Olympic federations and a similar number of non-Olympic federations and which requires the co-operation of over one hundred or so governments who have a significant number of athletes participating in international competition. The dynamism of the policy area is best reflected in the constant, and largely successful, search on the part of drug-abusing athletes for new substances and practices which are more difficult to detect. One might also point to the global mobility of athletes, to the ambivalence of many doctors and other professionals towards doping, and to the willingness of some governments to view international sporting success as a convenient resource in international relations.

An acknowledgement of the novelty, complexity and dynamism of the policy issue is important in any assessment of progress in developing a response to the problem of doping in sport. With this caveat in mind it would be fair to claim that much has been achieved if measured in terms of agreement on what to test for, what procedures to adopt in the administration of anti-doping policies, and how to deal with doping infractions. From a position in the early 1960s where those, admittedly few, federations concerned with drug abuse were developing separate lists of proscribed substances, there is now a strong consensus constructed around the IOC list which has rapidly established itself as the benchmark. Indeed, one sign of the growing maturity of the policy discussions is that sports federations are beginning to refine the IOC list to meet the specific character and problems of their own sport. However, the content of the list is only significant if federations and countries intend to develop a programme of testing of which it is a part. Adopting the IOC, or similar, list does not in itself constitute an anti-doping policy. A much more tortuous process has been that of establishing a broad agreement on the process of anti-doping policy implementation. Progress has been painfully slow in reaching agreement on a large number of procedural questions including who to test, how many tests to conduct, the balance between in-competition and out-of-competition testing, the appropriate distribution of tests between sports, whether and how sampling officers should be trained and who should pay them and for their training, under what conditions should urine samples be collected, what constitutes the maintenance of an effective "chain of custody", which laboratories are suitable to undertake sample analysis, when should positive results be announced, when and under what circumstances is a positive result declared to be a doping infraction, and what appeals procedures are appropriate. It should come as no surprise that a high priority has been given by WADA in its current five-year plan to the development of a "universally harmonised anti-doping code and the harmonisation of anti-doping rules, regulations and legislation" prior to the 2004 Athens Olympic Games.[1]

The difficulty of achieving agreement on procedural questions is amply illustrated by the history of penalties for doping infractions. The emerging consensus regarding penalties for the use of steroids appears to be for a two-year ban for a first offence followed by a life ban for a subsequent offence. However, the fragility of this consensus is illustrated by the continuing debate among international federations and the periodic attempts by athletes to challenge the decisions of federations in the courts. On the positive side, there is a growing concern within federations to tailor the range of penalties to suit the characteristics of particular sports. For some sports, such as some disciplines in gymnastics, a two-year ban for steroid use would represent exclusion from a substantial part of an athlete's career: for other sports, such as middle-distance running, a two-year ban would be far less damaging as the career tends to be considerably longer. The concern to achieve a greater degree of equity between sports is hampered by a number of factors not least of which is the periodic challenge to federation decisions in domestic courts. The increasing adoption of a two-year ban for a first offence involving a major drug such as steroids is a retreat from an earlier preference for a four-year ban and was due to the mounting of a successful legal challenge in the German courts and the threat of litigation elsewhere.

---

1. WADA Press Release, 21 August 2001.

Table 6.3 : The evolution of anti-doping policy

	Policy focus	Level and scope of support for anti-doping policy	Technological development	Development of implementation infrastructure
1950s	Highly generalised, but concern is focused on one or two sports such as cycling.	Debate largely confined to specialists within specific sports and a small number of sports	Little specifically directed at drug testing in sport.	Almost none.
1960s	Early definitions of the problem are produced but are confused.	Widespread collusion among governments in doping, for example in the former GDR and Soviet Union. Still only a minority of major federations involved in anti-doping activity.	Testing refined for amphetamines.	Limited in-competition testing, but few international federations had anti-doping regulations. Few countries had laws relating to the misuse of drugs in sport. IOC Medical Commission (re)-established in 1967.
1970s	Focus on amateur rather than professional sport; some concern with addictive drugs in professional sport; start of a process of locating doping within the broader values of sport, e.g. "Sport for All".	Most governments at best lukewarm in their support for anti-doping; others ambivalent towards emerging anti-doping policy. Wide variation in the level of commitment to anti-doping among federations.	Testing developed for narcotic analgesics and stimulants. Later, in 1976, testing developed for steroids by radioimmunoassay.	Increase in testing, but still unreliable consequently few positives declared. IAAF Medical Committee established in 1972. IAAF & IOC accreditation of laboratories in mid 1970s. Still many weaknesses in procedure e.g. regarding the "chain of custody".
1980s	Shift of emphasis from deterrence alone to deterrence plus education.	Series of major scandals prompting sharp increase in government and federation interest.	Testing available for caffeine. Testing also available for betablockers and blood-doping in 1985 and for diuretics in 1987. GC/MS testing for steroids in late 1980s.	Mid to late 1980s increase in government legislation against steroid trafficking; 1985 laboratory re-accreditation by the IOC introduced. Out-of-competition testing introduced in late 1980s.
1990s	Increasing concern to locate doping within an articulation of the ethics of sport; shift (or broadening) of focus from the athlete alone to the athlete and entourage (i.e. penalties for coaches, doctors and even for domestic governing bodies); debate about athletes as victims or villains. Increasing concern with broad policy harmonisation.	Increasing sophistication of debates within the federations and the IOC, and also within governmental organisations such as the Council of Europe. Increasing awareness of the complexity of the issue leading both to greater commitment by some policy actors and to greater uncertainty and weakening of resolve among others.	Testing for growth hormone by 2000	IOC established Court of Arbitration. Increase in the number of international forums in which to discuss doping policy (e.g. Permanent World Conference on Doping, Nordic Group, CE and EU). Increase in government-funded research into drug testing.
2000s	Emphasis on harmonisation of doping control management. An increasing concern to balance testing, detection and sanctions with education.	Increasingly prominent role for governments and their anti-doping agencies. Increasing interest in doping issues from within the EU.	Test for EPO available, but research still continuing on hGH test.	The formation of IICGAD and WADA.

In addition to tracing the level of agreement on particular aspects of policy, it was suggested earlier in this chapter that the development of anti-doping policy could also be traced along four main dimensions namely, clarification of policy focus, generation and maintenance of political commitment, technology development and establishment of the necessary resource infrastructure. Table 6.3 provides a summary of change and indicates both the areas of progress, but also the areas where substantial difficulties remain.

As regards the clarity of policy focus, it is possible to trace the interweaving of a series of policy strands over the last forty years. One strand relates to the particular sports seen as most "at risk" and consequently acting as a focus for policy debates. In the 1950s and 1960s, cycling was the main source of concern followed in the 1970s by the throwing events and weightlifting: more recently, swimming, track events and again cycling have been seen as the sports most vulnerable to doping. The significance for policy makers of the association of the problem with particular sports is that each sport or cluster of sports generates distinct public perceptions. Doping infractions in élite-level football and cycling, as largely professional sports, rarely generate the intensity of public condemnation as doping cases in the "amateur" sports of track and field. Similarly, doping in swimming and track events have generated a greater intensity of condemnation than doping in weightlifting and field events, possibly because the former sports are perceived as more truly symbolic of the Olympic values. A second strand in defining the current focus of policy is the steady shift from the athlete to the athlete's entourage and an increasingly common debate as to whether the athlete was best seen as the villain, victim or co-conspirator. The third policy strand is closely related to the previous theme and concerns the debate about the degree to which the domestic governing body should be held responsible for the drug abuse of its members. The international federations responsible for weightlifting and swimming have both considered suspending domestic governing bodies when breaches of doping regulations by their athletes are considered unacceptably high. In November 2001, the International Weightlifting Federation suspended the Nigerian team from international competition for one year after a positive drug test.

The second dimension to doping policy is the generation and maintenance of political commitment. In many respects, the emergence of the issue of doping in sport and its transformation from a private issue to a public problem is a classic example of agenda setting through crisis. Although there was an awareness of drug abuse in sport as a fringe aspect of the broader problem of social drug abuse it was marginal to the concerns of anti-drug strategists largely because drug abuse in sport was seen as minor in extent, largely involving non-addictive drugs and substances that were legally available. In addition, there was, and remains, an understandable reluctance to add to the burden of anti-drug policing by criminalising a new set of drugs and users especially when there was not the extensive association between sports drug use and crimes such as smuggling, street crime and violence. For most international federations and domestic governing bodies, commitment to anti-doping has been slow to develop partly because of a reluctance to acknowledge the problem as specific to sport, partly due to an awareness of the resource implications of developing and implementing an anti-doping strategy, and partly, for some federations at least, the result of an unwillingness to recognise doping as a challenge to sports ethics. For some domestic governing bodies there is an additional motive for remaining unenthusiastic about anti-doping, namely a fear of alienating star athletes on whom they depend for the success of sports competitions. The recent example concerning USA Track and Field (USATF) provides an insight into the behaviour and attitudes of a major domestic federation for an Olympic sport. In a report into allegations made during the Sydney Olympic Games that USATF "had concealed information about US athletes who may have tested positive for the use of performance-enhancing drugs".[1] Although the commission found no evidence that anyone at USATF had "covered up" positive drug tests it none the less reached a series of highly critical conclusions, including that:

- "USATF interpreted and applied its own confidentiality regulations ... so restrictively that its effect was to prevent the IAAF from enforcing its own doping controls on an international level."[2]

- "USATF did not comply with certain of its own doping control regulations, including deadlines and reporting requirements."[3]

- "USATF did not meet its obligations to provide the USOC and the IAAF with accurate and current information about athletes' whereabouts, thereby impairing the effectiveness of those organisations' out-of-competition testing programmes."[4]

However, it is not just governing bodies that are reluctant to name those who produce positive test results. Earlier, in 1996, it was alleged that the IOC had failed to announce four positive test results, in addition to the two that were reported at the time of the Atlanta Games.

With some notable exceptions the ambivalence of many federations towards doping was a reflection of the often highly ambiguous attitude of governments to the issue. The blatant hypocrisy, for much of the post-war period, of the governments in the communist countries of eastern and central Europe was matched by the casual indifference of many, if not most, governments in non-communist industrialised countries. The level of state-supported doping has declined but there have been more recent accusations of

---

1. Report of the Independent International Review Commission on Doping Control – USA Track and Field, 11 July, Indianapolis, USATF, 2001, p. 1.
2. Ibid., p. 6.
3. Ibid., p. 12.
4. Ibid., p. 12.

state complicity in doping directed towards the People's Republic of China (PRC). Until the series of positives at the Perth World Swimming Championships in January 1998, it had been thought that the Chinese Government had become aware of the damage to the PRC's reputation and to the prospects of hosting future major track and field events that resulted from its weak stand on anti-doping. That three Chinese athletes tested positive in early 1997 for steroids might have suggested that nothing much had changed but the fact that they were identified by the domestic governing body rather than by international federation testing officers indicated a possible change of attitude. However, the Perth episodes once again raised serious doubts about the sincerity of the Chinese authorities' protestations of commitment to drug-free sport. For most countries, policy-making was scandal-driven with the stimulus for many governments being the desire to maintain the utility of international sports as a tool of foreign policy and general positive public relations. It remains to be seen whether the recent scandals will prompt the Chinese authorities to demonstrate a stronger commitment to anti-doping if for no other reason than to retain the diplomatic utility of international sport.

The third dimension of policy relates to the pace of technological development. The IOC has generally been reluctant to place a substance on its list of banned drugs until a reliable testing method had been identified. The development of radioimmunoassay analysis in the mid-1970s enabled steroids to be added to the IOC list and the more recent refinement of gas chromatography/mass spectrometry analysis proved to be major developments in the detection of traces of steroids forcing drug users to allow a much longer clearance period. Although technological and analytical developments have been significant, there is a major concern that the techniques of drug detection will be unable to keep pace with the increasing sophistication of newer drugs and especially those that enhance or replicate the normal chemistry of the body. A major issue for the success of current anti-doping policy and also for the credibility of future policy is the ability of federations and governments to fund research into detection techniques. Finally, there has been considerable progress in the development of an infrastructure to support policy implementation. On the one hand, the establishment and maintenance of a network of accredited laboratories is of major importance in reducing the likelihood of legal challenge to the laboratory analysis. However, the cost of maintaining an accredited laboratory continues to escalate as the analytic techniques increase in sophistication and greater sensitivity of measurement is needed. The distribution of laboratories is uneven with most being located in Europe and North America and with there being little likelihood of poorer countries ever having an accredited laboratory. The uneven distribution of laboratories also means that research into testing techniques is also confined to a small group of countries. A further element of the policy infrastructure is the regulatory framework operated by federations and governments. Although there is less diversity of regulatory practice than ten or twenty years ago, there is still substantial variation between federations on many aspects of sampling procedure and also variations between governments on matters such as the importation, sale and possession of steroids and the willingness of domestic courts to support bans for drug use.

In highlighting the weaknesses in current anti-doping policy implementation, one should not lose sight of the achievements. In a relatively short period of time, a basic policy infrastructure has been put in place and the issue of doping in sport is prominent on the agendas of federations and an increasing number of governments, many of whom have allocated considerable sums of public money to support anti-doping policy. It is probably fair to conclude that the initial stage of policy development is coming to an end and a new agenda of issues is emerging which will test the capacity of the international sporting community to maintain the policy commitment and momentum. At the forefront of the new agenda of issues is the question of policy harmonisation both across federations and sports and also across countries. It is this question that is considered more fully in the next chapter.

Chapter 7
Policy harmonisation : problems and prospects

For a number of years harmonisation has been accepted as the primary requirement for an effective global anti-doping policy. Until recently, it has been easy for sports organisations and governments who were lukewarm towards anti-doping policy to pay lip service to the goal of harmonisation as it was rarely defined and rested comfortably in the realm of policy aspiration rather than in the scope of practical policy. Such opposition as there was to harmonisation of anti-doping policy came from a variety of sources. Some established professional sports argued that they should not be expected to adhere to the same doping rules as "amateur" sports and some professional sportspeople argued that sport is their living and that they should be allowed more leeway in the range of permissible drugs particularly those used to control pain. Occasional challenges to harmonisation are also heard from the non-Olympic sports, which argue that it is both unnecessary and unfair to impose IOC standards on non-Olympic sports. From among the main Olympic sports, there was little opposition to progress to closer harmonisation although a number of federations expressed concerns at the prospect of losing some of their autonomy.

The primary stimulus for the current emphasis on harmonisation is the recognition of the global character of élite sports circuits and the high level of international mobility of élite athletes. There is little point in the government and domestic governing bodies of sport in one particular country having a clear set of regulations regarding doping if their élite athletes do not train in their home country nor participate in competition in that country. There are plenty of examples of world-class athletes, particularly from outside Europe, that have little or no contact with the anti-doping regime of their home country. Because the major cycling competitions are in Europe there are, for example, few world-class Australian or American cyclists who compete or train extensively in their home country. Much the same can be said regarding the top-class soccer players from South America and increasingly Africa who spend most of their careers in Europe. Given the multiplicity of sources of legitimate anti-doping regulation and the global nature of modern élite sport, it is important that there is minimum inconsistency between national anti-doping agencies, domestic governing bodies and international federations.

The drive for closer harmonisation was given significant additional momentum following the establishment of the World Anti-Doping Agency, which adopted the harmonisation of doping control procedures and policies as a central priority for its work programme. As Richard Pound, Chairman of the WADA Board, commented, "Achieving a unified code will be a true test of WADA's effectiveness. This represents a great opportunity to coalesce all the entities involved in anti-doping to collectively develop a harmonized approach to doping control. Such a code will allay most of the concerns the athletes have about the current state of affairs in doping control" (WADA Press Release, 21 August 2001). Despite the considerable resources and political weight that WADA will bring to the quest for closer harmonisation, formidable problems will need to be overcome including agreeing what har-monisation means, how we would recognise its achievement and how, when achieved, it will be maintained. Part of the continuing scepticism towards harmonisation lies in the deep ambiguity concerning its definition.

Harmonisation: depth, breadth and intensity of commitment

While the term harmonisation is used with increasing frequency there has been insufficient attempt to define its meaning or to set criteria which would indicate when it has been achieved.[1] On the one hand, harmonisation may be conceptualised as an objective or outcome and, on the other, it can be used to refer to the process by which the outcome is achieved. As an outcome, har-monisation has a variety of possible meanings including technical uniformity, proximity, compatibility and value consensus. As a process, harmonisation includes collective negotiation, external imposition and self-regulation. Identi-fying the criteria to be used for determining when the outcome of harmoni-sation has been achieved is far from easy and has at least three aspects that need to be taken into account namely, depth, breadth and intensity.

Depth has three distinct dimensions, the first of which refers to the extent of change required in national policies, for example in laws, administrative rou-tines and the allocation of resources. The second dimension concerns the degree to which international organisations such as the IOC and the interna-tional federations, but also governments, adopt policies that they would not otherwise have adopted. The importance of this dimension goes to the heart of any discussion of harmonisation as it concerns the cost of compliance. Clearly, harmonisation is easy to achieve if policy is specified in general terms and where thresholds are generous. For example, there has been a long debate among the major federations and with the IOC about the appropri-ate tariff of penalties for particular doping infractions. For many years, the norm in a number of key federations was four years for a first infraction con-cerning steroids and a life ban for a subsequent infraction. Recently the IOC recommended that the norm be reduced to two years for a first infraction. One view of the halving of the length of the ban is that it is an example of the formulation of policy according to the lowest common denominator where the policy is set at a point where even the least committed can com-ply with minimal cost. The view of the IOC was that a two-year ban was less likely to be challenged in domestic courts and therefore enabled consistency

1. For a fuller discussion of the problems of policy harmonisation in doping see Houlihan, B., "Policy Harmonisation: The Example of Global Anti-Doping Policy", *Journal of Sport Man-agement*, Vol. 13.3, 1999, pp. 197-215.

to be maintained. One could also argue that the prospect of having to impose a four-year ban made anti-doping authorities overly generous in giving athletes the benefit of the doubt. In addition, it can also be argued that depth of harmonisation on penalties counts for little if there is not equal depth in relation to the proportion of athletes selected for testing, the frequency of tests, etc. Moreover, the IOC argued that it was still a sufficient disincentive to break doping regulations. In other words, the aim was to set a standard that made the opportunity cost of defection higher than that of compliance. The third dimension of depth is the extent to which the specification of policy prescription extends beyond general statements of values and addresses matters of operational detail. With regard to the last dimension, it should be added that the specification of operational detail should be at the core of policy rather than in those aspects which might possess high visibility but are generally marginal to the central values of the policy. For example, the depth of specification of urine-sample laboratory analysis counts for little if there is not equal rigour in the selection of athletes for drug testing.

Breadth refers to the proportion of potential parties to an agreement that is deemed to be sufficient for satisfactory compliance. What is the critical mass required in order to maintain the commitment of the supporters of harmonisation? At the Sydney Olympic Games, 199 countries participated of which 80 won at least one medal.

Table 7.1: Distribution of medals at the 2000 Olympic Games between the 80 medal-winning countries

% of medal-winning countries	% of medals won
Most successful 10% (n = 8)	52.6% (n = 456)
Most successful 20% (n = 16)	72.5% (n = 629)
Most successful 40% (n = 32)	90% (n = 780)
Least successful 20% (n = 16)	2.6% (n = 23)

Table 7.2: Distribution of medals at the 2000 Olympic Games between the 199 participating countries

% of participating countries	% of medals won
Most successful 10% (n = 20)	77.5% (n = 672)
Most successful 20% (n = 40)	94.7% (n = 821)
Most successful 40% (n = 80)	100% (n = 869)

As Table 7.1 shows, of the total of 869 medals awarded almost 75% were won by 16 of the 80 countries that won at least one medal and 90% were won by just 32 countries. Table 7.2 illustrates even more dramatically the extent to which success is confined to an extremely small group of countries. Of the 199 countries that took part in the 2000 Games, 60% won no medals and 20% accounted for just under 95% of all medals. With this distribution in mind, it is possible to argue that as long as the thirty or so most successful medal-winning countries comply with anti-doping policy there will be little concern about failures of compliance by the others. Thus, breadth can be defined in terms of compliance by key "sports powers" rather than in terms of all countries that participate in major sports competitions.

Breadth can also refer to the scope or pervasiveness of the policy. If Olympic sports constitute the core focus for anti-doping policy, how far beyond that core should the policy extend? Should non-Olympic sports be included, professional team sports, single-country sports, "entertainment" sports, etc? The third dimension, intensity, refers to the level of commitment of key organisations and governments. Both sports organisations and governments have a wide range of responsibilities and demands on their resources. Inevitably, the issue of doping will not remain as their primary concern over the long term. If it is accepted that the intensity of interest and commitment of time and other resources will vary, the acceptable limits of that variation need to be specified. In other words, what is the maximum acceptable level of under-compliance.

Varieties of harmonisation

Apart from the small number of simple problems, such as which side of the road to drive on, most problems require a clear acknowledgement of their dynamic nature and a recognition that there may well be exceptional cases that need to be catered for. The dynamic aspects of doping include the emergence of new sports, changes in national laws, the development of new drugs or banned practices, and the development of new analytical techniques. The cumulative effect of complexity, dynamism and regard for exceptional cases in the pursuit of harmonisation is that a policy framework is required that applies different notions of harmonisation to different aspects of the problem. Within doping there are major clusters of decisions concerning issues such as athlete selection, sample-collection procedure, transport and analysis of samples, treatment of positive test results, and disciplinary and appeals procedures. Within each of these clusters, there are a similar number of discrete aspects of the overall process where decisions have to be made regarding the precise nature of the harmonisation required.

Broadly, there are four distinct interpretations or perceptions of harmonisation, namely as uniformity, proximity, compatibility and consensus (see Table 7.3). Uniformity is most appropriate in technical areas such as the process of urine or blood sample collection, transport and analysis. In recent years, there have been a number of successful appeals by athletes based on flaws in the collection, transport or laboratory analysis of samples. As a result, the process by which laboratories are accredited and re-accredited has become steadily more exacting, and the specification of the sample-collection process and the training of doping control officers have become increasingly detailed. Indeed, one of the tasks that WADA has set for itself is to achieve uniformity in a number of crucial areas of laboratory accreditation and re-accreditation.

Table 7.3: Varieties of harmonisation

Intended outcome	Description	Possible examples
Uniformity	Identical standards or processes	Same testosterone epitestosterone ratio accepted as indicating a doping infraction across all domestic federations and across all sports Standards for accreditation and re-accreditation of laboratories.
Proximity	Very close similarity in standards and processes with variation justified by the particularities of countries, sports or events	List of banned substances and practices Distribution of tests between sports in different countries
Compatibility	Difference is allowed up to the point where it undermines the credibility of standards, processes and objectives	Variation in practices between sports regarding the point at which a doping positive is made public Variation in the practices between sports regarding the point at which a domestic federation informs its international federation of a positive test result
Consensus	Agreement on values and ends which allows variation in means	Ensuring that an athlete's rights are respected may be through agreement to settle any disputes between the athlete and his/her federation at the Court of Arbitration for Sport, a domestic tribunal or the domestic courts

Proximity best describes the harmonisation of lists of banned substances and practices across different sports. Although most international federations have adopted the IOC list of banned substances and practices, uniformity is absent because some federations have taken the decision to vary the IOC list in order to take account of the particular characteristics of their sport. For example, beta blockers are not banned in basketball whereas alcohol is banned in motor sports (Vrijman, 1995). However, the extent of variation is very low and a high degree of proximity to the IOC standard is achieved across the world's major fifty or so sports (Vrijman, 1995: pp. 15-18). Harmonisation, defined as proximity, would also be an appropriate objective regarding the number/proportion of athletes to be tested, the frequency of testing, the extent of testing of junior athletes and the position in the ranking list where testing should begin. With regard to many of these elements of anti-doping policy, uniformity would be hard to achieve even if it were considered desirable. Such is the degree of variation, even within one sport, in terms of the composition and strength of a squad, and such is also the variation in the resources of domestic federations and governments that proximity of policy within agreed bounds of tolerance regarding under-compliance is a more realistic objective.

Compatibility allows variation up to the point where the procedures/policies adopted by the various bodies come into conflict with the broad goals of anti-doping policy. For example, it is accepted that it is incompatible with broad-policy goals for one national federation to allow an athlete to register and participate in competition if he or she has been banned by another federation for a doping infraction: for example, to transfer from rugby union to rugby league. The final interpretation of harmonisation is as consensus, whether of values or regarding goals, and might concern the process by which athletes' rights are protected in any doping-control process and generally how principles of natural justice are incorporated into anti-doping procedures.

The need for closer harmonisation: the problems of inconsistency

Bearing in mind the different interpretations of harmonisation, its importance to the future success of anti-doping efforts is easily illustrated through reference to four recent cases each of which highlights different consequences of inconsistency. The first concerns three German athletes, Katrin Krabbe, Silke Müller and Grit Breuer. In January 1992, the three athletes were tested at their winter training camp in South Africa. The out-of-competition tests were requested by the German athletic federation, Deutscher Leichtathletik Verband (DLV), and were carried out by the South African Amateur Athletic Federation. The analysis, at the IOC-accredited laboratory in Cologne, revealed that the urine samples were identical. The athletes were suspected of breaching regulations concerning the manipulation of samples. The decision of the DLV Presidium was to suspend the athletes for a breach of regulations. However, the athletes appealed on a number of grounds including that the DLV lacked the authority to conduct out-of-competition tests and that the sanctions imposed were not allowable under the terms of the DLV constitution. The subsequent review of the decision by the DLV Legal Committee found in favour of the athletes and the suspension was lifted. The investigation of the two decisions of the DLV by the IAAF concluded that the legal committee had been correct. The key weakness in the DLV Presidium decision was the fact that the doping rules of the association had not been incorporated into the constitution of the federation but were contained in a separate document. This being the case, it was accepted that under German law the testing lacked constitutional validity and no legitimate penalty could be imposed. The lesson to be learned from the episode was that "In order for each (inter)national federation to be able to conduct effective anti-doping controls, the authority of the (inter)national federation to conduct such testing, should be firmly supported by a provision to this effect in the constitution of the (inter)national federation in question".[1] In other words, the domestic governing body to which the athlete belongs must explicitly recognise the authority of the domestic federations of other countries and that of the international federation to conduct tests on its members.

The second case also involves Katrin Krabbe. In July of the same year, the DLV decided to drop its case against Krabbe after she tested positive for steroids. The IAAF announced the doping infraction in August and the DLV imposed a four-year suspension on the athlete. However, Krabbe successfully undermined the DLV decision by threatening to challenge the decision in the German courts on the grounds that the scale of penalty was too severe. Facing the prospect of a potentially costly legal battle, the DLV reduced the penalty to one year's suspension. If the lesson of the previous episode was to ensure consistency between federations, the lesson of this case was to ensure that there was greater consistency between the scale of penalties deemed appropriate by the international federation and those accepted as fair by domestic legal systems.

The third case concerns the Australian athlete Martin Vinnicombe, a cyclist who was tested in Canada at the request of the Australian Sports Drug Agency (ASDA) in May 1991. At first glance, the procedures appeared to have been followed meticulously: ASDA had sent a letter of authorisation to the Canadian authorities and when the sample was taken, Vinnicombe signed a declaration of satisfaction with the procedures. The samples were analysed at an IOC-accredited laboratory in Montreal where traces of the steroid stanozolol were found whereupon Vinnicombe was suspended from competition for two years, a period consistent with the rules of both the domestic governing body and the international federation. As de Pencier noted "Vinnicombe never denied that he had in fact used stanozolol".[2] However, this did not prevent him challenging the suspension in the Australian court on the grounds that "the test results ought to be invalidated because of the variations between doping control set out in the ASDA Act and ASDA Regulations and as set out in the *Canadian Doping Control Standard Operating Procedures*".[3] The judge in the federal court suggested mediation with Bob Ellicott, a former minister responsible for sport, acting as mediator. "Ellicott ultimately found that, although it was clear that Vinnicombe had taken steroids, the sanctions imposed on him were invalid because the strict ASDA procedures for doping control had not been followed".[4] Bearing in mind that this incident took place only three years after a major overhaul of the doping control procedures in the wake of the AIS scandal, it demonstrates the

1. Council of Europe and European Union, "Clean Sport Guide", 1995, section B, module 8, p. 3.
2. De Pencier, J., "Law and Athlete Drug Testing in Canada", *Marquette Sports Law Journal*, Vol. 4.2, 1994, p. 295.
3. Ibid., p. 296.
4. Ibid., p. 296.

difficulty of ensuring that the regulations governing drug testing are water-tight and fulfil the purpose for which they were drafted.

The final case concerns the large number of positive tests for nandrolone in 1998 and 1999, seventeen alone in 1999, in the UK and the response of UK Athletics, the domestic track and field governing body. In a number of cases, including those concerned with Linford Christie and Dougie Walker, the domestic governing body decided to exonerate both athletes. Given that the predecessor of UK Athletics, the British Athletics Federation, had been involved in a costly and bruising court battle with the athlete Diane Modahl, which had been partly responsible for its bankruptcy, there was understandable caution within UK Athletics in risking further legal challenges. However, the decision by UK Athletics was rejected by the IAAF, which imposed a ban on both athletes and suggested that the UK governing body along with one or two more in other European countries was avoiding its responsibilities in relation to doping. This case not only draws attention to the apprehension of many domestic governing bodies in relation to doping, but also to the more substantial problem of ensuring consistency in the treatment of positive test results between domestic federations and their parent international federation.

The level of inconsistency reflected in these four cases has serious consequences for anti-doping policy. First, it increases the risk of costly litigation not only from the innocent but also from the guilty who appear increasingly willing to initiate legal proceedings to defend their income if not their innocence. Second, and clearly linked to the first consequence, is the heightened level of nervousness among governing bodies resulting in a welcome enhancement in attention to the detail of the testing procedures, but also in a reluctance to take action against athletes suspected of a doping infraction. The readiness of athletes to seek damages against governing bodies and federations and the financial weakness of most sports organisations provides added urgency for the achievement of harmonisation. Without greater harmonisation there is a risk that doping policy will atrophy as the evident tentativeness among sports authorities gives way to a paralysis based on fear of making decisions vulnerable to legal challenge.

Third, just as there is the risk that the current level of inconsistency may lead to a decline in morale among anti-doping authorities, there is also the danger that athletes will lose confidence in anti-doping policies and procedures. Whereas athletes should be at the heart of discussions regarding anti-doping policy, it has often been the case that they are relegated to the margins of policy debates to an extent that they feel that little sense of ownership of the policy and a growing sense of alienation.[1] Fourth, the lack of harmonisation, particularly regarding the announcement of doping positives by domestic

---

1. PMP Consultancy report to the European Union, "The Effects of Doping on Young Sports-people", Manchester: PMP Consultancy, 2001.

governing bodies and the treatment of positive results, may well encourage those considering using drugs to decide that the risk is worth taking especially if their domestic governing body has demonstrated a lack of enthusiasm for the policy in the past. Finally, the lack of consistency in the treatment of positive test results undermines public confidence in anti-doping policy and fuels the suspicion that anti-doping efforts are at best half-hearted and at worst purely cosmetic.

If WADA is to make progress towards closer harmonisation, it will need to draw heavily on the resources and support of national and international governing bodies of sport and governments. The engagement of governments with the issue of doping is not just part of the general trend towards greater government intervention in sport in modern society, it is also a consequence of the current character of the issue of doping involving, as it does, the use of many substances that are already illegal or else tightly regulated and the maintenance of the often delicate balance between an athlete's rights and his or her responsibilities. It is therefore not surprising that the impetus for harmonisation can be traced to two sources, one within governmental organisations and the other among sports organisations. Governmental efforts to improve harmonisation have centred for a number of years on the activity of the Council of Europe, while the IOC has been the focus for discussions among the international federations.

The international response to doping and the Council of Europe

In general, the division of function that has emerged in recent years between federations and governments is that the former are responsible for determining, among other things, the list of banned substances and practices, selecting athletes for testing, the penalties for doping infractions and the management of disciplinary and appeals systems. In some countries, federations also have responsibility for determining the number of tests and the balance between in-competition and out-of-competition testing, but in others these responsibilities rest with government. Governments tend to take responsibility for funding the testing regime and providing a legal context for the prohibition of certain drugs. In addition, governments are often heavily involved in underwriting the cost of research into anti-doping methods, providing training for sampling officers and providing elements of the administrative infrastructure for doping control. Broadly speaking, governments provide important elements of the administrative, financial and legal framework within which the anti-doping policies of the federations and domestic governing bodies function.

The growth in concern with policy harmonisation is best indicated by the marked growth, over the last ten years or so, in the involvement of governments in international discussions regarding doping. Governments have played a significant role as initiators of international forums, and multilateral and bi-lateral links which provide opportunities for the discussion and monitoring of anti-doping policy. The Council of Europe is the primary example, although the EU and, more recently, the International Intergovernmental Consultative Group on Anti-Doping in Sport (IICGADS) provide further arenas for information exchange and policy debate. In addition to these permanent forums, a number of governments, usually through their anti-doping agency, have entered into bi-lateral agreements often involving the sharing of expertise, research, training of personnel and testing of partner countries' athletes. The bi-lateral agreement between Australia and China is a good example of an agreement designed to pool expertise and research, and to develop training programmes in doping control. Similar bi-lateral agreements exist between Norway and China, France and Germany, Canada and Cuba and also between Canada and France. The Nordic Anti-Doping Agreement links a range of northern European countries including Denmark, Iceland, Finland, Sweden and Norway and provides not only for the testing of signatories' athletes, but also the sharing of expertise and research. Furthermore, the Nordic group of countries is committed to the harmonisation of rules and penalties as well as common action to limit the availability of drugs. The Nordic agreement was opened for accession in 1996 with Germany being one of the first countries to be invited to accede. The more recent Baltic Anti-Doping Agreement is intended to fulfil a broadly similar function within its region. Since 1989 there has been a series of Permanent World Conferences on Doping providing an opportunity largely for government anti-doping agencies and specialist groups such as scientists and doctors to exchange information, but also involving representatives from sports organisations.

Finally, there is a group of countries that subscribe to the International Anti-Doping Agreement (formerly the Memorandum of Understanding Group) which shares similar objectives to the Nordic group, namely the mutual testing of members' athletes, shared research and progress on harmonisation. The membership of the group currently includes Australia, Canada, New Zealand, Norway, Sweden and the United Kingdom. France was a member until recently. The primary focus of the efforts of the group is on harmonisation and specifically the need to agree objective quality standards as a secure basis for mutual trust and confidence building. To this end, a four-year plan (adopted in 1995) was agreed which aimed to "ensure the development and harmonisation of the domestic programmes of the signatories and thus by example of good practice, positively influence the international sporting community". The main vehicle for achieving this aim was through the development of a set of protocols for the doping control process which met the thresholds for such standards set by the International Standards Organisation (ISO). The intention of the group was to produce a quality manual that covered all the major stages of the doping control process from the selection and notification of athletes for doping control through sample analysis to hearings, sanctions and appeals. The value of ISO standards as a basis for further harmonisation is explored more fully in the next chapter.

While it is true that many intergovernmental agreements can be a substitute for action or are initiated because of broader diplomatic imperatives, the pattern of agreements that now exist, with the Council of Europe's Anti-Doping Convention at its heart, provides an important element of the policy framework on which WADA, in particular, can build. Forty-four states have signed the Council of Europe convention, of which all but five have ratified the convention and brought it into force (see Appendix C). Interestingly, the Council deliberately and unusually left the word "European" out of the title of the convention in order to make it clear that there was no geographical restriction and in the hope that the convention would become a global standard.

The driving force behind the implementation of the convention has been the Anti-Doping Convention Monitoring Group which meets twice a year and operates through a series of working parties responsible for science, education and information, legislative measures and, finally, technical co-operation. Some of the recent topics and projects undertaken by the working groups are tightly focused on current problems such as the development of standard procedures for blood sampling, the interpretation of testosterone epitestosterone ratios, compliance with the convention and the applicability of the convention to the non-sports use of prohibited substances. Other topics are much more broadly focused on issues associated with harmonisation and include the development of an education and information folder "The Clean Sports Guide", which provides guidance on best practices in doping control and the sanctions that should be taken with regard to an athlete's entourage following a doping infraction. However, even where the working parties are dealing with tightly focused issues, they function within the context of three overlapping and dominant concerns of the monitoring group, namely harmonisation, information dissemination and organisational networking.

At the first meeting of the monitoring group, it was agreed that each contracting partner and observer would provide an annual report on domestic developments in anti-doping policy. The exchange of information through the system of annual reports and the establishment of a database have identified many of the issues that have become subjects for working group discussion. If the exchange of information is one obvious prerequisite for harmonisation then another is the construction of an effective interorganisational network for the dissemination of information and the discussion of policy. The greatest success of the monitoring group has been in consolidating membership within the new post-communist Europe and in extending contacts beyond Europe. Among the most recent signatories to the Anti-Doping Convention are a number of countries of central and eastern Europe including Croatia, the Czech Republic, Estonia, Latvia and the Russian Federation. Both Australia and Canada have ratified the convention and a range of other countries including the United States, Peru and Brazil, South Africa, New

Zealand and, most recently, China and Japan have participated in the discussions of the monitoring group.

The monitoring group has also been relatively successful in building links with a number of key governmental bodies including Unesco, the World Health Organisation, the European Union and the International Intergovernmental Consultative Group on Anti-Doping in Sport, with the last two being of especial importance. The Council of Europe has generally a co-operative relationship with the European Union. In 1991, when the European Union meeting of health ministers proposed a code of conduct relating to doping, an invitation to participate in discussions was extended by the EU to the monitoring group. In general, the discussions of European Union Ministers for Sport are fairly closely informed of the work of the Council of Europe on sports matters. However, this does not prevent occasions when there has been the risk of duplication of work as in 1994 when the European Parliament passed a resolution on doping and sport which, if implemented in full, would have overlapped substantially with the Council's convention. More recently, the Council and the European Union have co-operated closely on the production of the education and training pack, "The Clean Sports Guide", for distribution among federations and domestic governing bodies. The relationship between the Council and IICGADS is much more recent, but the early signs are that the relationship is proving to be mutually supportive. The consultative group was able to draw on the experience of the Council when addressing the many practical problems that arise in managing a global intergovernmental organisation. Not surprisingly, the Council was closely involved with the formation of IICGADS and with the establishment of WADA.

Where the group has been less successful is in bringing sports organisations such as the IOC and the major federations into the network. The involvement of the IOC has been generally consistent and its representatives have on occasions made significant contributions to the work of the group. However, the committee seemed to be content to provide encouragement for the work of the Council of Europe and to maintain a watching brief on the activities of the monitoring group rather than acknowledge the Council as the primary policy-making forum and thereby sacrifice its own claims to policy leadership. A similar relationship existed between the international federations and the monitoring group. Although there is a clear awareness on the part of the governmental representatives and on the part of those from the federations that they share many fundamental concerns and objectives, there is also an acute wariness felt by the federations that control over their sports may be irretrievably undermined if policy leadership on anti-doping is ceded too readily to governments. For example, some federations were, and indeed still are, unhappy with national anti-doping authorities carrying out drug tests at federation competitions without consultation, and argue that this was interference in their sphere of responsibility and that they would not consider themselves bound by the outcome of any result from a national anti-doping agency. One of the federations representing a major team sport expressed a reluctance to take a greater responsibility for the conduct of out-of-competition testing, arguing that the workload would be too great. Given that the sport was one of the more affluent this was a surprising and worrying claim, but one that reflected the growing tensions within an increasingly commercialised sport where leagues, clubs, players and their domestic governing bodies are jockeying for control over the sport.

A different, but equally significant, objection to harmonisation was expressed by the representative of another major sport who, in response to a challenge that the federation had not yet subscribed to the 1994 Lausanne Agreement with the IOC concerning harmonisation, argued that it wished to retain its own schedule of sanctions which are generally lighter than those supported by the IOC, partly on the grounds that heavy sanctions breached the convicted athlete's "right to work". Although the record of this second federation in developing and implementing an anti-doping strategy is stronger than that of the federation referred to in the first example, both federations share a common concern to protect their autonomy, not just in relation to perceived encroachment by governments and governmental organisations such as the Council of Europe, but also in relation to other sports bodies such as the IOC. It took the dramatic events at the 1998 Tour de France and the risk of being marginalised from future policy discussions that prompted the international federations and the IOC to accept that they had little option but to co-operate with public authorities through WADA.

The response to doping from international sports organisations

Contact between the two sets of interests has generally been limited and characterised on the part of governments by a degree of scepticism about the level of commitment to anti-doping among federations, and a corresponding wariness on the part of sports federations that governments were seeking to undermine their control over their sports. The reluctance among key sports federations and organising bodies such as the IOC to become too closely integrated into the agenda of the Council of Europe and other governmental bodies was paralleled by a degree of mutual suspicion among federations which made interfederation co-operation, at times, difficult to achieve. The failure of the IOC and the major federations to engage in debate with public authorities or even to work closely with each other on doping issues was the product of a series of deeply rooted tensions. Many federations considered, with substantial justification, that many governments of leading "sporting powers" were not to be trusted, that they bore much of the responsibility for stimulating doping and undermining the early anti-doping efforts of the IOC and the major federations, and that their motives for their current enthusiasm for drug-free sport were unclear. However, there were also significant tensions between federations due to increasing competition for talented sportspeople, sponsorship, government support, and television revenue as well as a much more serious division between the federations, on the one hand, and the IOC, on the other. In 1997, the IAAF, for example, made it clear that it did not intend to recognise the Court of Arbitration for Sport in Lausanne as superior to its own arbitration panel. Furthermore, the IAAF's Secretary General, Istvan Gyulai, expressed fundamental reservations about IOC claims to anti-doping policy leadership arguing that "The IOC acts like a world government, but we do not want to be dominated in this way".[1] In addition, there is frequently tension within the Olympic movement over the division of sponsorship and television income arising from the Olympic Games.

Aware of the risk of losing the initiative in the formation of anti-doping policy, the IOC and the major federations made a belated attempt to address the issue of harmonisation. However, by the late 1990s progress had been limited. In 1995, the Council of Europe published an evaluation of the status of harmonisation among the federations[2] based on the collection of data by the British Sports Council's Doping Control Unit.[3] The conclusion of the report, prepared by Emile Vrijman, the then Dutch representative in the Council's Monitoring Group, drew attention to a catalogue of weaknesses in the anti-doping rules of the major sports and highlighted the lack of harmonisation in a number of important areas of policy.

There were a number of attempts, mainly in the mid to late 1980s, to achieve greater harmonisation of anti-doping rules among the federations, and between the federations and the IOC. One such attempt was in January 1994 when a meeting, which included the IOC along with the organisations representing the Summer and Winter Olympic Federations, decided to "unify their respective anti-doping rules and procedures".[4] Vrijman's review was indeed timely as it was based on the anti-doping rules in force in 1993 and consequently provided a clear indication of the scale of challenge facing the IOC. Vrijman analysed the anti-doping rules of fifty-four international federations paying especial attention to their rules regarding the definition of doping; the list of banned drugs and methods of doping, forms of doping control; laboratory arrangements; penalties; recognition of sanctions imposed by other sports bodies; the right to a hearing; and the treatment of minor procedural mistakes. Apart from assessing the extent of harmonisation between the rules of the federations when compared to the anti-doping rules of the IOC, Vrijman's analysis was also concerned with assessing the extent to which federation rules were secure from legal challenge. In 1997, the UK Sports Council's Ethics and Anti-Doping Directorate published the third edition of its survey of current anti-doping regulations therefore providing

---

1. Quoted in *Sport Intern*, Vol. 29.11, 30 June 1997, p. 6.
2. Vrijman, E.N., "Harmonisation: Can it Ever Really be Achieved?", Strasbourg: Council of Europe, 1995.
3. Doping Control Unit, United Kingdom Sports Council, *Directory of Anti-Doping Regulations of International Sports Federations*, 2nd edn., London: UK Sports Council, 1993.
4. Ibid., p. 5.

useful data on the progress that has been made in the three years since the Lausanne Agreement.[1] More recently, in 1999, an analysis of anti-doping regulations was undertaken by the TMC Asser Instituut, which provides a further point of comparison.[2]

As should be evident from the discussion of definitions of doping in Chapters 5 and 6 there is no easy, let alone legally secure, answer to the question "What is doping in sport?". Charles Dubin argued that a definition was "impossible to achieve"[3] and quoted approvingly Arthur Gold's comment that "to define doping is, if not impossible, at best extremely difficult, and yet everyone who takes part in competitive sport or who administers it knows exactly what it means. The definition lies not in words but in integrity of character".[4] While many would sympathise with the sentiments expressed by Dubin and Gold a workable definition of doping is essential given the accelerating rate of legal challenge to the decisions of federations on doping infractions. "Integrity of character" provides the moral basis for the anti-doping policy but it is the words used to express that morality that will be scrutinised by lawyers. The importance of a clearly worded definition was reinforced by the judge who heard the case brought by Sandra Gasser against the IAAF, in which she challenged their definition of doping as one of strict liability. The judge defended the IAAF definition and referred approvingly to the IAAF representative's concern that "if a defence of moral innocence were open, the floodgates would be opened and the IAAF's attempts to prevent drug taking by athletes would be rendered futile".[5] Mark Gay, in a presentation to the 4th Permanent World Conference on Anti-Doping in Sport, provided ample support for a definition based on strict liability by demonstrating the flaws in a wide range of definitions that were based on criteria such as "intent" and "use in competition" rather than being based on the simple presence of banned substances in the urine or blood sample.[6]

---

1. Ethics and Anti-Doping Directorate, United Kingdom Sports Council, *Directory of Anti-Doping Regulations of International Sports Federations*, 3rd edn., London: UK Sports Council, 1997.
2. Siekmann, R.R.C, Soek, J. & Bellani, A. (eds.), *Doping Rules of International Sports Organisations*, The Hague: TMC Asser/Kluwer, 1999.
3. Dubin Inquiry, 1990, op. cit., p. 77.
4. Quoted in Dubin Inquiry, 1990, op. cit., p. 78.
5. Gay, M., "Constitutional Aspects of Testing for Prohibited Substances, London: unpublished paper, no date.
6. A definition based on "strict liability" would mean that a doping offence had been committed if a prohibited substance is present in an athlete's urine sample irrespective of whether the drug was taken knowingly or whether the drug was capable of enhancing performance. The IAAF definition of doping is as follows: "The offence of doping takes place when either (i) a prohibited substance is found to be present within an athlete's body tissue or fluids; or (ii) an athlete uses or takes advantage of a prohibited technique; or (iii) an athlete admits having used or taken advantage of a prohibited substance or prohibited technique" (*IAAF Handbook*, 1992-93, Rule 55). According to Wise, the "strict liability" definition means that an athlete can be found guilty of a doping infraction "without the sports governing body proving culpable intent, knowledge or fault; or without the athlete being allowed to prove he or she was faultless" (Wise, A.N., "'Strict liability' Drug Rules of Sports Governing Bodies, *New Law Journal*, 2 August 1996, p. 1 161).

Vrijman reports Gay's advice that all federations should make doping an offence not dependent on proving an intention to cheat but rather based on strict liability. The IAAF is one of a small but growing number of federations that have adopted a "strict liability" definition. Writing in 1995 and using the IAAF definition as the benchmark, Vrijman reviewed the definitions of thirty-three other federations and found, first, that all of them had definitions that were potentially vulnerable to legal challenge and, second, that there was very little uniformity between sports. Many sports such as squash and badminton did not provide a definition of doping, while others included a sentence in their rules that associated them with the IOC rules on doping. Of those that did provide a definition many were unclear and confused and, as mentioned earlier, vulnerable to legal challenge. By 1999, there has been some progress in amending anti-doping rules to make them less vulnerable to legal challenge. Seven federations, including those for gymnastics and ice hockey, had adopted definitions similar to that used by the IAAF, but the vast majority have left their definitions unrevised.

Despite the case quoted by Gay, there is some doubt regarding the value of a "strict liability" definition particularly in the United States. In 1995, the swimmer Jessica Foschi tested positive for the anabolic steroid mesterolone and was penalised under the rules of the international federation (FINA). She appealed against the penalty to the American Arbitration Association (AAA), the body prescribed under the terms of the United States Amateur Sports Act 1978. The AAA was emphatic in its rejection of the FINA decision and the application of the concept of "strict liability". The arbitrators argued that "Having concluded that the claimant and all those connected with her are innocent and without fault, we unanimously conclude that the imposition of any sanction on the claimant so offends our deeply rooted and historical concepts of fundamental fairness so as to be arbitrary and capricious".[1] Similar rejections of the concept of strict liability have been provided by the Swiss courts and the Legal Committee of the German track and field federation with the latter arguing that "the maxim *nulla poena sine culpa* [no penalty without fault] has the status of a constitutional principle since the principle of the State Rechtsstaatlichkeit is infringed, the corresponding provision in that case is grossly unfair and thus unenforceable".[2] "Strict liability" may well be the preferred definition in terms of security from legal challenge, but is clearly not without problems.

Vrijman found greater consistency regarding the adoption of a common list of banned substances and practices. Most federations have adopted the IOC list, although eight out of thirty-eight had adopted a specific, earlier list rather than the current list. Where there are variations they tend to be relatively minor modifications of the IOC list and often involve the specification

1. Ibid., p. 1 161.
2. Ibid., p. 1 162.

of additional drugs that have a particular relevance to their sport. For example, the motor sport federation, FISA (Fédération internationale du Sport automobile), adds alcohol and marijuana to the IOC list of banned substances. In contrast, the federation responsible for basketball, FIBA (Fédération internationale de Basketball amateur), varies the IOC list by allowing the use of beta blockers. The results suggest that there is a minority of federations that are examining the IOC list and making minor modifications to ensure that it is appropriate to the specific requirements of their sport.

Between 1993 and 1999, there had been significant movement towards greater uniformity around the IOC list. Of the twenty-nine sports surveyed in 1999, all but one had adopted the current IOC list. However, as Vrijman observed, "it should be noted that it took the IFs almost five years to achieve an almost 100% degree of harmonisation on a limited technical issue".[1] Moreover, it is unclear whether the increasing standardisation of anti-doping regulations around the IOC list represents a recognition of the universal applicability of the list or simply reflects a convenient response by federations seeking to shelter under the authority of the IOC irrespective of the appropriateness of the list to their sport.

Much the same can be said for the relative uniformity among federations in their use of IOC-accredited laboratories for the analysis of samples. The fact that an increasing majority of federations use IOC-accredited laboratories provides little evidence of the extent of commitment to anti-doping policy. Agreeing to have samples analysed by IOC-accredited laboratories imposes few significant obligations. What matters more is the commitment to carry out a sufficient number of tests to make the analysis worthwhile.

One of the most pronounced trends in recent years has been the extension of testing into the out-of-competition period. Begun in the mid-1980s and given a boost as a result of the Ben Johnson case, the extension of out-of-competition testing was a priority of the signatories to the Lausanne Agreement. At the time of the second survey of anti-doping regulations in 1993, only sixteen out of fifty-four sports operated both in-competition and out-of-competition testing indicating the scale of the problem that the supporters of the Lausanne Agreement faced. Moreover, some thirty-eight federations would have needed to change their rules in order to introduce out-of-competition testing. By the time of the third survey in 1997, there had been a significant increase, from sixteen to twenty-five, in the number of federations undertaking in- and out-of-competition testing. Among the sports that had changed their rules were netball, squash, tae kwon do and cycling. However, it needs to be borne in mind that the balance between in- and out-of-competition testing will, of necessity, vary between sports with

---

1. Vrijman, E. N., "Harmonisation: A Bridge Too Far? A Commentary on Current Issues and Problems" in O'Leary, J. (ed.), *Drugs and Doping in Sport: Socio-Legal Perspectives*, London: Cavendish, 2001, p. 154.

199

some sports with a very long season, such as soccer, understandably being less convinced of the value of out-of-competition tests. This still leaves a large number of sports, such as triathlon, wrestling and bobsleigh, which have a closed season and which are comparable to those sports where steroid use is well known. In relation to the balance between in- and out-of-competition testing, one would need to apply a more subtle measure of harmonisation than mere uniformity. Unfortunately, a significant proportion of federations are still some way from harmonisation on this aspect of policy. Vrijman found that, in 1999, only twelve of the twenty-nine international federations surveyed had rules which allowed out-of-competition testing.[1]

Many similar points may be made regarding the basis on which athletes are selected for testing and the number of athletes that are selected for testing. On the one hand, given the individual characteristics of each sport one should not expect uniformity: on the other hand, an analysis of the regulations of the federations suggests that while most sports have a selection process that is derived (albeit loosely in some cases) from the character of the sport some appear arbitrary. The two most common procedures for the selection of athletes to be tested are either by lot or on the basis of finishing position. Generally, selection by lot is used in team games (soccer, rugby league and volleyball) and selection on the basis of finishing position is used in individual sports (triathlon, mountaineering and fencing). Other criteria for identifying athletes for tests include world record breakers (swimming), and those athletes whose behaviour has aroused suspicion (motor sports). The weakness in the testing policy of many federations is most evident in relation to the number of tests conducted with many sports, including ice hockey, tae kwon do, yachting and university sports, leaving it to officials at competitions to determine the details of selection for testing. What is particularly interesting to debate is what would be the appropriate criteria for determining whether harmonisation had been achieved with regard to the selection of athletes. Again, uniformity would be inappropriate but the importance of identifying a set of criteria by which sports as diverse as soccer, tennis and motor racing can be judged is a significant challenge and one that the federations seem far from accepting.

One of the most difficult and sensitive aspects of policy harmonisation concerns the sanctions imposed following a doping infraction. As part of the Lausanne Agreement, federations were exhorted to make rapid progress towards the adoption of an agreed set of minimum sanctions for doping infractions, but progress has been extremely slow. Vrijman noted that the IOC established a benchmark for penalties in the late 1980s, suggesting that the penalty for a serious violation of doping rules (anabolic steroids, amphetamines, etc.) should be a two-year ban for a first offence and a life ban for a second offence. For less serious doping infractions, involving ephedrine or

---

1. See footnote 1, p. 199 *ante*. Ibid.

codeine for example, the IOC recommended a maximum ban of three months for a first offence, two years for a second and a life ban for a third offence. The strong lead given by the IOC did little to stimulate a consistent approach to sanctions with a number of federations maintaining lighter penalties and some federations, such as the IAAF in 1991 following the Ben Johnson case, establishing a harsher penalty of four years for a serious doping infraction. The hawkish stance of the IAAF has, however, proved extremely difficult to sustain with resistance coming from a number of domestic affiliates of the federation and from the legal systems of a small number of major athletic countries including Germany and Russia.[1] The difficulty of establishing the initial penalty of four years led the IAAF, in mid-1997, to retreat to a two-year initial ban for steroid use.

On the basis of data available in 1993, Vrijman compared current sanctions with the IOC recommendation and concluded that "Only 12 of [the federations] have incorporated the IOC recommended sanctions, while at the same time 11 international sports governing bodies don't seem to apply any sanctions at all! The remaining 31 international sports governing bodies have sanctions different from the IOC recommended ones".[2] According to the 1997 survey, the number incorporating the IOC sanctions (or at least very close versions of them) into their rules had risen substantially from twelve to twenty-one but still leaving the majority of major federations with sets of sanctions that differed from the IOC benchmark or else no sanctions at all. It would be reassuring to establish that the cause of the variation from the IOC standard is due to federations tailoring penalties to suit the particular character and attributes of their sport. To an extent, there is evidence to suggest that this is the case. Some federations, such as body building, have harsher penalties, others highlight particular drugs for severe sanctions, such as motor sports with alcohol, and still others have relatively minor variations on the IOC standard. In general, it is a relatively small number of sports that give an impression of neglect or disdain towards the issue. However, the lack of commitment by some federations prompted IOC President Samaranch to raise the issue at the opening of the IOC session prior to the start of 1998 Nagano Winter Olympic Games. He drew attention to the failure of some federations to establish effective out-of-competition testing programmes and appropriately severe sanctions for those guilty of doping infractions.[3]

While it would appear that an increasing number of federations are adopting the IOC set of sanctions, there has been far less progress in persuading

---

1. Not all legal challenges to the IAAF four-year ban have been overturned by national courts. In Britain in 1995, Paul Edwards argued that a four-year ban imposed in 1994 for testing positive for steroids should be reduced to two years on the grounds that there were countries where a two-year ban was the maximum allowed and the action of the IAAF was consequently discriminatory. The challenge was rejected with the judge concluding that not only was the four-year ban reasonable but also that the action of the federation was not discriminatory (*The Times*, law report, 30 June 1995).
2. Vrijman, op. cit., p. 29.
3. Reuters news report 2 February 1998.

federations to recognise the sanctions imposed by other federations. The purpose of such mutual recognition of sanctions is to prevent an athlete banned from participating in one sport simply moving to another sport. In 1993, only five out of fifty-four federations recognised the sanctions imposed by others and even those five did not recognise the sanctions imposed by government anti-doping agencies; by 1999, the figures were still low having risen to only ten out of twenty-nine federations.

For those federations that have adopted effective testing regimes and adhere to a set of sanctions, it is increasingly important that they also acknowledge the imperatives of natural justice in policy implementation. One central requirement of any set of anti-doping rules is not simply that the analysis of the urine sample is reliable but that the investigation of the allegation of doping be fair and particularly that the athlete has a right to a hearing. Gay acknowledges that many may conclude that if "the offence of doping is constituted merely by the detection of the presence of a prohibited substance in the urine of an athlete and that prohibited substance has been detected by an accredited laboratory, then there is little point in having a hearing".[1] Gay emphasises that this is a seriously mistaken and dangerous view and argues that "no matter how futile it may seem, every athlete must be given the right, enshrined in the constitution of the governing body, to have the opportunity of a hearing before any final decision is taken as to whether any disciplinary sanctions should be imposed upon that athlete".[2] Vrijman found that in 1995 only fourteen international federations studied did include the right to a hearing in their respective anti-doping rules and regulations, although by 1999 the figure had risen to twenty-one out of twenty-nine.[3]

Conclusion

Policy harmonisation is never easy to achieve. When harmonisation involves such a wide range of governmental and private interests, the challenge that harmonisation presents is formidable indeed. Given that the international anti-doping effort depends so heavily on standardisation of practices and close co-operation between agencies, it is not surprising that harmonisation has been endorsed by WADA as the central priority within the policy area. Over the last ten years, much has been achieved, particularly as regards the technical aspects of anti-doping procedures. The list of banned substances and practices, the procedures by which samples are collected and analysed, the penalties applied for doping infractions and the basis on which appeals can be made are becoming increasingly comparable across a broad range of Olympic and non-Olympic sports and across a broad range of countries. The effect of this trend has been such that international federations that do not conform to these standards feel obliged to justify their distinctive position.

1. Gay, op. cit., p. 5.
2. Ibid., p. 6.
3. Vrijman, 2001, op. cit.

Growing technical uniformity in anti-doping policy is balanced by a much greater degree of variation in the broader implementation of policy. Agreement on substances to be tested for, the training of sampling officers and the accreditation of laboratories has proved much easier to achieve than agreement on the number of athletes to be tested, the frequency of testing and the action to be taken following a positive test result. It is also possible to argue that the progress towards harmonisation has been attained at the expense of the autonomy of sports organisations. It is significant that the strengthening of the international anti-doping policy framework has relied heavily on government action. Over the last ten years, governments have fulfilled a key role in providing the organisational framework, finance and legislative powers for anti-doping initiatives. Anti-doping agencies, established by government and staffed by public officials, with access to public funds to carry out tests and research, and with a legislative basis for their activities are an increasingly common feature of the apparatus of policy implementation.

Needless to say, the problems facing governmental and sports organisations and WADA in implementing an effective anti-doping policy are formidable. Not least of which is the long-standing mutual suspicion between the IOC, the federations and governmental bodies. Other problems include the fragmentation within sport between, for example, commercial and non-commercial sport, and between Olympic and non-Olympic sport; the difficulty of establishing criteria by which an acceptable level of harmonisation may be recognised; and the process by which compliance with established standards may be monitored. These questions and the general prospects for the campaign against doping in sport are examined in the chapter that follows.

Chapter 8

The future of anti-doping policy: issues and challenges

Anti-doping policy is at one of its regular watersheds. It is as though the individuals and organisations involved in the campaign against doping embarked on a sprint only to be told that the race has now become a marathon. Over the last twenty-five years, and especially over the last ten years, there has been substantial progress towards the development of a global anti-doping policy, but each refinement in policy has been accompanied by a sharper insight into the issues and aspects of policy that remain unresolved. There is an unfortunate number of examples of the identification of a problem which prompts a period of enthusiastic debate and policy-making, but which slows considerably when the analysis of the problem leads to a greater awareness of the complexity of the issue or the cost of resources required for its resolution. Initial enthusiasm is dissipated, and energy and commitment are sapped creating a situation where, at worst, problems are quietly dropped and attention is given to other more amenable issues.

The initial burst of activity on the issue of doping in sport in the 1970s resulted in a number of important policy developments within a broad range of sports and at major sporting events such as the Olympic Games. Among the most significant developments were the establishment of medical committees across a range of sports, the investment in research to develop testing methods for drugs such as amphetamine, the training of sampling officers, and the effective organisation of drug testing at major sports events all of which are examples of the achievements of the early enthusiasm to deal effectively with drug abuse in sport. As the previous chapter showed, the energy and commitment of the 1980s and 1990s has produced many of the necessary technical requirements for the successful implementation of policy. The widespread acceptance of the IOC list of banned substances and practices, the systematic training of sampling officers, the high level of standardisation of sample collection methods, the increasingly routine use of IOC-accredited laboratories for sample analysis and the widespread adoption of the IOC-recommended sanctions for doping infractions are all illustrations of the progress in the elaboration of a global anti-doping strategy.

The recent establishment of WADA would appear to be further evidence of the steady progress towards a comprehensive global anti-doping policy. While neither the significance of the decision to form WADA nor the potential of the agency to maintain the policy momentum so evident at the Sydney Olympic Games should be underestimated the challenges that remain should not be dismissed lightly. Some of the challenges are technical and others are financial, while some are more abstract and concern the maintenance of commitment. Starkly, it may well be possible to perfect a series of effective tests for the current crop of new drugs, it may also be possible to establish publicly verifiable quality standards for the sampling and analysis process, and it may be possible to reach a consensus on a scale of penalties for particular doping infractions, but these achievements will count for little if there is not a harmonisation of commitment to tackle the problem of drug abuse by athletes. In other words alongside the technical questions is a parallel set of questions concerning the values, beliefs and attitudes that are necessary to ensure the maintenance of momentum for implementation. The depth of support for the anti-doping effort among sports organisations and governments is regrettably matched by an equal depth of equivocation and, at times, duplicity among some federations and a diminishing, but still significant, number of governments. There is an abundance of evidence that many domestic governing bodies, international federations and governments maintained, during the 1980s in particular, a public commitment to the anti-doping campaign while either simply refusing to enquire too deeply into practices within their own sports or countries or conspiring to subvert the anti-doping strategy of the IOC and the federations.[1]

The first part of this chapter examines some of the current challenges facing the sports community in sustaining the anti-doping campaign, namely the need to know more about the drug users, the threats posed by the rising number of legal challenges to positive test results, the value of ISO Standards in facilitating closer harmonisation of doping control procedures, harmonisation of penalties and tensions arising from the overlapping jurisdiction of anti-doping agencies. The second part of the chapter discusses the potential contribution of WADA and the prospects for maintaining the political momentum required to improve upon the present level of success.

Understanding drug use and the role of education

It is a truism that policy-making should be informed by an understanding, based on research, of the nature of the problem to be addressed. While there has been a considerable investment in researching the problem of drug abuse, it has been skewed heavily in favour of scientific research directed towards the specification of the ergogenic properties of particular drugs and the development of methods for identifying the presence of prohibited drugs in the athlete's system. This emphasis on the scientific aspects of the problem is understandable but underscores the relative paucity of understanding of the psychological and social aspects of drug use. Thus, although it is possible to answer questions with reasonable confidence about the effects of particular drugs on an athlete's performance and the reliability of the tests designed

---

1. See Houlihan, 1997, op. cit., for an overview, but see also Government of Australia, 1989, op. cit.; Government of Australia, "Drugs in Sport", Second Report of the Senate Standing Committee on the Environment, Recreation and the Arts, Canberra: Australian Government Publishing Service, 1989a; Dubin Inquiry, 1990, op. cit.; Voy, 1991, op. cit.; Simson, V. & Jennings, A., The Lords of the Rings, London: Simon and Schuster, 1992; and Jennings, 1996, op. cit.

to detect drugs, it is far more difficult to answer the question why athletes take drugs. Evidence about the motives of athletes is generally anecdotal and offers little beyond the bland assertion that athletes take drugs in order to improve their chances of winning. We know relatively little about how athletes start taking drugs, who introduces them to drugs, and how drug use varies by sport, age, gender or country. We also have at best sparse information about when athletes stop taking drugs, and the drug-taking patterns and motivations in non-élite sport and in fringe sporting activities such as body building. Finally, we know little about the level of knowledge of drug abusers about the drugs they take or how they acquire that information.

It would be unfair to suggest that there has been an overemphasis on the detection and punishment of drug use at the expense of the prevention of the onset of drug use, although it would be fair to argue that it is only comparatively recently that anti-doping agencies have recognised the importance of the provision of information and education as potentially valuable tools in responding to the problem. Over the last eight years or so, there has been a much greater investment in the production of information packs and also educational material accompanied by a shift in emphasis in this material away from reliance on appeals to the sense of fair play of athletes to an emphasis on providing information about the serious health risks associated with drug abuse. National anti-doping agencies are gradually accumulating more information about athletes' attitudes towards doping, their knowledge of anti-doping procedures and their experience of doping, although the depth of understanding of athletes' attitudes towards doping is still limited. One of the best examples of increasing sophistication in the understanding of the social context of drug use is the research carried out by the Australian Sports Drug Agency (ASDA). ASDA has conducted a series of surveys of athletes and of coaches designed to gather data, for example, about the level of knowledge about drugs, the perceived effectiveness of the current anti-doping programme, the extent to which coaches are involved in anti-doping activity, and where athletes and coaches obtain their information about drugs. On the basis of these data, ASDA has been able to refine and target more precisely its educational programme.

Although education is slowly being accepted as a key aspect of an anti-doping strategy, it is surprising how little attention has been paid to the evaluations of similar approaches in the field of recreational drug use. There is a wealth of evidence that suggests that:

- anti-drugs education needs to start young;[1]

1. See, for example, McBride, N. et al., "Early Results from a School Alcohol Harm Minimiztion Study: The School Health and Alcohol Harm Reduction Project", Addiction, 95.7, 2000, pp. 1 021-42; Hurry, J. et al., "Long-Term Effects of Drug Education in Primary School", Addiction Research, 8.2, 2000, pp. 183-202; and White, D. & Pitts, M., "Educating Young People about Drugs: A Systematic Review", Addiction, 93.10, 1998, pp. 1 475-87.

- the young athlete's community needs to be involved;[1]
- media campaigns are of limited use in isolation, but can be effective in reinforcing more broadly based campaigns;[2]
- attention needs to be paid to developing the capacity of the young person to withstand peer pressure.[3]

Although there are some examples of excellent educational materials aimed at the young athlete, many international federations make little effort to design material for their young sportspeople. However, even if appropriate educational material were available the evidence from drug abuse outside sport suggests strongly that it will have only limited effect unless it is reinforced by key figures in the young person's community. For the young athlete those key figures would probably include parents, coaches and schoolteachers, and there is mixed evidence of anti-doping authorities attempting to involve these groups as part of a comprehensive anti-doping strategy.

Furthermore, there is also a need to examine more closely the stages in an athlete's career and ensure that the educational material is appropriate to their current concerns and that it is also adjusted to take account of their evolving community. Table 8.1 draws on research by PMP Consultancy which suggests that there are five clear stages in the athlete's career each of which has distinctive characteristics, especially in terms of pressures and immediate community and which consequently requires an equally distinctive and focused anti-doping campaign.

Although the profile will obviously vary from sport to sport, the value of the table is that it prompts us to consider whether existing anti-doping policies address the particular circumstance of athletes at different stages of their career and whether the focus should indeed be the athlete or his/her parents, teachers, coaches, doctor, etc.

Defining doping and the continuing threat of legal challenge

As the previous chapter made clear, the basic question of the definition of doping remains problematic. In an analysis of the current Olympic Movement Anti-Doping Code, Foster highlights the series of overlapping themes that are woven through the preamble and the definition of doping.[4] The code

---

1. See, for example, Montonen, M., "Educational Approaches", *Addiction*, 92, Supplement 1, 1997, pp. S121-5; and Holder, H.D. et al., "A Community Prevention Trial to Reduce Alcohol-Involved Accidental Injury and Death: Overview", *Addiction*, 92, Supplement 2, 1997, pp. S155-71.
2. See, for example, Holder, H.D. & Treno, A.J., "Media Advocacy in Community Prevention: News As a Means to Advance Policy Change", *Addiction*, 92, Supplement 2, 1997, pp. S189-99.
3. Goldberg, L. et al., "The Adolescents Training and Learning to Avoid Steroids (ATLAS) Prevention Program", *Archives of Pediatrics and Adolescent Medicine*, 150, 1996, pp. 713-21.
4. Foster, K., "The Discourses of Doping: Law and Regulation in the War Against Drugs" in O'Leary, 2001, op. cit.

Table 8.1 Drugs in an athlete's career

Stage	Characteristics	Implications for anti-doping policy
Foundation	• age around 8 to 16 • emphasis on basic skills acquisition and development • school and junior club important • teachers, parents and possibly junior coaches important figures	• a crucial opinion-forming stage • only limited knowledge of doping • heavy reliance on parents, teachers and junior coaches for information and positive values • **A key opportunity for influencing athlete's values**
Development	• age around 14 to 19 • talented athletes being identified • athletes specialising in one sport or team role • involved in regular training and coaching with a club • competition and championships increasingly important	• coach of increasing importance • peers an important part of the athlete's community • athlete increasingly aware of the limits of their body • heavy reliance on coaches and peers for value reinforcement • **A high-risk stage where peer values and those of the coach are crucial**
Transition	• athlete is highly specialised • may be training full time • competition a central focus of training regime • training is intensive and possibly training with élite athletes	• decline in the athlete's rate of improvement and may even reach a plateau • peers increasingly seen as rivals rather than training partners • immediate community will include coach, team/squad doctor and sports scientists • **A high-risk stage as there is often intense pressure to make the grade and enter the élite squad**
Peak	• highly skilled • focus is on optimal preparation for competition • training intensively and full time • may just be one "key" competition each year	• community is increasingly closed • intense pressure to succeed • the threat of injury is a constant concern • intense pressure not to miss the premier competition: for example, World Championships or Olympic Games • **High risk as there may be a temptation to take short cuts to ensure success or to aid recovery from injury for the one "golden opportunity"**
Decline	• moving out of the élite squad/team • aware of next generation of athletes moving through the system • competitive orientation still extremely strong	• beginning to lose contact with élite coaches and other support staff • much looser community • **Temptation to use drugs to prolong a career**

Source: PMP Consultancy, *Studies to Combat Doping in Sport, Lot 2, Final Report*, Brussels: European Commission, 2001 refers to the "duty" of the Olympic movement to protect the health of athletes, to the importance of maintaining the "ethical concepts implicit in fair play" and to the prohibited nature of doping practices thus combining themes of health, welfare, ethics and criminality. While these overlapping themes are an important part of the context for the definition of doping, the definition itself should be as concise and clear as possible.

Doping is defined in Article 2 of the code as follows:

"1 the use of an expedient (substance or method) which is potentially harmful to athletes' health and/or capable of enhancing their performance, or

2 the presence in the athlete's body of a Prohibited Substance or evidence of the use thereof or evidence of the use of a Prohibited Method."[1]

As Foster notes, "this is an extremely wide definition".[2] First, not only is the list of substances referred to a long one, it is also an open-ended list which introduces considerable uncertainty by stating that it contains "examples" and that it also covers "related substances". Second, in attempting to be comprehensive, the definition appears to suggest that "anything that improves performance can be considered to be doping and anything that harms the health of the athlete is also doping".[3] The definition reflects an uneasy, and potentially disastrous, balance between the desire for the precision of a criminal definition with a medical discourse that seeks to maintain sufficient flexibility to take account of pharmacological advances. Foster concludes that the definition has the "makings of a legal minefield".[4]

Not surprisingly, WADA has made a review of the definition of doping one of its priorities as an accepted, clear and legally defensible definition is crucial given the increasing litigiousness of athletes and the greater willingness of courts to accept jurisdiction in sports matters. In general, the courts in many countries have been disinclined to intervene in matters concerning the organisation and conduct of sport whether it involves matters of eligibility or athlete behaviour. Nevertheless, the courts have steadily (even if reluctantly) extended their involvement with sport. In part, this is the result of a broader trend in many countries to seek redress through the courts as a first course of action rather than as a last resort, but it is also the result of the rapid commercialisation of sport and the fact that there are an increasing number of athletes who stand to lose substantial earnings if their careers are interrupted through suspension. Added to these reasons is the reluctance among commercial clubs and businesses, such as television companies, to lose star players due to positive drug tests. In the previous chapter, mention was made of the recent spate of high-profile challenges to the decisions of anti-doping agencies and domestic and international federations. What is striking about

1. IOC, 1999, op. cit.
2. Foster, 2001, op. cit., p. 191.
3. Ibid., p. 191.
4. Ibid., p. 192.

recent cases is not just the number of them but the variety of bases on which legal challenges are being mounted. First, there are those, like Martin Vinnicombe, who are admitted drug takers and who avoid sanctions due to inconsistencies between the regulations of the anti-doping agencies. Second, there are those, like Katrin Krabbe, who mount successful challenges to the scale of penalty applied for the doping infraction. Thirdly, there are those, such as Diane Modahl, who having establish their innocence, have then used the courts to seek damages against the responsible sports organisation.[1] Fourth, Harry "Butch" Reynolds' successful appeal in a US district court against suspension was based on general grounds of natural justice. The court concluded that "the IAAF hearing was not conducted in good faith, was not conducted by an unbiased decision maker, was not in accordance with the IAAF's own rules and regulations, and did not accord Reynolds a full and fair opportunity to participate ..."[2] Finally, there are a large number of potential legal challenges from athletes penalised for doping infractions in the early years of the anti-doping campaign for whom the current crop of challenges provide a powerful demonstration of the possible grounds for disputing earlier decisions. For example, it was reported in 1997 that the American swimmer Rick DeMont attempted to sue the United States Olympic Committee for $12 million in connection with the USOC's decision in 1972 to strip him of his Olympic gold medal following a positive test for ephedrine, a drug contained in an asthma treatment he was using at the time.[3]

To these well-publicised cases that have reached, or are likely to reach, the courts must be added the large number of cases in which findings have been overturned by sports arbitration panels or tribunals. In 1994, in the United Kingdom, seven cases were overturned or shelved by governing bodies often due to a rejection of, or lack of confidence in, laboratory results. In the same year, there were also two cases in Austria including one where an athlete sued the international federation for loss of earnings because it had applied a four-year ban, one year longer than the domestic governing body. Similar cases, where sanctions had not been applied for doping infractions, were reported from the Netherlands, where cases have been dropped because the testosterone/epitestosterone ratios were considered "borderline", and from Norway, where a positive result was not deemed to be a doping infraction because of a lack of "intent" on the part of the athlete and a lack of proven "effect" of the drug. It is not just the growing number of appeals against the decisions in doping cases that is notable but also the variety of grounds on

1. It is interesting to note that the IAAF expects national governing bodies to deal with the hearing and all the related expenses, but reserves the right to arbitrate in a decision of the national federation. The settlement of Diane Modahl's claim is complicated by the recent bankruptcy of the British Athletics Federation which was partly the result of the costs associated with the Modahl case.
2. Quoted in Buti, T. & Fridman, S., "Drug Testing in Sport: Legal Challenges and Issues", *University of Queensland Law Journal*, 20.2, 1999, pp. 153-85.
3. Reported in *The Times*, London, 28 July 1997.

which appeals are based, both factors which reinforce the need for clearly and precisely worded anti-doping regulations and for adherence to a set of rigorous standards covering the sampling and analytical processes. The increasing prevalence of legal challenge to test results and the decisions of anti-doping authorities provide a powerful imperative for greater harmonisation among federations and national anti-doping agencies. Closer harmonisation should reduce the opportunities for successful legal challenge arising from inconsistency between the rules of different agencies. In addition, the process of harmonisation should enable a diffusion of best practice and the consequent reduction in appeals that exploit the inadequacies of federation rule books.

Setting quality standards

One of the most secure ways of ensuring comparability of standards and procedures, and gaining a degree of protection from legal challenges is to establish quality standards and benchmarks external to any one specific anti-doping organisation. One attempt to establish international standards was by the signatories to the International Anti-Doping Arrangement (IADA)[1] who agreed in 1995 to formulate a Standard for Doping Control. The aim of the quality policy was stated as follows:

> "Through the implementation of quality systems for doping control which satisfy the requirements in the IADA Standards for Doping Control, the doping control procedures and practices will be consistent and reliable in all phases of the doping control process."[2]

The IADA standard contains three elements, the first of which is a set of policies and standards for the management of the doping control process intended to "represent world best practices for doping control in sport and will be essential in harmonising doping control procedures and practices in the international sport community".[3] This element identifies seven phases, such as the selection and notification of athletes, and the management of results. The second element relates to the establishment of supporting conditions (organisational, legal and procedural for example) which enable national anti-doping organisations, for example, to function effectively and implement the IADA standard effectively. The final element concerns the introduction of quality management principles through compliance with ISO 9002, which is not just concerned with the formulation of good practice, but is equally concerned with the processes for the continual review of procedures. The ISO 9000 series of standards define quality systems and have been adopted in over seventy countries. The adoption by IADA of the ISO 9000 series of standards as a tool for achieving harmonisation of standards and

---

1. IADA membership comprises Australia, Canada, Norway, Sweden and the UK.
2. IADA, "The IADA Standard for Doping Control", Version 2.0, March 1998.
3. Ibid., p. 4.

procedures in doping has had a significant impact on the discussions on harmonisation within the monitoring group and WADA. Most of the IADA members have achieved ISO 9002 accreditation with Canada, for example, doing so in December 2000.

The use of ISO standards is not confined to the management of the control procedure but has been discussed in the context of establishing a reference laboratory and using ISO 17025 as the basis for identifying good practice in laboratory procedures. It is envisaged that the adoption of ISO 17025 will greatly support the work of the proposed reference laboratory.[1] The increasing use of ISO standards should not only help to harmonise practices, but also help to enhance the level of confidence that athletes have in the doping control system.

Harmonisation of sanctions

One of the most awkward issues facing WADA and its partners is the harmonisation of sanctions. At the heart of the issue is a debate concerning the appropriateness of a uniform set of sanctions as opposed to allowing international federations and their domestic affiliates greater discretion to vary penalties. It has long been argued that harmonisation defined as uniformity was overly crude as it attempted to treat all sports in the same way, as was the division of drugs into two or at most three excessively broad categories. Rather than seeking uniformity of penalties it was argued that sanctions should be more sensitive to the particular characteristics of the sport, especially the typical length of a career, and also sensitive to the differential benefit of the same drug in different sports.

Within most legal systems, punishment is a mix of mandatory penalties (usually for the minor crimes, such as motoring offences, and for the most serious crimes, such as murder) and penalties which can be imposed at the discretion of the judge, but usually within legislative guidelines. With regard to doping, there are some sports, such as cycling and athletics, that developed a bespoke set of penalties, but generally federations were content to adopt the IOC recommended tariff of sanctions. However, for some federations the willingness to adopt the IOC tariff was a mark of apathy rather than commitment, while for others it reflected an acknowledgement of the risks associated with applying penalties to athletes and the security to be gained from applying a penalty that had a legitimacy based on common action with the IOC and other major federations.

The challenge facing the IOC was to establish a set of sanctions that were effective in deterring drug users and which commanded sufficient respect among athletes and federations to act as a reference point for debates within

1. De Merode, A. & Schamasch, P., "Harmonisation of Methods and Measures in the Fight Against Doping in Sport", Final Report, Brussels: European Union, DG XII.

individual sports about the refinement of sanctions to meet the precise characteristics of their sport. To this end, and following considerable debate
among sports organisations, the IOC developed in the early 1990s such a set
of reference sanctions with a two-year ban for a first offence involving
steroids being a key aspect. However, the decisions by individual international federations are shaped by a number of factors in addition to the lead given
by the IOC. Some international federations, such as the IAAF in particular,
but also the International Weightlifting Federation and FINA, wished to
adopt or retain a stronger sanction for a first offence involving steroids. However, the wishes of the international federations have often been undermined
by the actions of domestic courts. The IAAF experience is a good example.
The federation argued strongly in favour of a four-year suspension for a first
offence concerning steroids, but was forced to retreat from this position to
the IOC recommendation of two years by a series of legal challenges, the
most important of which was that made by the Munich Regional Appeal
Court in March 1995, which declared that Katrin Krabbe's suspension for a
three-year period for steroid use was invalid because a suspension of "more
than two years contravenes... the constitutional principle of proportionali-
ty".[1] Even though there were contrary decisions being made in other courts
in the UK and in Canada, the IAAF considered that its four-year suspension
was unsustainable.

During the 1999 Lausanne conference on doping, the IOC made a further
attempt to achieve a consensus around a set of standard penalties which
aimed to combine a set of minimum sanctions with a degree of discretion.
The 1999 Olympic Movement Anti-Doping Code implies a distinction
between intentional and unintentional doping. For the latter, the period of
suspension, for a first offence, can be from two to eight years if a minor drug
is involved, but from four years to life if a more serious drug such as steroids
is involved. There is a second category of offence, where one assumes that
intent is not evident, where the penalties, for a first offence, include a period
of suspension of between one and six months and, for a more serious drug,
such as steroids, a period of suspension of at least two years. However, the
suggestion of two years is qualified as follows: "However, based on specific,
exceptional circumstances to be evaluated in the first instance by the competent IF bodies, there may be a provision for a possible modification of the
two-year sanction".[2] No indication is given of what might constitute "exceptional circumstances", but it did provide a convenient escape clause for those
international federations, such as tennis, football and road cycling, that were
more equivocal about the imposition of a two-year suspension. UEFA, for
example, has imposed much lighter penalties on footballers who tested

---

1. Vieweg, K., "A Legal Analysis of the German Situation", paper presented to the international Symposium on Doping in Sport and its Legal and Social Control, Birmingham, Alabama,
1996, p. 6.
2. IOC, 1999, op. cit., p. 13.

positive for steroid use than is the case in athletics. Three players for Perugia were recently given sixteen-month suspensions after testing positive for nandrolone, Edgar Davids of Juventus was given a five-month suspension and Frank de Boer of Barcelona was given a one-year suspension which was later reduced to four months by UEFA's court of appeal.

There is little evidence that international federations are using the discretion offered by the Olympic movement code to fine-tune sanctions to suit either the particular characteristics of their sport or the circumstances of the individual athlete. It is much more likely that some federations, especially those faced by rich and litigious clubs, leagues or individual athletes, are using their discretion to disguise the fact that they have been successfully intimidated. The challenge facing WADA is to support the international federations when they are faced by powerful commercial interests in their sport and thus prevent anti-doping policy being undermined by profit.

The jurisdiction of anti-doping bodies

A further crucial aspect of current policy which needs clarification if progress to greater harmonisation is to be maintained concerns the management of the overlapping jurisdictions of the various organisations involved in anti-doping. Given the widespread public condemnation of doping by sports bodies and governments, it is surprising the speed with which organisations will protest at what they perceive to be an invasion of their jurisdiction. The view of UEFA is not uncommon. Not only has UEFA argued in the past that it was not able to undertake out-of-competition testing because the workload was too great, but it also objected to national doping agencies carrying out tests at UEFA competitions. The problem of overlapping jurisdictions is the product of the fragmented evolution of anti-doping policies in different countries and sports. Clashes of jurisdiction are unlikely to occur during major international competitions, such as the Olympic Games, when there is a long-established precedent of testing by the organising body. Jurisdictional friction is more likely where a competition takes place over a long period of time, such as a cricket test match series, the Tour de France, Giro d'Italia or a soccer competition where there is a clear need for agreement between the domestic doping agency and the international federation about jurisdiction. Conflict is even more likely in the case of out-of-competition testing by international federations which may take place without the national anti-doping authority being informed.

Leaving aside the territorial concerns of the various agencies, the range of testing bodies is confusing for athletes who may be tested by officers of their international federation, by the officers of the anti-doping agency of the country in which they are currently located and by officers of the organising body of the competition in which they participate. Superficially, the problem of overlapping jurisdiction can be easily solved through a combination of greater courtesy by agencies in informing others of their intentions and actions, and the fostering of a higher level of mutual confidence. At a more fundamental level, the prescription for the resolution of the problem may be far less easy to achieve. Raising the level of mutual confidence is likely to be especially problematic. Greater mutual confidence is required not just in the capacity of agencies to undertake drug testing effectively, but also in the motives of other agencies. For the federations, the maintenance of jurisdictional boundaries reflects a deeper concern to prevent an erosion of control over their sport and taps a deeply held suspicion of the long-term commitment of governments to sport. Developing a degree of mutual confidence sufficient to encourage federations to cede authority to national doping agencies is a long-term project and one that must provide federations (and not just the sport for which they are responsible) with a tangible benefit.

While the establishment of WADA provides a forum for debating this issue and for generating a greater degree of mutual confidence, it must be acknowledged that WADA may well be perceived as adding to the problem of multiple jurisdictions. For example, at the Sydney Olympic Games there was some ambiguity regarding the respective roles of the IOC Medical Commission, the Australian anti-doping agency, ASDA, and the team of WADA observers.

The athlete's entourage

Just at the time when the harmonisation of primary aspects of anti-doping policy such as sanctions and jurisdiction are becoming more problematic other issues, including the punishment of members of the athlete's entourage for involvement in doping, are being added to the harmonisation agenda. In 1994, it was agreed by members of the Council of Europe's monitoring group to raise the profile of the issue of the role of an athlete's entourage in doping. The Anti-Doping Convention refers to the importance of encouraging sports organisations to harmonise their "procedures for the imposition of effective penalties for officials, doctors, veterinary doctors, coaches, physiotherapists and other officials or accessories associated with infringements of the anti-doping regulations by sportsmen and women".[1] Over recent years, this aspect of the convention has grown in importance particularly as a result of the steady reduction in the age of élite athletes in many sports such as gymnastics, swimming, skating and tennis, and the occurrence of positive drug tests among minors. The concern with the behaviour of the athlete's entourage in relation to doping is thus reinforced by the increasing concern to curtail incidents of abuse of young athletes through, for example, manipulation of diet and over-training. However, the problems involved in punishing an athlete's entourage are substantial even when the athlete is a minor. The current anti-doping policy is focused on the athlete and there has been little discussion, let alone experience, of establishing a procedure for

---

1. Council of Europe, Anti-Doping Convention, 1989, Article 7.2.e. See Appendix B.

examining the involvement of others.[1] In addition, as part of the drive for greater harmonisation, federations are being encouraged to define doping purely in terms of strict liability, a concept that is difficult to apply to the athlete's entourage, with the possible though arguable exception of those associated with athletes who are minors. Thirdly, athletes accused of a doping infraction have a right to a hearing which is investigative and clarifying in nature: any hearings involving others would, of necessity, be adversarial in nature. Fourthly, the current Olympic Movement Anti-Doping Code obscures rather than clarifies the position of members of the athlete's entourage. On the one hand, the code defines "participant" as "any athlete, coach, trainer, official, medical or paramedical personnel working with or treating athletes" while, on the other hand, referring, in the section on sanctions, to the "competitor".[2] Finally, and of overwhelming importance, there is the stark fact that federations, even with the injection of WADA funding, barely have the resources to support anti-doping programmes aimed at athletes and are unlikely to be able to produce the additional resources that an extension of the policy would require. As a result, the recommendation published by the Council of Europe regarding the involvement of an athlete's entourage in doping is an example of policy as aspiration rather than as substance.[3]

One suggestion that emerged during the discussion of the ways in which young athletes could be protected from doping and other forms of exploitation was to place a heavier responsibility on the domestic governing body to safeguard actively the interests of children. The notion that domestic governing bodies should take greater responsibility for the actions of their athletes and officials is one that is gaining some support as a strategy in the campaign against doping. The threat by FINA to suspend domestic governing bodies whose athletes had an especially poor record of drug offences was partly responsible for the greater openness in China about its recent drug record. This followed a similar policy adopted by the International Weightlifting Federation. Such strategies for encouraging compliance by domestic governing bodies can be effective but depend obviously on the commitment of the international federation to opposing doping. A source of pressure on international federations comes from the governing bodies in countries where there exists a government-resourced anti-doping policy or where there has been a tradition of success in the particular sport which is being threatened by weaker anti-doping policies in other countries. Canada would

---

1. Cycling and swimming are two exceptions.
2. IOC, 1999, op. cit., pp. 9 & 15.
3. A further source of concern is the apparent willingness of countries to employ coaches from the former GDR. Australia has recently appointed Ekkart Arbeit as its head coach despite the fact that Arbeit is under investigation for his involvement in government-sanctioned doping. According to Werner Franke, the German parliamentary investigator, Arbeit was "a major person responsible for the use of anabolic steroids" (*Guardian*, newspaper, 3 October 1997). However, Germany employs the former east German swimming coach, Winfried Leopold, despite his admission that he was involved in doping in the 1980s.

be a good example of the former and the United States an example of the latter. The United States' governing body for swimming strongly supported the proposed suspension of the Chinese from international competition for two reasons: first, it strongly suspected the Chinese governing body of either actively or passively supporting drug abuse by its swimmers and, second, because the rapid success of the Chinese swimmers was challenging the traditional American dominance resulting in fewer Olympic medals and consequently a smaller share of USOC finance.

The future of anti-doping

The substantial progress that has been made over the last twelve years or so in refining anti-doping policy and its implementation has to be balanced against the emergence of a series of new issues (genetic manipulation) and new aspects of longer established issues (jurisdictional friction, retreat on sanctions, and doping and minors). It would not be over-dramatising the current state of policy to suggest that anti-doping policy is at a crucial stage in its evolution. One way of conceptualising the challenge facing anti-doping authorities is to view progress on anti-doping as a linear progression along the upward curve of a graph. According to this model, the goal is both clear and within sight but each succeeding move towards the goal is more difficult to achieve, but progress is sustained by a consensus among interested parties over the policy goal and also over the means by which it is to be attained. Although accurate in indicating the progressive difficulty in making headway, an alternative model is one which is three-dimensional rather than linear, which is stepped rather than represented by a smooth curve and where the goal is occasionally clear but at other times lost in a fog of re-negotiation. The three-dimensional aspect takes account of the continuing debates about the best means of achieving anti-doping objectives and would include debates over complementing urine tests with blood sampling, the proper balance between in-competition and out-of-competition tests, and the respective roles and jurisdictions of national anti-doping agencies, WADA, the IOC and the federations. The periodic indistinctness of policy goals represents the admittedly occasional disagreements over whether to include particular drugs, test particular groups of athletes and extend the remit beyond élite competitive sport. The steps are by far the most important element in the model as they represent a quantum break or watershed in policy development where continued progress is no longer possible with the current level of resources. The late 1980s was one such watershed and occurred when the limitations of in-competition testing had become all too apparent and the extension of out-of-competition testing required considerable additional, and qualitatively different, resources such as authority, money and technical expertise. The watershed of the late 1990s was rather less focused than that of the late 1980s and included the delay and cost in developing reliable tests for some of the hormone-based drugs and EPO, the likely escalation in the cost of conducting tests should blood sampling be more widely adopted, the increasing volume of litigation initiated by athletes, and the sensitivity among federations that their role in anti-doping is being usurped by governmental agencies. Central to all these elements was the concern that the necessary organisational commitment from governments, the IOC and the federations to achieve the quantum change in policy was lacking, as was an infrastructure for facilitating global harmonisation of policy and practices.[1]

To a significant degree, these policy and organisational weaknesses were addressed through the formation of IICGADS and WADA. However, there still remains substantial concern regarding the depth and strength of commitment among governments and sports bodies to the goal of drug-free sport. Allegations persist of unreported positives, on the one hand and, on the other, reported positives where no action was taken. The recent highly critical enquiry into the treatment of a series of positive test results by USA Track and Field during 2000 clearly showed that the problem has not diminished and the USATF did not meet its obligations to either the USOC or IAAF in relation to prompt reporting of positives. Many commentators have detected a lack of enthusiasm among senior members of the IOC for an intensive anti-doping programme. A similar impression of muted enthusiasm is formed when assessing the commitment of the federations. Federations have to cope with increasingly assertive athletes and clubs, and, globally, are under intense pressure to retain their authority and control over major events and competitions. Some federations, such as those for rugby (both union and league) and soccer, are definitely the weaker partner in the relationship with élite clubs mirroring the erosion of federation power that has already taken place in golf, tennis and some motor sports.

It would be of some comfort to be able to feel confident that governments share a higher level of collective commitment to anti-doping policy, but while a number have adopted a lead in providing the political and tangible resources required to maintain policy momentum, there is also a number whose failure to reinforce their rhetoric with action arouses and sustains suspicion regarding their intentions. Even among those governments which are actively supportive of the goals of the anti-doping effort, they generally possess a highly instrumental attitude towards sport – seeing it as a useful tool to help achieve a series of non-sporting objectives. It is also not so long ago that a number of major "sports powers" in central and eastern Europe were among a highly disruptive group of subversive countries that were actively undermining the anti-doping strategy. It is consequently hard not to feel

---

1. One cost which is of growing concern relates to the maintenance of accredited laboratories. There are seventeen accredited labs in Europe but many of the smaller ones are finding it difficult to survive. Laboratories are estimated to need between 10 000 and 30 000 samples for analysis each year in order to be economically viable. As a result, there might only be scope for five or six laboratories in Europe. In addition, there is the increasing cost of laboratory equipment and staff. For example, a high-resolution mass spectrometer costs approximately $600 000, is expensive to run and needs highly qualified (and well-paid) staff to operate it.

some sympathy for the scepticism shown by many international sports organisations towards the newly discovered evangelical enthusiasm of some governments. The legal and economic resources of IICGADS members has gained them a leading role in the policy-making process but they still have much to do in order to earn the confidence and respect of many international sports organisations.

It is within this context of rapid organisational innovation through WADA and IICGADS, of pressing technical and scientific problems and variable political and organisational support that efforts towards greater harmonisation are taking place. Despite the challenging context for harmonisation, there are a number of positive developments which augur well for the future. Most notable is the establishment of WADA, providing, at last, a permanent forum which is both truly global and which brings together all the major interests in doping policy. However, it should be borne in mind that in many ways WADA is the product of the extensive, pre-existing web of bi-lateral and multilateral agreements, such as IADA, between governments. It is also the product of the numerous examples of co-operation on anti-doping issues between governmental and sports organisations. At the scientific level, the GH2000 project aimed at developing a test to identify the presence of growth hormones relies on joint funding of £1.8 million by the IOC and the European Union. The European Union was also involved in the joint production of "The Clean Sport Guide" along with the Council of Europe. The 1994 Lausanne Agreement is further example of co-operation between sports organisations being supported by all the key organisations within the Olympic movement including the associations of both Summer and Winter Olympic Federations (ASOIF and AIWF), the International Olympic Federations, the Association of National Olympic Committees and the various continental associations of national Olympic committees. More importantly, the IOC-sponsored working group (Harmonisation of Rules on Doping Control) inspired by the Lausanne Agreement draws its membership from federations, national governmental doping control agencies and from the Council of Europe.

The above examples provide illustrations of the extent to which an inter-organisational infrastructure is emerging which enables contact and discussions between the different interests. It also draws attention to the number of different clusters of interests that need to be involved in the harmonisation process. Harmonisation involves at least two parallel processes, the first within the various clusters and the second between clusters. Among the clusters of interests that may be readily identified are the international federations, governments and the IOC. The first process focuses on the harmonisation of policy within individual sports between domestic governing bodies and the parent federation, among federations and among governments, while the second process involves the harmonisation between governmental and non-governmental sports organisations. Even with three major clusters, the problems of harmonisation would be formidable but in reality each cluster can be further divided into sub-sets of interests. For example, the federations may be divided between the Olympic and non-Olympic, the rich and poor, the established and the new, and those that are commercially successful and those that are not. Each main cluster is, at best, a loose and sometimes uneasy coalition of interests all generally capable of withholding their support from proposals of which they are suspicious. One could be forgiven for asking whether the harmonisation project is overambitious as the issue is too complex and there are just too many organisations with a capacity to prevaricate and veto policy. However, rather than this line of questioning leading to a concern about the prospects for policy success, it prompts a reflection on the importance of establishing criteria against which progress towards harmonisation may be measured and also a set of broad agreements about the extent of harmonisation that would constitute successful policy implementation. In other words, specifying the depth, breadth and intensity of harmonisation that is required.

The establishment of an appropriate organisational infrastructure, focused around WADA, the commitment of resources by sports organisations and governments, and the clear specification of the objectives and extent of the harmonisation project are all crucial to the future success of the anti-doping effort. However, of key importance is the continued support of the sports fans and the general public for the ideal of drug-free sport. Possibly the greatest threat to the anti-doping campaign is that the public loses interest in the issue. As was made clear in Chapter 5, arguments to underpin the anti-doping policy based on notions of fairness, health, paternalism and role model behaviour are too vulnerable to charges of inconsistency to provide a sufficient justification for the present policy. The foundation of existing policy and the determining factors in assuring closer harmonisation are sustained disapproval of doping by the majority of those involved in sport and the continuing vocal public support for current anti-doping efforts.

Possibly the greatest danger at the present time is that the debate on the future direction of policy becomes too esoteric for the public, too much the province of experts, and too disassociated from the sports that the mass of the public play and events that the public enjoy watching. The current attention being paid to the array of legal, technical and scientific issues generated by the harmonisation debate is a necessary step in policy refinement, but it is also important not to lose sight of the importance of keeping the public educated about the issues in order to ensure continued support. The Modahl, Krabbe and Vinnicombe cases are all in their various ways policy failures that give added urgency to the drive for closer harmonisation. These cases have the effect of, at best, confusing the public and, at worst, sowing the seeds of cynicism so evident in public attitudes to drug abuse by American football players and which result in each new positive result producing a shrug of the shoulders rather than an emphatic condemnation.

Appendices

Appendix A

New reference list of prohibited pharmacological classes of doping agents and doping methods[1] and its explanatory document[2]

Date of entry into force: 1 September 2001

Prohibited classes of substances and prohibited methods (2001-02)

I. Prohibited classes of substances

A. Stimulants

Prohibited substances in class (A) include the following examples:

amineptine, amiphenazole, amphetamines, bromantan, caffeine,* carphedon, cocaine, ephedrines,** fencamfamin, formoterol,*** mesocarb, pentetrazol, pipradrol, salbutamol,*** salmeterol,*** terbutaline,*** … and related substances.

* For caffeine, the definition of a positive is a concentration in urine greater than 12 micrograms per millilitre.

** For cathine, the definition of a positive is a concentration in urine greater than 5 micrograms per millilitre. For ephedrine and methylephedrine, the definition of a positive is a concentration in urine greater than 10 micrograms per millilitre. For phenylpropanolamine and pseudoephedrine, the definition of a positive is a concentration in urine greater than 25 micrograms per millilitre.

*** Permitted by inhaler only to prevent and/or treat asthma and exercise-induced asthma. Written notification by a respiratory or team physician that the athlete has asthma and/or exercise-induced asthma is necessary to the relevant medical authority prior to the competition.

At the Olympic Games, athletes who request permission to inhale a permitted beta agonist will be assessed by an independent medical panel.

NOTE: All imidazole preparations are acceptable for topical use. Vasoconstrictors may be administered with local anaesthetic agents. Topical preparations (e.g. nasal, ophtalmological, rectal) of adrenaline and phenylephrine are permitted.

---

1. Previously amended on 1 September 1990, 24 January 1992, 1 August 1993, 1 July 1996, 1 July 1997, 15 March 1998, 15 March 1999 and 31 March 2000.
2. Appendix to the Council of Europe Anti-Doping Convention.

B. Narcotics

Prohibited substances in class (B) include the following examples:

buprenorphine, dextromoramide, diamorphine (heroin), methadone, morphine, pentazocine, pethidine, ... and related substances.

NOTE: codeine, dextromethorphan, dextropropoxyphene, dihydrocodeine, diphenoxylate, ethylmorphine, pholcodine, propoxyphene and tramadol are permitted.

C. Anabolic agents

Prohibited substances in class (C) include the following examples:

1. Anabolic androgenic steroids

a. clostebol, fluoxymesterone, metandienone, metenolone, nandrolone, 19-norandrostenediol, 19-norandrostenedione, oxandrolone, stanozolol, ... and related substances.

b. androstenediol, androstenedione, dehydroepiandrosterone (DHEA), dihydrotestosterone, testosterone,* ... and related substances.

Evidence obtained from metabolic profiles and/or isotopic ratio measurements may be used to draw definitive conclusions.

* The presence of a testosterone (T) to epitestosterone (E) ratio greater than six (6) to one (1) in the urine of a competitor constitutes an offence unless there is evidence that this ratio is due to a physiological or pathological condition, e.g. low epitestosterone excretion, androgen producing tumour, enzyme deficiencies.

In the case of T/E higher than 6, it is mandatory that the relevant medical authority conducts an investigation before the sample is declared positive. A full report will be written and will include a review of previous tests, subsequent tests and any results of endocrine investigations. In the event that previous tests are not available, the athlete should be tested unannounced at least once per month for three months. The results of these investigations should be included in the report. Failure to co-operate in the investigations will result in declaring the sample positive.

2. Beta-2 agonists

bambuterol, clenbuterol, fenoterol, formoterol,* reproterol, salbutamol,* salmeterol,* terbutaline,* ... and related substances.

* Authorised by inhalation as described in Article (I.A).

For salbutamol, the definition of a positive under the anabolic agent category is a concentration in urine greater than 1 000 nanograms per millilitre.

D. Diuretics

Prohibited substances in class (D) include the following examples:

acetazolamide, bumetanide, chlorthalidone, ethacrynic acid, furosemide, hydrochlorothiazide, mannitol,* mersalyl, spironolactone, triamterene, ... and related substances.

* Prohibited by intravenous injection.

E. Peptide hormones, mimetics and analogues

Prohibited substances in class (E) include the following examples and their analogues and mimetics:

1. **Chorionic Gonadotrophin** (hCG) prohibited in males only;

2. **Pituitary and synthetic gonadotrophins** (LH) prohibited in males only;

3. **Corticotrophins** (ACTH, tetracosactide);

4. **Growth hormone** (hGH);

5. **Insulin-like Growth Factor** (IGF-1);

    and all the respective releasing factors and their analogues;

6. **Erythropoietin** (EPO);

7. **Insulin**;

    permitted only to treat athletes with certified insulin-dependent diabetes. Written certification of insulin-dependent diabetes must be obtained from an endocrinologist or team physician.

The presence of an abnormal concentration of an endogenous hormone in class (E) or its diagnostic marker(s) in the urine of a competitor constitutes an offence unless it has been proven to be due to a physiological or pathological condition.

II. Prohibited methods

The following procedures are prohibited:

1. Blood doping: means the administration of blood, red blood cells and/or related blood products to an athlete, which may be preceded by withdrawal of blood from the athlete, who continues to train in such a blood-depleted state;

2. Administering artificial oxygen carriers or plasma expanders;

3. Pharmacological, chemical and physical manipulations.

III. Classes of prohibited substances in certain circumstances

A. Alcohol

Where the rules of a responsible authority so provide, tests will be conducted for ethanol.

B. Cannabinoids

Where the rules of a responsible authority so provide, tests will be conducted for cannabinoids (e.g. marijuana, hashish). At the Olympic Games, tests will be conducted for cannabinoids. A concentration in urine of 11-nor-delta 9-tetrahydrocannabinol-9-carboxylic acid (carboxy-THC) greater than 15 nanograms per millilitre constitutes doping.

C. Local anaesthetics

Injectable local anaesthetics are permitted under the following conditions:

a. bupivacaine, lidocaine, mepivacaine, procaine, and related substances, can be used but not cocaine. Vasoconstrictor agents may be used in conjunction with local anaesthetics;

b. only local or intra-articular injections may be administered;

c. only when medically justified.

Where the rules of a responsible authority so provide, notification of administration may be necessary.

D. Glucocorticosteroids

The systemic use of glucocorticosteroids is prohibited when administered orally, rectally, or by intravenous or intramuscular injection. When medically necessary, local and intra-articular injections of glucocorticosteroids are permitted. Where the rules of a responsible medical authority so provide, notification of administration may be necessary.

E. Beta blockers

Prohibited substances in class (E) include the following examples:

acebutolol, alprenolol, atenolol, labetalol, metoprolol, nadolol, oxprenolol, propranolol, sotalol, … and related substances.

Where the rules of a responsible authority so provide, tests will be conducted for beta blockers.

Summary of urinary concentrations above which IOC-accredited laboratories must report findings for specific substances

caffeine	> 12 micrograms/millilitre
carboxy-THC	> 15 nanograms/millilitre
cathine	> 5 micrograms/millilitre
ephedrine	> 10 micrograms/millilitre
epitestosterone	> 200 nanograms/millilitre
methylephedrine	> 10 micrograms/millilitre
morphine	> 1 microgram/millilitre
19-norandrosterone	> 2 nanograms/millilitre in males
19-norandrosterone	> 5 nanograms/millilitre in females
phenylpropanolamine	> 25 micrograms/millilitre
pseudoephedrine	> 25 micrograms/millilitre
salbutamol	
(as stimulant)	> 100 nanograms/millilitre
(as anabolic agent)	> 1 000 nanograms/millilitre
T/E ratio	> 6

IV. Out-of-competition testing

Unless specifically requested by the responsible authority, out-of-competition testing is directed solely at prohibited substances in class I.C (anabolic agents), I.D. (diuretics), I.E. (peptide hormones, mimetics and analogues), and II (Prohibited Methods).

List of examples of prohibited substances and prohibited methods

CAUTION: This is not an exhaustive list of prohibited substances. Many substances that do not appear on this list are considered prohibited under the term "and related substances".

Athletes must ensure that any medicines, supplement, over-the-counter preparation or any other substances they use do not contain any Prohibited Substance.

STIMULANTS:

amineptine, amfepramone, amiphenazole, amphetamine, bambuterol, bromantan, bupropion, caffeine, carphedon, cathine, cocaine, cropropamide, crotethamide, ephedrine, etamivan, etilamphetamine, etilefrine, fencamfamin, fenetylline, fenfluramine, formoterol, heptaminol, mefenorex, mephentermine, mesocarb, methamphetamine, methoxyphenamine, methylendioxyamphetamine, methylephedrine, methylphenidate, nikethamide, norfenfluramine, parahydroxyamphetamine, pemoline, pentetrazol, phendimetrazine, phentermine, phenylephrine, phenylpropanolamine, pholedrine, pipradrol, prolintane, propylhexedrine, pseudoephedrine, reproterol, salbutamol, salmeterol, selegiline, strychnine, terbutaline.

NARCOTICS:

buprenorphine, dextromoramide, diamorphine (heroin), hydrocodone, methadone, morphine, pentazocine, pethidine.

ANABOLIC AGENTS:

androstenediol, androstenedione, bambuterol, boldenone, clenbuterol, clostebol, danazol, dehydrochlormethyltestosterone, dehydroepiandrosterone (DHEA), dihydrotestosterone, drostanolone, fenoterol, fluoxymesterone, formebolone, formoterol, gestrinone, mesterolone, metandienone, metenolone, methandriol, methyltestosterone, mibolerone, nandrolone, 19-norandrostenediol, 19-norandrostenedione, norethandrolone, oxandrolone, oxymesterone, oxymetholone, reproterol, salbutamol, salmeterol, stanozolol, terbutaline, testosterone, trenbolone.

DIURETICS:

acetazolamide, bendroflumethiazide, bumetanide, canrenone, chlortalidone, ethacrynic acid, furosemide, hydrochlorothiazide, indapamide, mannitol (by intravenous injection), mersalyl, spironolactone, triamterene.

MASKING AGENTS:

bromantan, diuretics (see above), epitestosterone, probenecid.

PEPTIDE HORMONES, MIMETICS AND ANALOGUES:

ACTH, erythropoietin (EPO), hCG,* hGH, insulin, LH,* clomiphene,* cyclofenil,* tamoxifen,* aromatase inhibitors.*

* Prohibited in males only

BETA BLOCKERS:

acebutolol, alprenolol, atenolol, betaxolol, bisoprolol, bunolol, carteolol, celiprolol, esmolol, labetalol, levobunolol, metipranolol, metoprolol, nadodol, oxprenolol, pindolol, propranolol, sotalol, timolol.

Explanatory document on the IOC list of prohibited substances and prohibited methods 2001-02

1. Beta-2 agonists

At the Olympic Games, athletes who require an inhaled beta-2 agonist to treat asthma and/or exercise-induced bronchoconstriction (exercise-induced "asthma") in Salt Lake City will be required to submit to the IOC-MC clinical and laboratory (including respiratory function tests) evidence that justifies such treatment. This must be received by the IOC-MC at least one week prior to the athlete's first competition. A panel of scientific and medical experts will review the submitted information. In doubtful cases, the panel has the authority to perform appropriate scientifically validated tests. Inhaled formoterol and terbutaline are permitted with notification prior to the competition.

2. Blood doping

The definition of blood doping as stated in the Olympic Movement Anti-Doping Code is included in the list.

3. Glucocorticosteroids

Glucocorticosteroids administered by local or intra-articular injection remain permitted, but International Federations may require written notification of such injection.

4. Expanded list of examples

Bupropion: is added on this list as a prohibited stimulant.

Aromatase inhibitors: is added to the list and are prohibited in males only.

Appendix B

Anti-Doping Convention (ETS No. 135)

Strasbourg, 16 November 1989

Preamble

The member states of the Council of Europe, the other states party to the European Cultural Convention, and other states, signatory hereto,

Considering that the aim of the Council of Europe is to achieve a greater unity between its members for the purpose of safeguarding and realising the ideals and principles which are their common heritage and facilitating their economic and social progress;

Conscious that sport should play an important role in the protection of health, in moral and physical education and in promoting international understanding;

Concerned by the growing use of doping agents and methods by sportsmen and sportswomen throughout sport and the consequences thereof for the health of participants and the future of sport;

Mindful that this problem puts at risk the ethical principles and educational values embodied in the Olympic Charter, in the International Charter for Sport and Physical Education of Unesco and in Resolution (76) 41 of the Committee of Ministers of the Council of Europe, known as the "European Sport for All Charter";

Bearing in mind the anti-doping regulations, policies and declarations adopted by the international sports organisations;

Aware that public authorities and the voluntary sports organisations have complementary responsibilities to combat doping in sport, notably to ensure the proper conduct, on the basis of the principle of fair play, of sports events and to protect the health of those that take part in them;

Recognising that these authorities and organisations must work together for these purposes at all appropriate levels;

Recalling the resolutions on doping adopted by the Conference of European Ministers responsible for Sport, and in particular Resolution No. 1 adopted at the 6th Conference at Reykjavik in 1989;

Recalling that the Committee of Ministers of the Council of Europe has already adopted Resolution (67) 12 on the doping of athletes, Recommendation No. R (79) 8 on doping in sport, Recommendation No. R (84) 19 on the "European Anti-Doping Charter for Sport", and Recommendation No. R (88) 12 on the institution of doping controls without warning outside competitions;

Recalling Recommendation No. 5 on doping adopted by the 2nd International Conference of Ministers and Senior Officials responsible for Sport and Physical Education organised by Unesco at Moscow (1988);

Determined, however, to take further and stronger co-operative action aimed at the reduction and eventual elimination of doping in sport using as a basis the ethical values and practical measures contained in those instruments,

Have agreed as follows:

Article 1 – Aim of the convention

The Parties, with a view to the reduction and eventual elimination of doping in sport, undertake, within the limits of their respective constitutional provisions, to take the steps necessary to apply the provisions of this convention.

Article 2 – Definition and scope of the convention

1. For the purposes of this convention:

    a. "doping in sport" means the administration to sportsmen or sportswomen, or the use by them, of pharmacological classes of doping agents or doping methods;

    b. "pharmacological classes of doping agents or doping methods" means, subject to paragraph 2 below, those classes of doping agents or doping methods banned by the relevant international sports organisations and appearing in lists that have been approved by the monitoring group under the terms of Article 11.1.b;

    c. "sportsmen and sportswomen" means those persons who participate regularly in organised sports activities.

2. Until such time as a list of banned pharmacological classes of doping agents and doping methods is approved by the monitoring group under the terms of Article 11.1.b, the reference list in the appendix to this convention shall apply.

Article 3 – Domestic co-ordination

1. The Parties shall co-ordinate the policies and actions of their government departments and other public agencies concerned with combating doping in sport.

2. They shall ensure that there is practical application of this convention, and in particular that the requirements under Article 7 are met, by entrusting, where appropriate, the implementation of some of the

provisions of this convention to a designated governmental or non-governmental sports authority or to a sports organisation.

Article 4 – Measures to restrict the availability and use of banned doping agents and methods

1. The Parties shall adopt where appropriate legislation, regulations or administrative measures to restrict the availability (including provisions to control movement, possession, importation, distribution and sale) as well as the use in sport of banned doping agents and doping methods and in particular anabolic steroids.

2. To this end, the Parties or, where appropriate, the relevant non-governmental organisations shall make it a criterion for the grant of public subsidies to sports organisations that they effectively apply anti-doping regulations.

3. Furthermore, the Parties shall:

    a. assist their sports organisations to finance doping controls and analyses, either by direct subsidies or grants, or by recognising the costs of such controls and analyses when determining the overall subsidies or grants to be awarded to those organisations;

    b. take appropriate steps to withhold the grant of subsidies from public funds, for training purposes, to individual sportsmen and sportswomen who have been suspended following a doping offence in sport, during the period of their suspension;

    c. encourage and, where appropriate, facilitate the carrying out by their sports organisations of the doping controls required by the competent international sports organisations whether during or outside competitions; and

    d. encourage and facilitate the negotiation by sports organisations of agreements permitting their members to be tested by duly authorised doping control teams in other countries.

4. Parties reserve the right to adopt anti-doping regulations and to organise doping controls on their own initiative and on their own responsibility, provided that they are compatible with the relevant principles of this convention.

Article 5 – Laboratories

1. Each Party undertakes:

    a. either to establish or facilitate the establishment on its territory of one or more doping control laboratories suitable for consideration for accreditation under the criteria adopted by the relevant international sports organisations and approved by the monitoring group under the terms of Article 11.1.b; or

b. to assist its sports organisations to gain access to such a laboratory on the territory of another Party.

2. These laboratories shall be encouraged to:

a. take appropriate action to employ and retain, train and retrain qualified staff;

b. undertake appropriate programmes of research and development into doping agents and methods used, or thought to be used, for the purposes of doping in sport and into analytical biochemistry and pharmacology with a view to obtaining a better understanding of the effects of various substances upon the human body and their consequences for athletic performance;

c. publish and circulate promptly new data from their research.

Article 6 – Education

1. The Parties undertake to devise and implement, where appropriate in co-operation with the sports organisations concerned and the mass media, educational programmes and information campaigns emphasising the dangers to health inherent in doping and its harm to the ethical values of sport. Such programmes and campaigns shall be directed at both young people in schools and sports clubs and their parents and at adult sportsmen and sportswomen, sports officials, coaches and trainers. For those involved in medicine, such educational programmes will emphasise respect for medical ethics.

2. The Parties undertake to encourage and promote research, in co-operation with the regional, national and international sports organisations concerned, into ways and means of devising scientifically based physiological and psychological training programmes that respect the integrity of the human person.

Article 7 – Co-operation with sports organisations on measures to be taken by them

1. The Parties undertake to encourage their sports organisations and through them the international sports organisations to formulate and apply all appropriate measures, falling within their competence, against doping in sport.

2. To this end, they shall encourage their sports organisations to clarify and harmonise their respective rights, obligations and duties, in particular by harmonising their:

a. anti-doping regulations on the basis of the regulations agreed by the relevant international sports organisations;

b. lists of banned pharmacological classes of doping agents and banned doping methods on the basis of the lists agreed by the relevant international sports organisations;

c. doping control procedures;

d. disciplinary procedures, applying agreed international principles of natural justice and ensuring respect for the fundamental rights of suspected sportsmen and sportswomen; these principles will include:

i. the reporting and disciplinary bodies to be distinct from one another;

ii. the right of such persons to a fair hearing and to be assisted or represented;

iii. clear and enforceable provisions for appealing against any judgment made;

e. procedures for the imposition of effective penalties for officials, doctors, veterinary doctors, coaches, physiotherapists and other officials or accessories associated with infringements of the anti-doping regulations by sportsmen and sportswomen;

f. procedures for the mutual recognition of suspensions and other penalties imposed by other sports organisations in the same or other countries.

3. Moreover, the Parties shall encourage their sports organisations:

a. to introduce, on an effective scale, doping controls not only at, but also without advance warning at any appropriate time outside, competitions, such controls to be conducted in a way which is equitable for all sportsmen and sportswomen and which include testing and retesting of persons selected, where appropriate, on a random basis;

b. to negotiate agreements with sports organisations of other countries permitting a sportsman or sportswoman training in another country to be tested by a duly authorised doping control team of that country;

c. to clarify and harmonise regulations on eligibility to take part in sports events which will include anti-doping criteria;

d. to promote active participation by sportsmen and sportswomen themselves in the anti-doping work of international sports organisations;

e. to make full and efficient use of the facilities available for doping analysis at the laboratories provided for by Article 5, both during and outside sports competitions;

f. to study scientific training methods and to devise guidelines to protect sportsmen and sportswomen of all ages appropriate for each sport.

Article 8 – International co-operation

1. The Parties shall co-operate closely on the matters covered by this convention and shall encourage similar co-operation amongst their sports organisations.

2. The Parties undertake:

   a. to encourage their sports organisations to operate in a manner that promotes application of the provisions of this convention within all the appropriate international sports organisations to which they are affiliated, including the refusal to ratify claims for world or regional records unless accompanied by an authenticated negative doping control report;

   b. to promote co-operation between the staffs of their doping control laboratories established or operating in pursuance of Article 5; and

   c. to initiate bilateral and multilateral co-operation between their appropriate agencies, authorities and organisations in order to achieve, at the international level as well, the purposes set out in Article 4.1.

3. The Parties with laboratories established or operating in pursuance of Article 5 undertake to assist other Parties to enable them to acquire the experience, skills and techniques necessary to establish their own laboratories.

Article 9 – Provision of information

Each Party shall forward to the Secretary General of the Council of Europe, in one of the official languages of the Council of Europe, all relevant information concerning legislative and other measures taken by it for the purpose of complying with the terms of this Convention.

Article 10 – Monitoring group

1. For the purposes of this convention, a monitoring group is hereby set up.

2. Any Party may be represented on the monitoring group by one or more delegates. Each Party shall have one vote.

3. Any state mentioned in Article 14.1 which is not a Party to this convention may be represented on the monitoring group by an observer.

4. The monitoring group may, by unanimous decision, invite any non-member state of the Council of Europe which is not a Party to the convention and any sports or other professional organisation concerned to be represented by an observer at one or more of its meetings.

5. The monitoring group shall be convened by the Secretary General. Its first meeting shall be held as soon as reasonably practicable, and in any case within one year after the date of the entry into force of the convention. It shall subsequently meet whenever necessary, on the initiative of the Secretary General or a Party.

6. A majority of the Parties shall constitute a quorum for holding a meeting of the monitoring group.

7. The monitoring group shall meet in private.

8. Subject to the provisions of this convention, the monitoring group shall draw up and adopt by consensus its own Rules of Procedure.

Article 11

1. The monitoring group shall monitor the application of this convention. It may in particular:

    a. keep under review the provisions of this convention and examine any modifications necessary;

    b. approve the list, and any revision thereto, of pharmacological classes of doping agents and doping methods banned by the relevant international sports organisations, referred to in Articles 2.1 and 2.2, and the criteria for accreditation of laboratories, and any revision thereto, adopted by the said organisations, referred to in Article 5.1.a, and fix the date for the relevant decisions to enter into force;

    c. hold consultations with relevant sports organisations;

    d. make recommendations to the Parties concerning measures to be taken for the purposes of this convention;

    e. recommend the appropriate measures to keep relevant international organisations and the public informed about the activities undertaken within the framework of this convention;

f. make recommendations to the Committee of Ministers concerning non-member states of the Council of Europe to be invited to accede to this convention;

g. make any proposal for improving the effectiveness of this convention.

2. In order to discharge its functions, the monitoring group may, on its own initiative, arrange for meetings of groups of experts.

Article 12

After each meeting, the monitoring group shall forward to the Committee of Ministers of the Council of Europe a report on its work and on the functioning of the convention.

Article 13 – Amendments to the articles of the convention

1. Amendments to the articles of this convention may be proposed by a Party, the Committee of Ministers of the Council of Europe or the monitoring group.

2. Any proposal for amendment shall be communicated by the Secretary General of the Council of Europe to the states mentioned in Article 14 and to every state which has acceded to or has been invited to accede to this convention in accordance with the provisions of Article 16.

3. Any amendment proposed by a Party or the Committee of Ministers shall be communicated to the monitoring group at least two months before the meeting at which it is to be considered. The monitoring group shall submit to the Committee of Ministers its opinion on the proposed amendment, where appropriate after consultation with the relevant sports organisations.

4. The Committee of Ministers shall consider the proposed amendment and any opinion submitted by the monitoring group and may adopt the amendment.

5. The text of any amendment adopted by the Committee of Ministers in accordance with paragraph 4 of this article shall be forwarded to the Parties for acceptance.

6. Any amendment adopted in accordance with paragraph 4 of this article shall come into force on the first day of the month following the expiration of a period of one month after all Parties have informed the Secretary General of their acceptance thereof.

Final clauses

Article 14

1. This convention shall be open for signature by member states of the Council of Europe, other states party to the European Cultural Convention and non-member states which have participated in the elaboration of this convention, which may express their consent to be bound by:

    a. signature without reservation as to ratification, acceptance or approval; or

    b. signature subject to ratification, acceptance or approval, followed by ratification, acceptance or approval.

2. Instruments of ratification, acceptance or approval shall be deposited with the Secretary General of the Council of Europe.

Article 15

1. The convention shall enter into force on the first day of the month following the expiration of a period of one month after the date on which five states, including at least four member states of the Council of Europe, have expressed their consent to be bound by the convention in accordance with the provisions of Article 14.

2. In respect of any signatory state which subsequently expresses its consent to be bound by it, the convention shall enter into force on the first day of the month following the expiration of a period of one month after the date of signature or of the deposit of the instrument of ratification, acceptance or approval.

Article 16

1. After the entry into force of this convention, the Committee of Ministers of the Council of Europe, after consulting the Parties, may invite to accede to the convention any non-member state by a decision taken by the majority provided for in Article 20.d of the Statute of the Council of Europe and by the unanimous vote of the representatives of the contracting states entitled to sit on the Committee.

2. In respect of any acceding state, the convention shall enter into force on the first day of the month following the expiration of a period of one month after the date of the deposit of the instrument of accession with the Secretary General of the Council of Europe.

Article 17

1. Any state may, at the time of signature or when depositing its instrument of ratification, acceptance, approval or accession, specify the territory or territories to which this convention shall apply.

2. Any state may, at any later date, by a declaration addressed to the Secretary General, extend the application of this convention to any other territory specified in the declaration. In respect of such territory, the convention shall enter into force on the first day of the month following the expiration of a period of one month after the date of receipt of such declaration by the Secretary General.

3. Any declaration made under the two preceding paragraphs may, in respect of any territory mentioned in such declaration, be withdrawn by a notification addressed to the Secretary General. Such withdrawal shall become effective on the first day of the month following the expiration of a period of six months after the date of receipt of the notification by the Secretary General.

Article 18

1. Any Party may, at any time, denounce this convention by means of a notification addressed to the Secretary General of the Council of Europe.

2. Such denunciation shall become effective on the first day of the month following the expiration of a period of six months after the date of receipt of the notification by the Secretary General.

Article 19

The Secretary General of the Council of Europe shall notify the Parties, the other member states of the Council of Europe, the other states party to the European Cultural Convention, the non-member states which have participated in the elaboration of this convention and any state which has acceded or has been invited to accede to it of:

>   a. any signature in accordance with Article 14;

>   b. the deposit of any instrument of ratification, acceptance, approval or accession in accordance with Article 14 or 16;

>   c. any date of entry into force of this convention in accordance with Articles 15 and 16;

>   d. any information forwarded under the provisions of Article 9;

>   e. any report prepared in pursuance of the provisions of Article 12;

f. any proposal for amendment or any amendment adopted in accordance with Article 13 and the date on which the amendment comes into force;

g. any declaration made under the provisions of Article 17;

h. any notification made under the provisions of Article 18 and the date on which the denunciation takes effect;

i. any other act, notification or communication relating to this convention.

In witness whereof the undersigned, being duly authorised thereto, have signed this convention.

Done at Strasbourg, the 16th day of November 1989, in English and French, both texts being equally authentic, in a single copy which shall be deposited in the archives of the Council of Europe. The Secretary General of the Council of Europe shall transmit certified copies to each member state of the Council of Europe, to the other states party to the European Cultural Convention, to the non-member states which have participated in the elaboration of this convention and to any state invited to accede to it.

Appendix

List of prohibited classes of substances and prohibited methods[1]

---

1. For the latest list, see Appendix A.

Appendix C

Chart of signatures and ratifications to the Anti-Doping Convention (ETS No. 135)

Opened for signature: Strasbourg, 16 November 1989

Entry into force: five ratifications, including four member states on 1 March 1990

Member states of the Council of Europe

Member states	Date of signature	Date of ratification or accession	Date of entry into force	R: Reservations D: Declarations T: Territorial Decl.
Albania	02/02/95			
Andorra				
Armenia	26/05/00			
Austria	10/05/90	10/07/91	01/09/91	
Azerbaijan				
Belgium	16/11/89	30/11/01	01/01/02	
Bulgaria	24/03/92	01/06/92	01/08/92	
Croatia		27/01/93 su	01/03/93	
Cyprus	20/06/91	02/02/94	01/04/94	
Czech Rep.	28/04/95 s	28/04/95 s	01/06/95	
Denmark	16/11/89 s	16/11/89 s	01/03/90	T
Estonia	14/05/93	20/11/97 a	01/01/98	
Finland	16/11/89	26/04/90	01/06/90	
France	16/11/89	21/01/91	01/03/91	T
Georgia	02/07/01			
Germany	27/05/92	28/04/94	01/06/94	
Greece	10/10/90	06/03/96	01/05/96	D
Hungary	29/01/90 s	29/01/90 s	01/03/90	
Iceland	25/03/91 s	25/03/91 s	01/05/91	
Ireland	25/06/92			
Italy	16/11/89	12/02/96	01/04/96	
Latvia	23/01/97	23/01/97	01/03/97	
Liechtenstein	16/11/89	22/05/00	01/07/00	
Lithuania	01/04/93	17/05/96	01/07/96	
Luxembourg	16/11/89	21/06/96	01/08/96	
Malta	09/09/94			
Moldova				
Netherlands	04/12/90	11/04/95	01/06/95	T
Norway	16/11/89 s	16/11/89 s	01/03/90	
Poland	16/11/89	07/09/90	01/11/90	
Portugal	14/06/90	17/03/94	01/05/94	
Romania	16/06/94	07/12/98	01/02/99	

Member states	Date of signature	Date of ratification or accession	Date of entry into force	R: Reservations D: Declarations T: Territorial Decl.
Russia[1]		12/02/91 a	01/04/91	
San Marino	16/11/89	31/01/90	01/03/90	
Slovakia	06/05/93 s	06/05/93 s	01/07/93	
Slovenia		02/07/92 su	01/09/92	
Spain	16/11/89	20/05/92	01/07/92	
Sweden	16/11/89	29/06/90	01/08/90	
Switzerland	16/11/89	05/11/92	01/01/93	
"the former Yugoslav Republic of Macedonia"		30/03/94 su	01/05/94	
Turkey	16/11/89	22/11/93	01/01/94	
Ukraine	02/07/98	29/11/01	01/01/02	
United Kingdom	16/11/89 s	16/11/89 s	01/03/90	T
Non-member states	Date of signature	Date of ratification or accession	Date of entry into force	R: Reservations D: Declarations T: Territorial Decl.
Australia		05/10/94 a	01/12/94	
Belarus				
Bosnia and Herzegovina		29/12/94 su	01/02/95	
Canada	6/03/96 s	06/03/96 s	01/05/96	
Holy See				
Monaco				
United States				
Yugoslavia		28/02/01 su	01/04/01	

Total number of signatures not followed by ratifications: 5

Total number of ratifications/accessions: 39

Notes:
[1]: Date of accession by the former Union of Socialist Soviet Republics.
a: accession; s: signature without reservation as to ratification; su: succession; r: signature ad referendum.
R: reservations; D: declarations; T: territorial application

Source: Treaty Office at http://conventions.coe.int

Appendix D

Selected anti-doping websites

International organisations

The World Anti-Doping Agency *(www.wada-ama.org)* is the most important Internet source for up-to-date information on doping policy. Available in both English and French.

The Council of Europe (www.coe.int)

The European Union *(http://europa.eu.int/comm/sport/index_en.html)*

International sports federations

Note: these are of highly variable quality and are useful mainly because of the access they give to federation handbooks and thus an insight into the ways in which the federations deal with the issue of doping in their administrative structures and constitutions.

- International Amateur Athletic Federation *(www.iaaf.org)*
- *Union Cycliste internationale (www.uci.ch)*
- *Fédération internationale de Natation (www.fina.org)*

National anti-doping agencies

The following national anti-doping agencies provide rich sources of up-to-date news and information about developments in anti-doping. A number of them also provide useful educational material for use by athletes and their entourage.

- The Netherlands Centre for Doping Affairs (NeCeDo) *(www.necedo.nl)*. Material is also available in English.
- The Anti-Doping Unit within UK Sport *(www.uksport.gov.uk)*
- The United States Anti-Doping Agency *(www.usantidoping.org)*
- The Canadian Centre for Ethics in Sport (CESS) *(www.cces.ca)*
- The Australian Sports Drug Agency (ASDA) *(www.asda.org.au)*
- The South African Institute for Drug-Free Sport *(www.drugfreesport.org.za)*
- *Conseil de Prevention et de Lutte contre dopage* (CPLD) *(www.cpld.fr)*

Other useful sites

- *www.dopage.com/fr*
- *www.drugtestingnews.com*

Sales agents for publications of the Council of Europe
Agents de vente des publications du Conseil de l'Europe

AUSTRALIA/AUSTRALIE
Hunter Publications, 58A, Gipps Street
AUS-3066 COLLINGWOOD, Victoria
Tel.: (61) 3 9417 5361
Fax: (61) 3 9419 7154
E-mail: Sales@hunter-pubs.com.au
http://www.hunter-pubs.com.au

AUSTRIA/AUTRICHE
Gerold und Co., Weihburggasse 26
A-1010 WIEN
Tel.: (43) 1 533 5014
Fax: (43) 1 533 5014 18
E-mail: buch@gerold.telecom.at
http://www.gerold.at

BELGIUM/BELGIQUE
La Librairie européenne SA
50, avenue A. Jonnart
B-1200 BRUXELLES 20
Tel.: (32) 2 734 0281
Fax: (32) 2 735 0860
E-mail: info@libeurop.be
http://www.libeurop.be

Jean de Lannoy
202, avenue du Roi
B-1190 BRUXELLES
Tel.: (32) 2 538 4308
Fax: (32) 2 538 0841
E-mail: jean.de.lannoy@euronet.be
http://www.jean-de-lannoy.be

CANADA
Renouf Publishing Company Limited
5369 Chemin Canotek Road
CDN-OTTAWA, Ontario, K1J 9J3
Tel.: (1) 613 745 2665
Fax: (1) 613 745 7660
E-mail: order.dept@renoufbooks.com
http://www.renoufbooks.com

CZECH REPUBLIC/
RÉPUBLIQUE TCHÈQUE
Suweco Cz Dovoz Tisku Praha
Ceskomoravska 21
CZ-18021 PRAHA 9
Tel : (420) 2 660 35 364
Fax : (420) 2 683 30 42
E-mail : import@suweco.cz

DENMARK/DANEMARK
Swets Blackwell A/S
Jagtvej 169 B, 2 Sal
DK-2100 KOBENHAVN O
Tel.: (45) 39 15 79 15
Fax: (45) 39 15 79 10
E-mail: info@dk.swetsblackwell.com

FINLAND/FINLANDE
Akateeminen Kirjakauppa
Keskuskatu 1, PO Box 218
FIN-00381 HELSINKI
Tel.: (358) 9 121 41
Fax: (358) 9 121 4450
E-mail: akatilaus@stockmann.fi
http://www.akatilaus.akateeminen.com

FRANCE
La Documentation française
(Diffusion/Vente France entière)
124 rue H. Barbusse
F-93308 Aubervilliers Cedex
Tel.: (33) 01 40 15 70 00
Fax: (33) 01 40 15 68 00
E-mail: commandes.vel@ladocfrancaise.gouv.fr
http://www.ladocfrancaise.gouv.fr

Librairie Kléber (Vente Strasbourg)
Palais de l'Europe
F-67075 STRASBOURG Cedex
Fax: (33) 03 88 52 91 21
E-mail: librairie.kleber@coe.int

GERMANY/ALLEMAGNE
UNO Verlag
Am Hofgarten 10
D-53113 BONN
Tel.: (49) 2 28 94 90 20
Fax: (49) 2 28 94 90 222
E-mail: bestellung@uno-verlag.de
http://www.uno-verlag.de

GREECE/GRÈCE
Librairie Kauffmann
Mavrokordatou 9
GR-ATHINAI 106 78
Tel.: (30) 1 38 29 283
Fax: (30) 1 38 33 967
E-mail: ord@otenet.gr

HUNGARY/HONGRIE
Euro Info Service
Hungexpo Europa Kozpont ter 1
H-1101 BUDAPEST
Tel.: (361) 264 8270
Fax: (361) 264 8271
E-mail: euroinfo@euroinfo.hu
http://www.euroinfo.hu

ITALY/ITALIE
Libreria Commissionaria Sansoni
Via Duca di Calabria 1/1, CP 552
I-50125 FIRENZE
Tel.: (39) 556 4831
Fax: (39) 556 41257
E-mail: licosa@licosa.com
http://www.licosa.com

NETHERLANDS/PAYS-BAS
De Lindeboom Internationale Publikaties
PO Box 202, MA de Ruyterstraat 20 A
NL-7480 AE HAAKSBERGEN
Tel.: (31) 53 574 0004
Fax: (31) 53 572 9296
E-mail: lindeboo@worldonline.nl
http://home-1-worldonline.nl/~lindeboo/

NORWAY/NORVÈGE
Akademika, A/S Universitetsbokhandel
PO Box 84, Blindern
N-0314 OSLO
Tel.: (47) 22 85 30 30
Fax: (47) 23 12 24 20

POLAND/POLOGNE
Głowna Ksiegarnia Naukowa
im. B. Prusa
Krakowskie Przedmiescie 7
PL-00-068 WARSZAWA
Tel.: (48) 29 22 66
Fax: (48) 22 26 64 49
E-mail: inter@internews.com.pl
http://www.internews.com.pl

PORTUGAL
Livraria Portugal
Rua do Carmo, 70
P-1200 LISBOA
Tel.: (351) 13 47 49 82
Fax: (351) 13 47 02 64
E-mail: liv.portugal@mail.telepac.pt

SPAIN/ESPAGNE
Mundi-Prensa Libros SA
Castelló 37
E-28001 MADRID
Tel.: (34) 914 36 37 00
Fax: (34) 915 75 39 98
E-mail: libreria@mundiprensa.es
http://www.mundiprensa.com

SWITZERLAND/SUISSE
BERSY
Route de Monteiller
CH-1965 SAVIESE
Tel.: (41) 27 395 53 33
Fax: (41) 27 395 53 34
E-mail: jprausis@netplus.ch

Adeco – Van Diermen
Chemin du Lacuez 41
CH-1807 BLONAY
Tel.: (41) 21 943 26 73
Fax: (41) 21 943 36 06
E-mail: mvandier@worldcom.ch

UNITED KINGDOM/ROYAUME-UNI
TSO (formerly HMSO)
51 Nine Elms Lane
GB-LONDON SW8 5DR
Tel.: (44) 207 873 8372
Fax: (44) 207 873 8200
E-mail: customer.services@theso.co.uk
http://www.the-stationery-office.co.uk
http://www.itsofficial.net

UNITED STATES and CANADA/
ÉTATS-UNIS et CANADA
Manhattan Publishing Company
468 Albany Post Road, PO Box 850
CROTON-ON-HUDSON,
NY 10520, USA
Tel.: (1) 914 271 5194
Fax: (1) 914 271 5856
E-mail: Info@manhattanpublishing.com
http://www.manhattanpublishing.com

Council of Europe Publishing/Editions du Conseil de l'Europe
F-67075 Strasbourg Cedex
Tel.: (33) 03 88 41 25 81 – Fax: (33) 03 88 41 39 10
E-mail: publishing@coe.int – Website: http://book.coe.int